The
Reference Shelf®

Representative American Speeches

2008–2009

Edited by Brian Boucher

The Reference Shelf
Volume 81 • Number 6
The H.W. Wilson Company
New York • Dublin
2009

The Reference Shelf

The books in this series contain reprints of articles, excerpts from books, addresses on current issues, and studies of social trends in the United States and other countries. There are six separately bound numbers in each volume, all of which are usually published in the same calendar year. Numbers one through five are each devoted to a single subject, providing background information and discussion from various points of view and concluding with a subject index and comprehensive bibliography that lists books, pamphlets, and abstracts of additional articles on the subject. The final number of each volume is a collection of recent speeches, and it contains a cumulative speaker index. Books in the series may be purchased individually or on subscription.

Library of Congress has cataloged this serial title as follows:

Representative American speeches. 1937 / 38–
    New York, H. W. Wilson Co.™
        v. 21 cm.—The Reference Shelf
Annual
Indexes:
    Author index: 1937/38–1959/60, with 1959/60; 1960/61–1969/70, with 1969/70; 1970/71–1979/80, with 1979/80; 1980/81–1989/90, 1990.
    Editors: 1937/38–1958/59, A. C. Baird.—1959/60–1969/70, L. Thonssen.—1970/ 71–1979/80, W. W. Braden.—1980/81–1994/95, O. Peterson.—1995/96–1998/99, C. M. Logue and J. DeHart.—1999/2000–2002/2003, C. M. Logue and L. M. Messina.—2003/2004–2005/2006, C. M. Logue, L. M. Messina, and J. DeHart.—2006/ 2007– , J. Currie, P. McCaffrey, L. M. Messina.—2007/ 2008–2008/2009, B. Boucher.
        ISSN 0197-6923 Representative American speeches.
            1. Speeches, addresses, etc., American. 2. Speeches, addresses, etc.
                I. Baird, Albert Craig, 1883–1979 ed. II. Thonssen, Lester, 1904–III. Braden, Waldo Warder, 1911–1991 ed. IV. Peterson, Owen, 1924– ed. V. Logue, Calvin McLeod, 1935– , Messina, Lynn M., and DeHart, Jean, eds. VI. Series.
PS668.B3   815.5082   38-27962
                                                                                                        MARC-S

    Library of Congress [8503r85] rev4

Cover: Former Vice President Dick Cheney speaks at the American Enterprise Institute (AEI). Peter Holden Photography for AEI.

Visit H.W. Wilson's Web site: www.hwwilson.com

Printed in the United States of America

Contents

Preface

As the nation limped through 2008 and 2009, burdened by high unemployment and seeing few signs of a broad recovery, as salary caps and government bailouts continued to spur debate across the country, the main topic on many Americans' minds was the economy. While the current volume of Representative American Speeches does not include a chapter exclusively devoted to the subject, the sputtering economy serves as a backdrop to the five topics addressed this year: the efforts of the new administration, the future of journalism and the media, ongoing initiatives to "green" American energy, the plight of the U.S. auto industry, and the state of the American city.

January 20, 2009, saw the inauguration of Barack Obama, the first African-American president, and this volume offers a survey of speeches by members of the new administration, as well as assessments, approving and critical, by several commentators. Obama's inaugural address is included as well as talks by two key members of the administration: Vice President Joe Biden speaks at the 45th Munich Security Conference, and Secretary of State Hillary Clinton gives an address on foreign policy at the Council on Foreign Relations. All three stress a radical departure from the policies and tone of the previous administration. Representing that faction is Vice President Dick Cheney, who follows in the Al Gore tradition of high-profile vice presidents with a lecture at the American Enterprise Institute, arguing against the new administration's national-security policies. Also representing the loyal opposition is Louisiana's governor, Bobby Jindal, who delivered the Republican response to Obama's first State of the Union address. Providing a more approving view is the Brookings Institution's Thomas E. Mann, who evaluates the Obama presidency after its first 100 days in office.

Abundant evidence speaks to the troubled condition of the American newspaper. Ever a bellwether, the satirical newspaper *The Onion* published in October 2009 an item entitled "Report: Majority of Newspapers Now Purchased By Kidnappers To Prove Date." The American Society of News Editors, for the first time since 1945, canceled its annual convention in 2009 due to constrained budgets at so many of its members' papers. (The month before making that announcement, in an effort to broaden membership, the organization changed its name from Newspaper Editors to News Editors.) As another indication of the shifting ways people get their news, *The New York Post* pointed out on July 22, 2009, that a

Nielsen report indicated there are now more televisions in the country than there are people. Amid steep declines in circulation and revenue, according to *The New York Review of Books*, "newspapers lost 15,974 jobs in 2008 and another 10,000 in the first half of 2009." On an even more somber note, the passing in 2009 of Walter Cronkite, "the most trusted man in America," prompted many to reflect on the state of journalism today. In these pages, top industry figures, an academic, and a former reporter weigh in. Incoming National Public Radio (NPR) CEO Vivian Schiller discusses the lessons public and private media can learn from each other, while her former boss, Arthur Sulzberger, Jr., publisher of *The New York Times*, makes a case for the continued importance of old-fashioned journalism in new and traditional media. Former newspaperman and now television writer and producer David Simon, as well as Columbia University's Todd Gitlin, describe the crisis (or, as Gitlin puts it, "crises") facing journalism today, and both of them sketch out possible solutions.

Even as the dangers of climate change become more and more widely understood, global demand for energy grows. A chapter herein includes some highlights of the recent national discussion of green energy. An energy company CEO, a government administrator, and two academic scientists comment on how to reconcile the need to meet demand with a desire to change the way energy is provided, how government can foster innovation, and what forms of energy are most promising. James Mulva, the CEO of ConocoPhillips, calls for a national energy policy and outlines some of the principles that should define it. Shirley Ann Jackson, the president of Rensselaer Polytechnic Institute (RPI), introduces the term "energy security" as an alternative to "energy independence" and explains why the designation is more apt while offering a perspective that is informed by both international realpolitik and technical considerations. Lisa Jackson, the administrator of the U.S. Environmental Protection Agency (EPA), calls for big ideas to meet the challenge of climate change and points out the close links between environmental and other national dilemmas. Finally, Rockefeller University's Jesse H. Ausubel makes a case for natural gas as the most realistic option to provide power on a large scale and even argues against the term "fossil fuels," based on an evolving understanding of how energy is produced by the Earth.

Speeches in the subsequent chapter describe how the U.S. auto industry came to its current perilous state and ask whether and how it can be saved. During the credit crisis of 2008, Americans witnessed unprecedented—and highly controversial—government intervention in an industry that was on the brink of collapse. The addresses in this chapter trace the arguments over that intercession, including testimony by prominent figures such as United Auto Workers (UAW) President Ron Gettelfinger and Public Citizen's Joan Claybrook before the U.S. Senate and House, respectively. Also included is Barack Obama's announcement on the government's response to the automakers' appeals and remarks by the new General Motors (GM) president and chief executive officer (CEO) Fritz Henderson on "day one" of the new GM, post-government intervention.

As America becomes increasingly urbanized, the state of the American city has come under discussion. Three city officials and a Brookings Institution scholar herein offer their observations on America's urban areas and their changing relationship to the federal government. Brookings scholar Bruce Katz lobbies for a more integrated relationship between local, state, and federal governments. Mayor Greg Nickels of Seattle, in his State of the City address, points out the ways that cities have taken the lead on matters like environmental change. Jay Williams, the mayor of Youngstown, Ohio, meanwhile, discusses the ways that America's "shrinking cities," especially those hurt by the departure of heavy industry, can remake themselves. Departing Bronx Borough President Adolfo Carrión, Jr., who had been tapped to become director of the White House Office of Urban Affairs Policy, took advantage of his final State of the Borough speech to address New York City's status and to offer a preview of the new administration's urban policy.

Brian Boucher
December 2009

1

A New Administration Takes Office

Inaugural Address[*]

Barack Obama

President of the United States, 2009– ; born Honolulu, HI, August 4, 1961; early education in Jakarta, Indonesia, and Honolulu; B.A., Columbia University, 1983; J.D., Harvard Law School, 1992; first African-American president of the Harvard Law Review; *community organizer and civil rights lawyer in Chicago; senior lecturer, University of Chicago Law School, specializing in constitutional law; state senator, representing the South Side of Chicago, Illinois State Senate, 1997–2004; elected to U.S. Senate, 2004; U.S. senator (D), Illinois, 2005–08; U.S. Senate committees: Environment and Public Works, Foreign Relations, and Veterans' Affairs; organizations: Center for Neighborhood and Technology, Chicago Annenberg Challenge, Cook County Bar, Community Law Project, Joyce Foundation, Lawyers' Committee for Civil Rights Under the Law, Leadership for Quality Education, Trinity United Church of Christ; award, 40 Under 40,* Crain's Chicago Business, *1993; author,* Dreams from My Father: A Story of Race and Inheritance *(1995, reprinted 2004);* The Audacity of Hope: Thoughts on Reclaiming the American Dream *(2006).*

Editor's introduction: "Amidst gathering clouds and raging storms," as he characterizes the moment in history, and before a crowd estimated at well over a million people, President Barack Obama delivered his inaugural address, imploring all Americans to come together and "set aside childish things." Standing before the U.S. Capitol, in the soaring oratory that had become his hallmark during a long election campaign, he calls on the American people to transcend political divisions and lays out his administration's domestic brief: to improve access to health care, to change the way we create energy, to increase effective market oversight, and to protect the nation's citizens while upholding such ideals as "the rule of law and the rights of man." On the international front, Obama pledges to extend a hand to those countries willing to unclench their fists, to assist poor nations, and hold the prosperous to a high standard.

---

[*] Delivered on January 20, 2009, at Washington, D.C.

Barack Obama's speech: My fellow citizens:

I stand here today humbled by the task before us, grateful for the trust you have bestowed, mindful of the sacrifices borne by our ancestors.

I thank President Bush for his service to our nation as well as the generosity and cooperation he has shown throughout this transition.

Forty-four Americans have now taken the presidential oath.

The words have been spoken during rising tides of prosperity and the still waters of peace. Yet, every so often the oath is taken amidst gathering clouds and raging storms. At these moments, America has carried on not simply because of the skill or vision of those in high office, but because We the People have remained faithful to the ideals of our forebears, and true to our founding documents.

So it has been. So it must be with this generation of Americans.

That we are in the midst of crisis is now well understood. Our nation is at war against a far-reaching network of violence and hatred. Our economy is badly weakened, a consequence of greed and irresponsibility on the part of some but also our collective failure to make hard choices and prepare the nation for a new age.

Homes have been lost, jobs shed, businesses shuttered. Our health care is too costly, our schools fail too many, and each day brings further evidence that the ways we use energy strengthen our adversaries and threaten our planet.

These are the indicators of crisis, subject to data and statistics. Less measurable, but no less profound, is a sapping of confidence across our land; a nagging fear that America's decline is inevitable, that the next generation must lower its sights.

Today I say to you that the challenges we face are real, they are serious and they are many. They will not be met easily or in a short span of time. But know this America: They will be met.

On this day, we gather because we have chosen hope over fear, unity of purpose over conflict and discord.

On this day, we come to proclaim an end to the petty grievances and false promises, the recriminations and worn-out dogmas that for far too long have strangled our politics.

We remain a young nation, but in the words of Scripture, the time has come to set aside childish things. The time has come to reaffirm our enduring spirit; to choose our better history; to carry forward that precious gift, that noble idea, passed on from generation to generation: the God-given promise that all are equal, all are free, and all deserve a chance to pursue their full measure of happiness.

In reaffirming the greatness of our nation, we understand that greatness is never a given. It must be earned. Our journey has never been one of shortcuts or settling for less.

It has not been the path for the faint-hearted, for those who prefer leisure over work, or seek only the pleasures of riches and fame.

Rather, it has been the risk-takers, the doers, the makers of things—some celebrated, but more often men and women obscure in their labor—who have carried us up the long, rugged path towards prosperity and freedom.

For us, they packed up their few worldly possessions and traveled across oceans in search of a new life. For us, they toiled in sweatshops and settled the West, endured the lash of the whip and plowed the hard earth.

For us, they fought and died in places like Concord and Gettysburg; Normandy and Khe Sanh.

Time and again these men and women struggled and sacrificed and worked till their hands were raw so that we might live a better life. They saw America as bigger than the sum of our individual ambitions; greater than all the differences of birth or wealth or faction.

This is the journey we continue today. We remain the most prosperous, powerful nation on Earth. Our workers are no less productive than when this crisis began. Our minds are no less inventive, our goods and services no less needed than they were last week or last month or last year. Our capacity remains undiminished. But our time of standing pat, of protecting narrow interests and putting off unpleasant decisions—that time has surely passed.

Starting today, we must pick ourselves up, dust ourselves off, and begin again the work of remaking America.

For everywhere we look, there is work to be done.

The state of our economy calls for action: bold and swift. And we will act not only to create new jobs but to lay a new foundation for growth.

We will build the roads and bridges, the electric grids and digital lines that feed our commerce and bind us together.

We will restore science to its rightful place and wield technology's wonders to raise health care's quality and lower its costs.

We will harness the sun and the winds and the soil to fuel our cars and run our factories. And we will transform our schools and colleges and universities to meet the demands of a new age.

All this we can do. All this we will do.

Now, there are some who question the scale of our ambitions, who suggest that our system cannot tolerate too many big plans. Their memories are short, for they have forgotten what this country has already done, what free men and women can achieve when imagination is joined to common purpose and necessity to courage.

What the cynics fail to understand is that the ground has shifted beneath them, that the stale political arguments that have consumed us for so long, no longer apply.

The question we ask today is not whether our government is too big or too small, but whether it works, whether it helps families find jobs at a decent wage, care they can afford, a retirement that is dignified.

Where the answer is yes, we intend to move forward. Where the answer is no, programs will end.

And those of us who manage the public's dollars will be held to account, to spend wisely, reform bad habits, and do our business in the light of day, because only then can we restore the vital trust between a people and their government.

Nor is the question before us whether the market is a force for good or ill. Its power to generate wealth and expand freedom is unmatched.

But this crisis has reminded us that without a watchful eye, the market can spin out of control. The nation cannot prosper long when it favors only the prosperous.

The success of our economy has always depended not just on the size of our gross domestic product, but on the reach of our prosperity; on the ability to extend opportunity to every willing heart—not out of charity, but because it is the surest route to our common good.

As for our common defense, we reject as false the choice between our safety and our ideals.

Our founding fathers, faced with perils that we can scarcely imagine, drafted a charter to assure the rule of law and the rights of man, a charter expanded by the blood of generations.

Those ideals still light the world, and we will not give them up for expedience's sake.

And so, to all other peoples and governments who are watching today, from the grandest capitals to the small village where my father was born: know that America is a friend of each nation and every man, woman and child who seeks a future of peace and dignity, and we are ready to lead once more.

Recall that earlier generations faced down fascism and communism not just with missiles and tanks, but with sturdy alliances and enduring convictions.

They understood that our power alone cannot protect us, nor does it entitle us to do as we please. Instead, they knew that our power grows through its prudent use. Our security emanates from the justness of our cause; the force of our example; the tempering qualities of humility and restraint.

We are the keepers of this legacy, guided by these principles once more, we can meet those new threats that demand even greater effort, even greater cooperation and understanding between nations. We'll begin to responsibly leave Iraq to its people and forge a hard-earned peace in Afghanistan.

With old friends and former foes, we'll work tirelessly to lessen the nuclear threat and roll back the specter of a warming planet.

We will not apologize for our way of life nor will we waver in its defense.

And for those who seek to advance their aims by inducing terror and slaughtering innocents, we say to you now that, "Our spirit is stronger and cannot be broken. You cannot outlast us, and we will defeat you."

For we know that our patchwork heritage is a strength, not a weakness.

We are a nation of Christians and Muslims, Jews and Hindus, and nonbelievers. We are shaped by every language and culture, drawn from every end of this Earth.

And because we have tasted the bitter swill of civil war and segregation and emerged from that dark chapter stronger and more united, we cannot help but believe that the old hatreds shall someday pass; that the lines of tribe shall soon dissolve; that as the world grows smaller, our common humanity shall reveal itself; and that America must play its role in ushering in a new era of peace.

To the Muslim world, we seek a new way forward, based on mutual interest and mutual respect.

To those leaders around the globe who seek to sow conflict or blame their society's ills on the West, know that your people will judge you on what you can build, not what you destroy.

To those who cling to power through corruption and deceit and the silencing of dissent, know that you are on the wrong side of history, but that we will extend a hand if you are willing to unclench your fist.

To the people of poor nations, we pledge to work alongside you to make your farms flourish and let clean waters flow; to nourish starved bodies and feed hungry minds.

And to those nations like ours that enjoy relative plenty, we say we can no longer afford indifference to the suffering outside our borders, nor can we consume the world's resources without regard to effect. For the world has changed, and we must change with it.

As we consider the road that unfolds before us, we remember with humble gratitude those brave Americans who, at this very hour, patrol far-off deserts and distant mountains. They have something to tell us, just as the fallen heroes who lie in Arlington whisper through the ages.

We honor them not only because they are guardians of our liberty, but because they embody the spirit of service: a willingness to find meaning in something greater than themselves.

And yet, at this moment, a moment that will define a generation, it is precisely this spirit that must inhabit us all.

For as much as government can do and must do, it is ultimately the faith and determination of the American people upon which this nation relies.

It is the kindness to take in a stranger when the levees break; the selflessness of workers who would rather cut their hours than see a friend lose their job which sees us through our darkest hours.

It is the firefighter's courage to storm a stairway filled with smoke, but also a parent's willingness to nurture a child, that finally decides our fate.

Our challenges may be new, the instruments with which we meet them may be new, but those values upon which our success depends, honesty and hard work, courage and fair play, tolerance and curiosity, loyalty and patriotism—these things are old.

These things are true. They have been the quiet force of progress throughout our history.

What is demanded then is a return to these truths. What is required of us now is a new era of responsibility—a recognition, on the part of every American, that we have duties to ourselves, our nation and the world, duties that we do not grudgingly accept but rather seize gladly, firm in the knowledge that there is nothing so satisfying to the spirit, so defining of our character than giving our all to a difficult task.

This is the price and the promise of citizenship.

This is the source of our confidence: the knowledge that God calls on us to shape an uncertain destiny.

This is the meaning of our liberty and our creed, why men and women and children of every race and every faith can join in celebration across this magnificent mall. And why a man whose father less than 60 years ago might not have been served at a local restaurant can now stand before you to take a most sacred oath.

So let us mark this day in remembrance of who we are and how far we have traveled.

In the year of America's birth, in the coldest of months, a small band of patriots huddled by dying campfires on the shores of an icy river.

The capital was abandoned. The enemy was advancing. The snow was stained with blood.

At a moment when the outcome of our revolution was most in doubt, the father of our nation ordered these words be read to the people:

> Let it be told to the future world that in the depth of winter, when nothing but hope and virtue could survive, that the city and the country, alarmed at one common danger, came forth to meet it.

America, in the face of our common dangers, in this winter of our hardship, let us remember these timeless words; with hope and virtue, let us brave once more the icy currents, and endure what storms may come; let it be said by our children's children that when we were tested we refused to let this journey end, that we did not turn back nor did we falter; and with eyes fixed on the horizon and God's grace upon us, we carried forth that great gift of freedom and delivered it safely to future generations.

Thank you. God bless you.

And God bless the United States of America.

Speech at the 45th Munich Security Conference[*]

Joseph Biden, Jr.

Vice president of the United States, 2009– ; born Scranton, PA, November 20, 1942; B.A., University of Delaware, 1965; J.D., Syracuse University College of Law, 1968; attorney, private practice, 1968–1972; council member, New Castle City Council, 1970–72; U.S. senator (D), Delaware, 1973–2008; candidate for 1988 Democratic presidential nomination; adjunct professor, Widener University School of Law, 1991– ; candidate for 2008 Democratic presidential nomination; author, Promises to Keep: On Life and Politics *(2008).*

Editor's introduction: In this address to the 45th Munich Security Conference in the Hotel Bayerischer Hof, Vice President Biden sets a tone of cooperation and common goals between the American government and its European counterparts. This was part of a larger effort to repair relationships that many believed had become frayed in previous years. While acknowledging the U.S. financial crisis and the threat it posed to the nation and the world, he promises the new administration will work to uphold American values while meeting all threats both at home and abroad. Drawing a clear line between the Obama administration and its predecessor, he pledges to stress partnership over unilateralism, prevention over preemption, and tolerance over evangelism. More specifically, he addresses the international community's response to Iran's nuclear program, and calls for hitting "the reset button" on America's relationship with Russia.

Joe Biden's speech: Chancellor Merkel, Ambassador Ischinger, colleagues:

It is good to be back in Munich. I was honored to attend this conference as a United States Senator. Today, I am especially honored to represent a new American administration and the oldest American tradition: the peaceful, democratic transfer of power. I bring with me the regrets of two great Americans and two close friends—Senators John McCain and John Kerry. They had planned to be here, along with a bipartisan Congressional delegation, but they were detained in Washington by the debate on our economic recovery plan. I come to Europe on behalf of a new administration determined to set a new tone in Washington,

---

and in America's relations around the world. That new tone—rooted in strong partnerships to meet common challenges—is not a luxury. It is a necessity. While every new beginning is a moment of hope, this moment—for America and the countries represented in this room—is fraught with concern and peril. In this moment, our obligation to our fellow citizens is to put aside the petty and the political, to reject zero-sum mentalities and rigid ideologies, to listen to and learn from one another and to work together for our common prosperity and security. That is what this moment demands. That is what the United States is determined to do.

THE CHALLENGES WE FACE

For 45 years, this conference has brought together Americans and Europeans—and, in recent years, leaders from beyond the transatlantic community—to think through matters of physical security. This year, more than ever before, we know that our physical security and our economic security are indivisible. We are all confronting a serious threat to our economic security that could spread instability and erode the progress we've made in improving the lives of our citizens. In the United States, we are taking aggressive action to stabilize our financial system, jump start our economy and lay a foundation for growth. Working with Congress, we will make strategic investments that create and save over three million jobs and boost our competitiveness in the long run. Our plan includes doubling the production of alternative energy in the next three years; computerizing our citizens' medical records; equipping tens of thousands of schools and colleges with 21st century classrooms, labs, and libraries; expanding broadband access across America; and investing in science, research and technology to spur innovation. We're also working to stabilize our financial institutions by injecting capital, purchasing some assets, and guaranteeing others. These remedies will have an impact far beyond our shores, just as the measures other nations are taking will be felt beyond their borders, too. Because of that, to the greatest extent possible, we must cooperate, make sure that our actions are complementary, and do our utmost to combat this global crisis. The United States is doing its part and President Obama looks forward to taking this message to the G-20 meeting in London in April. Even as we grapple with an economic crisis, we must contend with a war in Afghanistan now in its eighth year, and a war in Iraq well into its sixth year.

And we must recognize new forces shaping this young century: the spread of weapons of mass destruction and dangerous diseases; a growing gap between rich and poor; ethnic animosities and failed states; a rapidly warming planet and uncertain supplies of energy, food, water; the challenge to freedom and security from radical fundamentalism.

THE FALSE CHOICE BETWEEN SECURITY AND VALUES

In meeting these challenges, the United States will be guided by this basic principle: There is no conflict between our security and our ideals. They are mutually reinforcing. The force of arms won our independence, and throughout our history, the force of arms has protected our freedom. That will not change. But the very moment we declared our independence, we laid before the world the values behind our revolution and the conviction that our policies must be informed by a "decent respect for the opinions of mankind." Our Founders understood then and the United States believes now—that the example of our power must be matched by the power of our example. That is why we reject as false the choice between our safety and our ideals. America will vigorously defend our security and our values, and in doing so we will all be more secure. As hard as we try, I know that we are likely to fall short of our ideals in the future, just as we have in the past. But I commit to you now: We will strive, every day, to honor the values that animate America's democracy . . . and that bind us to you. That is why, on one of the very first days of his presidency, Barack Obama reaffirmed America's most basic values. He made clear to the world: America will not torture. We will uphold the rights of those we bring to justice. And we will close the detention facility at Guantanamo Bay. Tough choices lie ahead. As we seek a lasting framework for our common struggle against extremism, we will have to work cooperatively with nations around the world—and we will need your help. For example, we will be asking others to take responsibility for some of those now at Guantanamo. Our security is shared. So, too, is our responsibility to defend it.

WHAT WE WILL DO—WHAT WE WILL ASK

That is the basis upon which we want to build a new approach to the challenges of this century.

America will do more, but America will ask for more from our partners. Here is what we will do and what we hope our partners will consider.

First, we will work in partnership whenever we can, alone only when we must.

The threats we face have no respect for borders. No single country, no matter how powerful, can best meet them alone. We believe that international alliances and organizations do not diminish America's power—they help us advance our collective security, economic interests and values. So we will engage. We will listen. We will consult. America needs the world, just as I believe the world needs America. But we say to our friends that the alliances, treaties, and international organizations we build must be credible and they must be effective. That requires a common commitment not only to live by the rules, but to enforce them.

That is the bargain we seek. Such a bargain can be at the heart of our collective efforts to convince Iran to forego the development of nuclear weapons. The Iranian people are a great people, and Persian civilization is a great civilization.

But Iran has acted in ways that are not conducive to peace in the region or to the prosperity of its people; its illicit nuclear program is but one manifestation. Our administration is reviewing policy toward Iran, but this much I can say: We are willing to talk.

We are willing to talk to Iran, and to offer a very clear choice: Continue down your current course and there will be pressure and isolation; abandon your illicit nuclear program and support for terrorism and there will be meaningful incentives.

Second, we will strive to act preventively, not preemptively, to avoid wherever possible a choice of last resort between the risks of war and the dangers of inaction.

We will draw upon all the elements of our power—military and diplomatic; intelligence and law enforcement; economic and cultural—to stop crises before they start. In short, we will recapture the totality of America's strength, starting with diplomacy. On his second full day in office, President Obama went to our State Department, where he stressed the centrality of diplomacy to our national security. That commitment can be seen in his appointments, starting with Secretary of State Hillary Clinton. It can be seen in the President's decision to name two of America's most tenacious diplomats—Senator George Mitchell and Ambassador Richard Holbrooke—to contend with two of the world's most urgent and vexing challenges: the need for a secure, just and lasting peace between Israel and the Palestinians and the imperative of stopping the mountains between Afghanistan and Pakistan from providing a haven for terrorists. In both of these efforts, America seeks your partnership. Senator Mitchell just completed his first trip to the Middle East. Above all, he went to listen. In the near term, we must consolidate the ceasefire in Gaza by working with Egypt and others to stop smuggling and developing an international relief and reconstruction effort that strengthens the Palestinian Authority, not Hamas.

Neither of these goals can be accomplished without close collaboration among the United States, Europe, and our Arab partners. Then, we must lay the foundation for broader peacemaking efforts. It is past time for a secure and just Two State solution. We will work to achieve it, and to defeat the extremists who would perpetuate the conflict. And, building on the positive elements of the Arab Peace initiative put forward by Saudi Arabia, we will work toward a broader regional peace between Israel and its Arab neighbors.

As we responsibly draw down our forces in Iraq, the United States will continue to work for a stable Afghanistan that is not a haven for terrorists. We look forward to sharing that commitment with the government and people of Afghanistan and Pakistan and with our allies and partners because a deteriorating situation in the region poses a security threat to all of us, not just the United States. President Obama has ordered a strategic review of our policy in Afghanistan and Pakistan to make sure that our goals are clear and achievable.

As we undertake that review, we seek ideas and input from you, our partners. The result must be a comprehensive strategy for which we all take responsibility that brings together our civilian and military resources that prevents a terrorist safe have and that helps Afghans develop the capacity to secure their own future.

No strategy for Afghanistan can succeed without Pakistan. We must all strengthen our cooperation with the people and government of Pakistan, help them stabilize the Tribal Areas and promote economic development and opportunity throughout the country. Third, America will extend a hand to those who unclench their fists.

We do not believe in a clash of civilizations. We do see a shared struggle against extremism—and we will do everything in our collective power to help the forces of tolerance prevail. In the Muslim world, a small number of violent extremists are beyond the call of reason. We will defeat them. But hundreds of millions of hearts and minds share the values we hold dear. We will reach them. President Obama has made clear that we will seek a new way forward based on mutual interest and mutual respect. It was not by accident that he gave his very first interview as President to Al-Arabiya.

To meet the challenges of this new century, defense and diplomacy are necessary—but not sufficient. We also need to wield development and democracy—two of the most powerful weapons in our arsenal. Poor societies and dysfunctional states can become breeding grounds for extremism, conflict, and disease. Non-democratic nations frustrate the rightful aspirations of their citizens and fuel resentment.

Our administration has set ambitious goals to increase foreign assistance—to cut extreme poverty in half by 2015; to help eliminate the global education deficit; to cancel the debt of the world's poorest countries; to launch a new Green Revolution that produces sustainable supplies of food and to advance democracy not through its imposition by force from the outside, but by working with moderates in government and civil society to build the institutions that will protect freedom.

We also are determined to build a sustainable future for our planet—and we are prepared to lead by example. America will act aggressively against climate change and in pursuit of energy security with like-minded nations. Our administration's economic stimulus includes long-term investments in renewable energy.

The President has directed our environmental protection agency to review how we regulate emissions, started a process to raise fuel efficiency and appointed a climate envoy—all in his first week in office. As America renews our emphasis on diplomacy, development, democracy and preserving our planet, we will ask our allies to rethink some of their own approaches—including their willingness to use force when all else fails.

When it comes to radical groups that use terror as a tool, radical states that harbor extremists, undermine peace and seek or spread weapons of mass destruction and regimes that systematically kill or ethnically cleanse their own people—we must stand united and use every means at our disposal to end the threat they pose.

None of us can deny—or escape—the new threats of the 21st century. Nor can we escape the responsibility to meet them.

RENEWING OUR ALLIANCE

Two months from now, the members of the North Atlantic Treaty Organization will gather for our Alliance's 60th anniversary. This Alliance has been the cornerstone of our common security since the end of World War II. It has anchored the United States in Europe and helped forge a Europe whole and free. Together, we made a pact to safeguard the freedom of our peoples, founded on the principles of democracy, individual liberty and the rule of law. We made a commitment to cooperate, to consult—and to act with resolve when the principles we defend are challenged.

There is much to celebrate. But we must do more. We must recommit to our shared security and renew NATO, so that its success in the 20th century is matched in the 21st. NATO's core purpose remains the collective defense of its members. But faced with new threats, we need a new resolve to meet them, and the capabilities to succeed. Our Alliance must be better equipped to help stop the spread of the world's most dangerous weapons, to tackle terrorism and cyber-security, to expand its writ to energy security, and to act in and out of area effectively.

We will continue to develop missile defenses to counter a growing Iranian capability, provided the technology is proven to work and cost effective.

We will do so in consultation with our NATO allies and Russia. As we embark on this renewal project, the United States, like other Allies, would warmly welcome a decision by France to fully participate in NATO structures. In a recent discussion with President Sarkozy, President Obama underscored his strong support for France's full participation in NATO, should France wish it. France is a founding member of NATO and a major contributor to its operations. We would expect France's new responsibilities to reflect the significance of its contributions throughout NATO's history and strengthen the European role within the Alliance.

We also support the further strengthening of European defense, an increased role for the European Union in preserving peace and security, a fundamentally stronger NATO-EU partnership, and deeper cooperation with countries outside the Alliance who share our common goals and principles.

The United States rejects the notion that NATO's gain is Russia's loss, or that Russia's strength is NATO's weakness. The last few years have seen a dangerous drift in relations between Russia and the members of our Alliance.

It is time to press the reset button and to revisit the many areas where we can and should work together. Our Russian colleagues long ago warned about the rising threat from the Taliban and Al Qaeda in Afghanistan. Today, NATO and Russia can and should cooperate to defeat this common enemy.

We can and should cooperate to secure loose nuclear weapons and materials and prevent their spread, to renew the verification procedures in the START treaty and then go beyond existing treaties to negotiate deeper cuts in our arsenals. The United States and Russia have a special obligation to lead the international effort to reduce the number of nuclear weapons in the world.

We will not agree with Russia on everything. For example, the United States will not recognize Abkhazia and South Ossetia as independent states. We will not recognize a sphere of influence. It will remain our view that sovereign states have the right to make their own decisions and choose their own alliances.

But the United States and Russia can disagree and still work together where our interests coincide.

CONCLUSION

This conference started in the shadow of the Cold War. Now it takes place in a new century with new threats. As a great poet once wrote, our world has changed utterly—a terrible beauty has been born. We must change too, while remaining true to the principles upon which our alliance was founded.

And we must have the courage and commitment of those who came before us to work together to build together—and to stand together. In sharing ideals and searching for partners in a more complex world, Americans and Europeans still look to one another before they look to anyone else.

Our partnership benefits us all. This is the time to renew it.

Americans Can Do Anything[*]

Piyush Amrit "Bobby" Jindal

Governor of Louisiana, 2008– ; born Baton Rouge, LA, June 10, 1971; B.A., biology/ public policy, Brown University, 1991; M.Litt, Oxford University, 1994; consultant, McKinsey and Company, 1994–95; secretary, Louisiana Department of Health and Hospitals (DHH), 1996–98; president of the University of Louisiana system, 1999–2001; assistant secretary, U.S. Department of Health and Human Services, 2001–04; U.S. Representative (R), Louisiana, 2004–08.

Editor's introduction: Providing the Republican Party's response to President Obama's first State of the Union Address, Governor Bobby Jindal of Louisiana delivered the following speech from the governor's mansion in Baton Rouge. In it, he acknowledges the historic quality of the moment and compares his own immigrant family's history to that of the president. However, he argues that solutions to America's problems will come not from the government, which he contends is the approach favored by the president and his fellow Democrats, but rather from the people. Jindal also criticizes what he calls runaway Democratic spending and plugs Republican proposals to reduce taxes and spending, lower energy prices, and improve access to health care and education. Jindal also states his belief that the Republican Party had lost its way in recent years and must work to regain the trust of Americans. While prior to this speech, Jindal's star had been on the ascent, and he was widely touted as a potential presidential candidate in 2012, his delivery was roundly criticized by Democrats and Republicans alike and the collective opinion held that the speech had damaged his prospects for higher office.

Bobby Jindal's speech: Good evening, and happy Mardi Gras. I'm Bobby Jindal, governor of Louisiana.

Tonight, we've witnessed a great moment in the history of our republic. In the very chamber where Congress once voted to abolish slavery, our first African-American president stepped forward to address the state of our union.

---

[*] Delivered on February 24, 2009, at Baton Rouge, LA.

With his speech tonight, the president completed a redemptive journey that took our nation from Independence Hall to Gettysburg to the lunch counter and now finally the Oval Office.

Regardless of party, all Americans are moved by the president's personal story, the son of an American mother and a Kenyan father who grew up to become leader of the free world.

Like the president's father, my own parents came to this country from a distant land. When they arrived in Baton Rouge, my mother was already four-and-a-half-months pregnant. I was what folks in the insurance industry now call a pre-existing condition.

To find work, my dad picked up the yellow pages and started calling local businesses. Even after landing a job, he still couldn't afford to pay for my delivery, so he worked out an installment plan with the doctor. Fortunately for me, he never missed a payment.

As I grew up, my mom and dad taught me the values that attracted them to this country, and they instilled in me an immigrant's wonder at the greatness of America.

As I—as a child, I remember going to the grocery store with my dad. Growing up in India, he had seen extreme poverty. As we walked through the aisles, looking at the endless variety on the shelves, he would tell me, "Bobby, Americans can do anything."

I still believe that to this day: Americans can do anything. When we pull together, there's no challenge we can't overcome.

As the president made clear this evening, we're now in a time of challenge. Many of you listening tonight have lost jobs; others have seen your college and your retirement savings dwindle. Many of you are worried about losing your health care and your homes. You're looking to your elected leaders in Washington for solutions.

Republicans are ready to work with the new president to provide these solutions. Here in my state of Louisiana, we don't care what party you belong to if you have good ideas to make life better for our people. We need more of that attitude from both Democrats and Republicans in our nation's capital.

All of us want our economy to recover and our nation to prosper. So where we agree, Republicans must be the president's strongest partners. And where we disagree, Republicans have a responsibility to be candid and offer better ideas for a path forward.

Today in Washington, some are promising that government will rescue us from the economic storms raging all around us. Those of us who lived through Hurricane Katrina, we have our doubts.

Let me tell you a story. During Katrina, I visited Sheriff Harry Lee, a Democrat and a good friend of mine. When I walked into his makeshift office, I had never seen him so angry. He was literally yelling into the phone. "Well, I'm the sheriff, and if you don't like it, you can come and arrest me." I asked him, "Sheriff, what's got you so mad?" He told me that he put out a call for volunteers to come with their boats to rescue people who were trapped on their rooftops by the flood-waters. The boats were all lined up and ready to go. And then some bureaucrat showed up and told him they couldn't go out in the water unless they had proof of insurance and registration.

And I told him, "Sheriff, that's ridiculous." Before I knew it, he was yelling in the phone. "Congressman Jindal's here, and he says you can come and arrest him, too." Well, Harry just told those boaters ignore the bureaucrats and go start rescuing people.

There's a lesson in this experience: The strength of America is not found in our government. It is found in the compassionate hearts and the enterprising spirit of our citizens.

We're grateful for the support we've received from across the nation for our ongoing recovery efforts. This spirit got Louisiana through the hurricanes, and this spirit will get our nation through the storms we face today.

To solve our current problems, Washington must lead. But the way to lead is not to raise taxes, not to just put more money and power in the hands of Washington politicians. The way to lead is by empowering you, the American people, because we believe that Americans can do anything.

That's why Republicans put forward plans to create jobs by lowering income tax rates for working families, cutting taxes for small businesses, strengthening incentives for businesses to invest in new equipment and to hire new workers, and stabilizing home values by creating a new tax credit for homebuyers. These plans would cost less and create more jobs.

But Democratic leaders in Congress, they rejected this approach. Instead of trusting us to make decisions with our own money, they passed the largest government spending bill in history, with a price tag of more than $1 trillion with interest.

While some of the projects in the bill make sense, their legislation is larded with wasteful spending. It includes $300 million to buy new cars for the government, $8 billion for high-speed rail projects, such as a magnetic levitation line from Las Vegas to Disneyland, and $140 million for something called volcano monitoring.

Instead of monitoring volcanoes, what Congress should be monitoring is the eruption of spending in Washington, D.C.

Democratic leaders say their legislation will grow the economy. What it will do is grow the government, increase our taxes down the line, and saddle future generations with debt.

Who amongst us would ask our children for a loan so we could spend money we do not have on things we do—we do not need? That is precisely what the Democrats in Congress just did. It's irresponsible. And it's no way to strengthen our economy, create jobs, or build a prosperous future for our children.

In Louisiana, we took a different approach. Since I became governor, we cut more than 250 earmarks from our state budget. To create jobs for our citizens, we cut taxes six times, including the largest income tax cut in the history of our state. We passed those tax cuts with bipartisan majorities.

Republicans and Democrats put aside their differences. We worked together to make sure our people could keep more of what they earn. If it can be done in Baton Rouge, surely it can be done in Washington, D.C.

To strengthen our economy, we need urgent action to keep energy prices down. All of us remember what it felt like to pay $4 at the pump. And unless we act now, those prices will return.

To stop that from happening, we need to increase conservation, increase energy efficiency, increase the use of alternative and renewable fuels, increase our use of nuclear power, and increase drilling for oil and gas here at home.

We believe that Americans can do anything. And if we unleash the innovative spirit of our citizens, we can achieve energy independence.

To strengthen our economy, we also need to address the crisis in health care. Republicans believe in a simple principle: No American should have to worry about losing their health care coverage, period. We stand for universal access to affordable health care coverage.

What we oppose is universal government-run health care. Health care decisions should be made by doctors and patients, not by government bureaucrats.

We believe Americans can do anything. And if we put aside partisan politics and work together, we can make our system of private medicine affordable and accessible for every one of our citizens.

To strengthen our economy, we also need to make sure that every child in America gets the best possible education. After Hurricane Katrina, we reinvented the New Orleans school system, opening dozens of new charter schools and creating a new scholarship program that is giving parents the chance to send their children to private or parochial schools of their choice.

We believe that with the proper education the children of America can do anything. And it shouldn't take a devastating storm to bring this kind of innovation to education in our country.

To strengthen our economy, we must promote confidence in America by ensuring ours is the most ethical and transparent system in the world. In my home state, there used to be saying: At any given time, half of Louisiana was said to be half underwater and the other half under indictment.

Nobody says that anymore. Last year, we passed some of the strongest ethics laws in the nation. And today, Louisiana has turned her back on the corruption of the past.

We need to bring transparency to Washington, D.C., so we can rid our capital of corruption and ensure that we never see the passage of another trillion-dollar spending bill that Congress hasn't even read and the American people haven't even seen.

As we take these steps, we must remember, for all of our troubles at home, dangerous enemies still seek our destruction. Now is no time to dismantle the defenses that have protected this country for hundreds of years or to make deep cuts in funding for our troops.

America's fighting men and women can do anything. If we give them the resources they need, they will stay on the offensive, defeat our enemies, and protect us from harm.

In all these areas, Republicans want to work with President Obama. We appreciate his message of hope, but sometimes it seems like we look for hope in different places.

Democratic leaders in Washington, they place their hope in the federal government. We place our hope in you, the American people.

In the end, it comes down to an honest and fundamental disagreement about the proper role of government. We oppose the national Democratic view that says the way to strengthen our country is to increase dependence on government. We believe the way to strengthen our country is to restrain spending in Washington, to empower individuals and small businesses to grow our economy and create jobs.

In recent years, these distinctions in philosophy became less clear. Our party got away from its principles. You elected Republicans to champion limited government, fiscal discipline, and personal responsibility.

Instead, Republicans went along with earmarks and big government spending in Washington. Republicans lost your trust, and rightly so.

Tonight, on behalf of our leaders in Congress and my fellow Republican governors, I say this: Our party is determined to regain your trust. We will do so by standing up for the principles that we share, the principles you elected us to fight for, the principles that built the greatest, most prosperous country on Earth.

You know, a few weeks ago, the president warned that our country is facing a crisis that he said, in quotes, "we may not be able to reverse." You know, our troubles are real, to be sure, but don't let anyone tell you that we cannot recover. Don't let anyone tell you that America's best days are behind her.

This is the nation that cast off the scourge of slavery, overcame the Great Depression, prevailed in two World Wars, won the struggle for civil rights, defeated the Soviet menace, and responded with determined courage to the attacks of September 11, 2001.

The American spirit has triumphed over almost every form of adversity known to man, and the American spirit will triumph again.

We can have confidence in our future because, amid all of today's challenges, we also count many blessings. We have the most innovative citizens, the most abundant resources, the most resilient economy, the most powerful military, and the freest political system in the history of the world.

My fellow citizens, never forget: We are Americans. And like my dad said years ago, Americans can do anything.

Thank you for listening. God bless you. God bless Louisiana. And God bless America.

From Campaigning to Governing[*]

Politics and Policymaking in the New Obama Administration

Thomas E. Mann

W. Averell Harriman Chair and Senior Fellow, The Brookings Institution, 1991– ; born Milwaukee, WI, September 10, 1944; B.A., 1966, University of Florida (Phi Eta Sigma, Phi Kappa Phi, political science honors program, cum laude); M.A., 1968, and Ph.D., 1977, University of Michigan; staff associate, assistant director and director, Congressional Fellowship Program, 1970–1981, American Political Science Association; visiting fellow and co-director, Congress Project, 1979–1981, and Adjunct Scholar, 1981–85, American Enterprise Institute for Public Policy Research; executive director, American Political Science Association, 1981–87; director, Governmental Studies Program, The Brookings Institution, 1987–1999; author, Unsafe at Any Margin: Interpreting Congressional Elections, *1978;* Vital Statistics on Congress, 1980, *with J. Bibby and N. Ornstein, 1980;* Vital Statistics on Congress, 1982, *with N. Ornstein, M. Malbin and J. Bibby, 1982;* The American Elections of 1982, *co-editor with N. Ornstein, 1983;* Vital Statistics on Congress, 1984–85, *with N. Ornstein, M. Malbin, J. Bibby, A. Schick, 1984;* Renewing Congress: A First Report, *with N. Ornstein, 1992;* Renewing Congress: A Second Report, *with N. Ornstein, 1993;* Vital Statistics on Congress, 1999–2000, *with N. Ornstein and M. Malbin, 2000;* Vital Statistics on Congress, 2001–2002, *with N. Ornstein and M. Malbin, 2002;* The New Campaign Finance Sourcebook, *with A. Corrado, D. Ortiz and T. Potter, 2005;* The Broken Branch: How Congress Is Failing America and How to Get It Back on Track, *with N. Ornstein, 2006;* Vital Statistics on Congress, 2008, *with N. Ornstein and M. Malbin, 2008.*

Editor's introduction: In this address, delivered at the University of Melbourne Law School, Brookings Institution scholar Thomas E. Mann discusses the new administration's performance after nearly 100 days in office, which he describes as an irresistible benchmark for observers to judge an administration's progress. He outlines its accomplishments, such as passage of a stimulus bill; the order to close the detention facility at Guantanamo Bay, Cuba; and initiatives to restructure

* Delivered on April 21, 2009, at Melbourne, Australia. Reprinted with permission.

the auto industry. He likewise describes the successes and missteps of staffing the administration, outlines Obama's relationship with Congress, and acknowledges criticisms of the president's philosophy and approach. In view of growing partisanship, he examines Obama's efforts to build popular support. He concludes that with an economic recovery, Obama has a strong chance to cement the Democratic Party's status as the majority party in the United States.

Thomas E. Mann's speech: Barack Obama's impressive victory in the 2008 American elections, the most decisive win for a new Democratic president since Franklin Roosevelt's in the depths of the Great Depression, raised high expectations—in the United States and around the globe—for significant changes in politics and policymaking. Obama's election came against the backdrop of an extended, deeply dispiriting and dysfunctional period in American public life, one characterized by a sharp ideological polarization of the political parties, a demise of genuine deliberation within and between the branches of government, a brutish tribalism among party and ideological activists and their media enablers, a public overwhelmingly of the view that the country was seriously off track and its government unable or unwilling to move it in the right direction, historically low presidential and congressional approval ratings, and a greatly diminished U.S. standing around the world.

While the country yearned to purge the political system of its pathologies and move on to a new era, Obama took the oath of office on January 20 facing a most daunting set of immediate policy challenges. A global financial meltdown and severe recession threatened to deteriorate into deflation and depression. Massive global trade and investment imbalances and huge inherited budget deficits complicated the task of emergency economic policymaking and constrained promised efforts to tackle widely acknowledged problems with health care, energy security, climate change and education. The foreign policy landscape was littered with dangers—a withdrawal of U.S. military forces from a far from stable Iraq, deteriorating conditions in Afghanistan and Pakistan, Iran apparently moving closer to achieving a nuclear weapons capacity, a moribund Middle East peace process, a bellicose Russia, a rising China not yet integrated into global economic and security systems, and Mexico threatened by drug cartels selling drugs and buying arms in the U.S.. The list goes on.

What are the prospects for President Obama healing and revitalizing a broken political system and successfully tackling these massive domestic and foreign policy problems? Near the end of the new leadership team's first hundred days in office, what can be surmised broadly from his achievements and setbacks and specifically from the organization and staffing of the administration, the setting of policy priorities and their sequencing, approaches to both parties in Congress, and strategies for building, maintaining and mobilizing public support?

THE FIRST HUNDRED DAYS—A USEFUL INDICATOR OF PRESIDENTIAL SUCCESS?

Ever since Franklin Roosevelt's remarkable launch of his presidency in 1933—fifteen major measures introduced and signed into law, unprecedented executive actions, and a riveting series of Fireside Chats—the first hundred day record has been an irresistible yardstick for measuring presidential progress. But as historian David Greenberg reminds us, no subsequent president has come close to matching FDR's record. The most successful—Lyndon Johnson in 1965 and Ronald Reagan in 1981—took much longer than one hundred days to achieve path-breaking but fewer and more limited policy initiatives. In Roosevelt's case, the incomparable sense of urgency from the dire circumstances of the Depression combined with the historic magnitude of his electoral victory muted the political opposition and made his early successes possible. Nothing approaching the magnitude of these economic and political conditions has materialized to provide the basis for a comparable episode of presidential leadership.

That is not to deny that how presidents begin their tenure importantly shapes their fortunes. There is something of a natural political dynamic in the presidency that dictates seizing opportunities created by their election as quickly as possible. Honeymoons with Congress and the media often end early and abruptly with some political miscue or aggressiveness by the opposition. The close proximity of the midterm election leads potentially vulnerable members of Congress to focus more intently on their own electoral fortunes by the end of the president's first year in office. The traditional loss of seats by the president's party in that midterm weakens his base of support in Congress for the final two years of his initial term. If re-elected, the president immediately becomes a lame duck.

In reality, each presidency has its own political dynamic, shaped by the size of the initial election victory, the contours of the economy, conditions of war or peace, public impressions, and legislative victories and defeats. Political capital is not a finite commodity generated in the election and then quickly depleted in battles to enact a policy agenda. It can be replenished through early legislative victories, reassuring leadership, and improving conditions at home and abroad. Presidents have often garnered significant policy victories well after their first year in office. The challenge is to begin one's presidency in a way that banks some initial achievable goals, avoids personal missteps and legislative defeats, and lays the political groundwork for sustained leadership throughout the life of his administration.

AN INITIAL TALLY

Not surprisingly, Obama's start does not come close to matching FDR's but his initial achievements stack up well with that of intervening occupants of the Oval Office. On the legislative front, he interceded with Congress even before taking office to head off a move to deny release of the second installment of funds under the increasingly unpopular $700 billion Troubled Assets Relief Program (TARP). Working with Congress on several legislative measures that were stymied in the previous year by filibusters or vetoes, he signed into law bills to ease the restrictions on wage discrimination lawsuits, expand the State Children's Health Insurance Program, and protect two million acres of public lands as wilderness areas. A very ambitious $787 billion fiscal stimulus package was enacted, albeit after painful negotiations with a small group of Senate moderates finally garnered the sixty votes needed to invoke cloture and end the Republican filibuster. The stimulus bill—unprecedented in its size and scope, totaling two percent of GDP—was passed into law less than four weeks into the Obama presidency, a very impressive achievement. It also incorporated substantial down payments on his campaign promises to cut middle class taxes and invest in health information technology, renewable energy, and education. And Obama delivered to Congress a $3.6 trillion fiscal year 2010 budget that incorporates the staggering costs of coping with the financial meltdown and deep recession as well as funds to launch his major initiatives in health, energy, and education. In spite of the sticker shock, the budget resolutions approved by the House and Senate largely accommodate Obama's priorities and keep his proposals alive to fight another day.

Drawing on his executive authority, Obama took a number of significant unilateral steps to deliver on campaign promises. He ordered the closing of the U.S. detention facility at Guantanamo Bay and banned torture by CIA interrogators. He struck the rule that prohibited the awarding of U.S. family-planning funds to any organization offering abortion or abortion counseling; removed limitations on federal support of embryonic stem cell research; reversed three previous orders governing labor unions and federal contractors; and increased transparency in government through new directives to agencies under the Presidential Records Act and the Freedom of Information Act.

In the foreign policy arena, he ordered a phased withdrawal of military forces from Iraq, announced a new strategy for and deployment of additional troops to Afghanistan, took new diplomatic initiatives with Iran, re-launched arms control negotiations with Russia, and outlined a vision of a nuclear weapons–free future. Obama came through his first international incident by successfully using military force to rescue the captain of a cargo ship taken hostage by pirates off the cost of Somalia. He also participated in the London G-20 summit to coordinate a global response to the financial meltdown and deep recession.

The latter came after the Administration first struggled at home to develop and unveil a strategy for stabilizing the financial markets and restoring liquidity to the economy. Treasury Secretary Tim Geithner was sharply criticized for announcing steps that were said to be too little and too vague—in part because the administration moved too slowly to get its top political appointees in place at Treasury to help Geithner put the package together. By the eve of the London meeting, however, the administration had in place the four pillars of its strategy to revive the banking system—stress tests and capital infusion of financial institutions, mortgage relief, easing credit for small business and consumer loans, and a public-private partnership to price toxic assets and remove them from financial institutions. Many critics remained deeply skeptical of the workability of these steps and convinced that a nationalization of troubled financial institutions was essential. But a plausible and politically achievable plan was in place and was soon followed by a serious plan for reducing systemic risks in the financial system. For the moment, at least, fear of a complete meltdown eased.

The other significant step taken by the Obama Administration during this period was to lay the groundwork for a major restructuring of the automobile industry. The provision of temporary life support to General Motors and Chrysler was tied to aggressive demands by federal officials. Chrysler was given thirty days to merge with Fiat or go bust. GM was allowed sixty days to meet the stringent conditions of the administration's auto task force. The CEO was fired and half the board designated for replacement. GM was effectively forced into a compressed bankruptcy process, either within sixty days with the administration calling the tune, or after with a judge supervising the restructuring.

Throughout his first few months in office, Obama has been deeply and visibly engaged in a number of big issues at home and abroad, not through passionate and aggressive presidential demands but instead with a leadership style that is cool, cerebral, and substantive—one designed to listen, inform and persuade, not proselytize. The scale of his policy ambitions could hardly be greater. He seeks to link responses to the immediate crisis with longer-term steps that in his view are essential for positioning the United States to prosper in rapidly changing global economic and security systems. He is aware of the considerable political and economic obstacles in his path and pragmatic enough to settle, where necessary, for something well short of those ambitions. He has a vision and a compass, as well as an abiding faith in the power of persistence. He is off to a quick start but is clearly banking on two full four-year terms to build a successful record.

ORGANIZING AND STAFFING THE ADMINISTRATION

Recent Democratic presidents (Bill Clinton and Jimmy Carter) were notoriously ineffective in using the long transition period to prepare to govern. Obama was a study in contrast. Months before the general election, he recruited former Clinton White House Chief of Staff John Podesta to plan for and build a transition team and charter. Lessons from previous transition failures and successes were codified. Plans for the order and timing of key personnel were set. The White House Chief of Staff would come first, not last, and key counselors, deputies, and office directors would follow shortly. Experience in Congress and in previous administrations was most welcome. The next priority was given to filling key economic and foreign policy Cabinet positions. Hillary Clinton was courted as Secretary of State. Robert Gates was asked to stay on at the Pentagon. Retired Marine General James Jones was selected as national security advisor. New York Fed Bank President Timothy Geithner was chosen for Treasury. Former Senate Majority Leader

Tom Daschle was picked to lead the health reform campaign as head of HHS and of a new White House office. Altogether, they comprised an impressive Obama team, strong on stature, experience, and moderation.

Just as most observers were concluding that Obama had managed the transition flawlessly, the first bumps were encountered. New Mexico Governor and former presidential candidate Bill Richardson withdrew from his appointment as Secretary of Commerce in the wake of a Justice Department investigation of an alleged pay-to-play scheme in the Governor's office. Geithner acknowledged that he failed to make timely payroll tax payments on income from the World Bank, turning a consensual choice into a very controversial one and delaying his Senate confirmation. Obama's choice for chief performance officer in the White House withdrew, presumably for failure to pay District of Columbia taxes on a household employee. Daschle's confirmation proceedings in the Senate stalled because of tax problems, in his case a failure to treat as taxable income a car and driver provided by an investment firm which employed him part-time. Days after it was first reported, Daschle withdrew from both his appointments.

The vaunted Obama team stumbled badly, souring what had been the sweetest of presidential transitions. Moreover, the vetting of potential nominees in the White House and Senate, which intensified after the Geithner and Daschle embarrassments, slowed the appointment process further and left key departmental secretaries bereft of sub-cabinet appointees. Tough new restrictions on lobbyists joining and leaving the Administration and increased fear of long delays and embarrassing publicity led a number of designees to withdraw from consideration. Geithner labored for almost two months without a single Senate-confirmed assistant; Clinton had no key undersecretaries or assistant secretaries in place during the same period.

To be sure, others were present to bear some of the workload during these early months. These included some holdovers from the Bush administration, senior career civil servants, and scores of political appointees not subject to Senate confirmation. Nonetheless, the costs of delay in filling these positions are real. Obama is doing no worse than Clinton and George W. Bush but that is a woefully inadequate standard. He faces a global financial and economic crisis and two hot wars demanding all hands on deck.

The organization and staffing of the new Administration reflects Obama's operating style and preferences. He is immensely self-confident, prepared to engage substantively a wide array of issues, open to debate and disagreement among senior advisors, more attracted to informal advice from individuals than formal reports from organizations, and ready to make decisions quickly and decisively. No surprise that he chose a number of individuals with independent political standing for his team; was attracted to the use of special envoys of considerable stature to deal with hotspots around the world; and further centralized power in the White House by appointing "czars" to lead policy initiatives on climate change and energy, health reform, the economy, and urban affairs. Obama also released a directive mandating formal procedures for the consideration of national security issues during his administration that appears to expand the reach of the National Security Council into areas now led by other senior White House officials expert in their respective fields. Mac Destler, co-author of *In the Shadow of the Oval Office*, questions the workability of this structure and the fit of General Jones. While he enjoys bipartisan respect for his integrity, Jones has never worked closely with Obama and is accustomed to operating within hierarchical structures, with business moving up and down the organization through reliable channels—a model that sounds a far cry from normal operating procedures in the White House and from Obama's open and fluid style of decision making.

SETTING PRIORITIES AND SEQUENCING POLICY INITIATIVES

New presidents who get off to a good start almost always have agenda control. They focus on a limited number of issues, keep extraneous matters from stepping on their priorities, and avoid overloading the circuits in Congress. Carter sent a flood of proposals to Capitol Hill with little concern for priority or sequencing. He reaped little in the way of legislative harvest from them and the public began to wonder if he was up to the job. Reagan focused relentlessly on cutting taxes and spending, ultimately succeeding in shifting policy for decades. Clinton allowed the issue of gays in the military to overwhelm his policy priorities at the outset of his administration and then misjudged the market for a small economic stimulus in the Senate and suffered a humiliating defeat.

Obama identified stabilizing the financial markets and shortening the recession as his highest initial priority. His early efforts to ensure the release of $350 billion in TARP funds, pass a large economic stimulus bill, and develop a new strategy for dealing with the troubled banking system reflected that priority. Nonetheless, he was widely criticized for diluting his focus on economic crisis management by linking it to reform of health policy, energy and education. Critics argued that his economic recovery leadership and proposals were not up to the seriousness of the crisis, that the staggering costs of the recession and bailout made health, energy and education reform wildly unrealistic, and that his huge agenda would overwhelm the capacity of Congress to deliver on its central components.

Obama insisted that the linkage was essential to long-term economic security and prosperity and refused to back down. At his insistence, the stimulus bill contained very generous allocations for health technology, renewable energy and education. The fiscal year 2010 budget he submitted to Congress made room for major health reform, a cap-and-trade carbon emissions system, and an expansion of federal investment in education from pre-K through college. He called on Congress to begin deliberations on legislation to deliver on his promise to overhaul health and energy policy. And to born-again deficit hawks alarmed by the massive increases in projected debt, he countered that the only credible way of dealing with the long-term fiscal imbalance is to spend generously now to increase aggregate demand and avoid an extended recession or depression and to make the investments essential to ultimately controlling exploding health care costs and to developing a new economy based on renewable energy.

My view is that Obama and his advisors are fully aware of the obstacles he faces in achieving his legislative ambitions. Neither ideological rigidity nor political naïveté are qualities I would associate with this White House. Nor is there any shortage of real-world experience working in and with Congress. Sticking with an ambitious agenda at this early stage does not mean Obama expects to achieve major reform on every element in six months or a year. Paying for an ambitious health reform package remains a daunting challenge. Congress has already signaled its unhappiness with several measures proposed by Obama to raise the necessary revenues. And administration officials very likely will not arrive in Copenhagen this December with cap-and-trade in hand. Banking what is possible in this first round will not exhaust the possibilities for policy change; indeed, in contrast to deferring action on all major policy goals not tied directly to the immediate economic crisis, it might well improve prospects for achieving his long-run objectives over the full course of his presidency.

APPROACHES TO CONGRESS

Several patterns are evident already in Obama's approaches to Congress. Unlike his immediate predecessor, he is respectful of the constitutional standing of Congress as the first branch of government and solicitous of the views of its members on both sides of the partisan divide. While careful not to compromise what he considers to be legitimate presidential prerogatives, Obama has pulled back from Bush and Cheney's expansive assertions of the inherent powers of the presidency (although not fully enough to mollify some critics). He already appears to have had personal meetings in the White House and on Capitol Hill with more members of Congress of both parties than Bush did during his eight years in office. Obama has been comfortable having Congress take the lead in drafting legislative language after he has publicly signaled the importance and general thrust of the policy initiative.

Critics see in these approaches signs of passivity and partisanship. By deferring to Congress to write the stimulus package, they allege, Obama allowed the Democratic leadership to highjack his vehicle and substitute its own priorities and interests. The 2009 omnibus spending bill, which contained thousands of earmarks, flouted the President's promise to reduce and reform such pork-barrel spending. The same pattern is likely to follow on health care and energy legislation, where he has declined to weigh in on most of the critical drafting decisions.

Those same critics see [in] his passivity with Congress a reflection of his underlying partisanship. In spite of his rhetoric of bipartisanship and symbolic gestures of meeting with and listening to Republicans in Congress, he has sought to govern almost entirely with his own party base. This, they say, has produced legislation incorporating only Democratic ideas and interests and party-line votes.

While Obama has been respectful of the independent role of Congress and of its leaders, Speaker Nancy Pelosi and Senate Majority Leader Harry Reid, I see little evidence of submissiveness in Obama's approach to Congress. The stimulus legislation, especially the version that passed the House, was almost entirely consistent with Obama's blueprint. That reality was obscured by Republican criticism of and media attention to a handful of minor measures included in the House leadership package that proved politically embarrassing. (I actually thought re-sodding the National Mall was a terrific idea: a shovel-ready, jobs-producing stimulus that produces a public good.) Key Obama aides worked before and after the inauguration with Democratic committee and party leadership staff on the dimensions and content of the package. The stimulus potency of the package was diluted in the Senate as a consequence of negotiations with a handful of moderate Democrats and Republicans whose support was necessary to garner sixty votes for cloture. The final conference report was reached with the active participation of the Chief of Staff Rahm Emanuel and Office of Management and Budget Director Peter Orszag. The 2009 spending bill priorities mirror those of Obama and substantial progress was made in reducing the number and costs of earmarks relative to the last Republican-controlled Congress.

Moreover, congressional assertiveness in writing legislation for presidential priorities is quite common in presidential-congressional relations. Medicare under Johnson and No Child Left Behind under George W. Bush are good examples. Clinton's unsuccessful experience with health care reform, in which he submitted a 1,342-page draft bill to Congress before engaging in serious negotiations with its members, is hardly the model Obama would choose to follow.

It is undeniable that the parties in Congress remain deeply polarized. As I shall argue shortly, this polarization is not simply an affectation of petty politicians in Washington; it reflects an ideological chasm between Democratic and Republican voters across the country. Obama's overtures to the opposition party have been unsuccessful to date because Republicans reject the central components of his agenda, including his economic recovery program. In less polarized times, the seriousness of the crisis and decisive nature of the Democratic electoral victory would have produced a significant number of Republican votes for the fiscal stimulus. But not a single Republican in the House and only three in the Senate voted for the stimulus; most have since gone on record supporting a repeal of the stimulus, a freeze on federal spending, and a massive, permanent, across-the-board tax cut—a combination of Herbert Hoover and Arthur Laffer—because that is what they believe. How can Obama split the difference with the Republican opposition without vitiating a stimulus he believes is the minimum required to avoid a serious risk of deflation and depression?

To be sure, Obama is likely to continue overtures to the Republicans on health care, energy, education and foreign policy and to court constituencies with high stakes in these policies that have traditionally aligned with the Republican party. Those overtures could eventually pay dividends that have been notably absent during his first months in office. Some of these issues do not break as readily along partisan lines. For example, Obama's approach to Afghanistan drew favorable reviews from many leading Republicans (including John McCain) who were critical of him on other fronts.

BUILDING AND MOBILIZING PUBLIC SUPPORT

Obama enjoyed the typical bounce in public support after his election and began his presidency with over two-thirds of the public approving of his performance. That early peak dropped to the low sixties—where it has held steady in spite of very difficult economic times and an aggressive political opposition. The number disapproving has doubled from fifteen to thirty percent, and is concentrated among Republican identifiers. In fact, the partisan pattern of approval or disapproval of Obama's performance is consistent with the increasing polarization of presidential assessments in recent decades. The partisan difference in ratings of the performance of new presidents in this early stage of their tenure increased sharply from Dwight Eisenhower and John F. Kennedy to Reagan, George H.W. Bush, and Clinton. George W. Bush proved to be the most polarizing president of them all, but by this early measure he is topped by Obama, who set a record of a sixty percentage point difference in approval between Democrats and Republicans. However, headlines suggesting Obama is more polarizing than Bush ignore an important fact: the number of Republicans has declined sharply since 2007, leaving a hard core of conservatives who disapprove deeply of Obama. The departees have mainly gone into the camp of independents, whose approval of the president remains robust.

This pattern of deep and growing partisan polarization extends to voting in presidential and congressional elections, ideological self-identification, and positions on the most salient issues. It reflects major shifts in the composition of the electorate and in the coalitional bases of the two parties. Democrats are increasingly a party of minorities and liberal whites, Republicans of conservative whites. *Washington Post* reporter Dan Balz reported that exit polls show that 64 percent of Republicans who voted in November 2008 called themselves conservatives. That compares with 54 percent in 2000 and 49 percent in 1992. The youngest cohort and well-educated professionals in metropolitan areas are increasingly attracted to the Democratic party, older and rural voters to the GOP. The Democrats' base is now larger than the Republicans' and growing, but they must compete successfully for enough support (not necessarily a majority) of white moderates to win elections and govern effectively.

Obama's approach to building and maintaining popular support is multi-faceted. First, the public's overriding concern about the dire state of the economy is the central focus of his administration. This entails reinforcing the prevalent public view that he has inherited an economic disaster from his predecessor and that it will take some time to turn things around; empathizing with and channeling the populist anger at economic elites; and taking bold steps to stabilize the financial system and revive the economy while projecting confidence that they will succeed.

Second, even in the face of the economic crisis, critical campaign commitments to the base are to be honored: ending the war in Iraq, restoring a respect for science in national policymaking, fighting for health reform, renewable energy and increased access to quality education, supporting key priorities of organized labor, and beginning the difficult journey to comprehensive immigration reform.

Third, the evident partisan shape of politics and policymaking, and his heavy reliance on Democrats in Congress, will not keep Obama from reaching out to Republicans in Congress and the country, talking about the need for a new kind of politics, and sticking with a rhetorical style absent of bluster and venom.

How best to reach the public? Obama has chosen to err on the side of overexposure. Hardly a day goes by without his public presence, including speeches, press conferences, and meetings with members of Congress, CEOs, policy experts, and ordinary citizens; exclusive interviews with network anchors and the national press; new access to minority media and sympathetic bloggers; an appearance on Jay Leno and a return to *60 Minutes*; weekly trips around the country, with extensive local and national news coverage; and an eight-day trip to Europe and Iraq jam-packed with news-worthy public appearances. If he keeps up this pace, he may wear out his welcome. But for now, all signs suggest that his public outreach is welcome and successful.

What of the promise of digital democracy? The transition from campaigning to governing has been far from seamless. The Obama campaign set a new standard in using the Internet for fundraising (a half billion dollars in online donations), social networking, video releases, campaign organization and policy discussions. Visions of high-tech transparency and accountability in government flowed naturally from that experience, but the effort is just getting off the ground.

The administration's Web presence, whitehouse.gov, is filled with useful information about the new administration and the business of government but a number of important executive orders and official presidential correspondence have gone un-posted and the promise to post non-emergency bills on the Web for five days of public comment before the President signs them has not yet been kept. Critics note that the site features more public persuasion than documentation, more interpretation of events than access to primary documents. On the other hand, Obama appears to be fully exploiting the video possibilities of the new media by producing and distributing a steady stream of online video clips that are now routinely picked up by YouTube and other major sites. A new website designed to provide the public with information on how funds are being spent under the $787 billion stimulus package—recovery.gov—is unprecedented in its scope and ambition. It is too early to know how accurate, complete and consequential that information will be.

The toughest challenge for Obama is figuring out how to utilize the thirteen million e-mail addresses he gathered in the campaign to mobilize public support on behalf of his legislative agenda. Because of legal restrictions on the use of public funds for lobbying and politicking, the effort is being led by Organizing for America, a new unit within the Democratic National Committee. Its first project—supporting the President's budget before a vote in Congress—generated only 214,000 signatures and swayed few, if any, members of Congress. Until these lists reach a critical mass in key congressional districts and states, they are unlikely to displace or importantly complement more traditional forms of persuasion.

CONCLUSION: PROSPECTS FOR 2009 AND BEYOND

The leitmotif of the 2008 election campaign—change—is clearly evident in the first months of the new administration. The most unpopular president in contemporary American history has been replaced by a very popular one—in the U.S. and around the globe. The percentage of Americans who believe that the country is headed in the right direction has soared from a trough of ten percent before the election to over forty percent today. In spite of dire economic news, a substantial number of Americans are feeling more upbeat about the economy than a few months ago. Even ratings of Congress have increased markedly under the new unified Democratic party government.

The sharply partisan structure and tone of politics and policymaking remains in place, reflecting the gaping ideological differences between the parties in Washington and around the country. The incendiary rhetoric of right-wing cable commentators Glen Beck, Sean Hannity, and Rush Limbaugh—portraying Obama as dangerously fascist and unpatriotic and openly hoping that he fails—is an extreme indicator of the passionate feelings of the political opposition. It turns out that it takes both parties to deliver a new kind of politics—one less partisan, more civil, respectful of policy differences and open to persuasion.

For the present, at least, Obama and the Democrats have the upper hand. The President is trusted over the Republican opposition to deal with the serious problems confronting the country by a margin of more than two-to-one. The Republican party has gotten smaller, more conservative, and less popular. The public sees its unified stance against Obama's proposals as political (the party of "no") and not constructive. That opposition stance has helped unify Democrats in support of their president and tilted Independents decisively in his direction. And that in turn makes Obama even more likely to rely heavily on his own party in moving important policy changes through Congress. For example, it makes inclusion of reconciliation instructions in the budget resolution—a procedure permitting a simple majority to approve bills in the Senate—even more likely. Health care reform, whose prospects have improved markedly since defeat of the Clinton plan in 1994, probably needs reconciliation as a threat to keep Republicans from filibustering it to death.

But there are good reasons to question whether this more partisan approach to governing, however necessary it may be now, is sustainable over the long haul. There are real limits to procedural end runs around the Senate's supermajority hurdle. No one appreciates that reality more than Senator Reid, who has worked assiduously to give Republicans ample opportunity to debate and amend proposals coming to the Senate floor during the first months of this year. Democrats will have difficulty holding their moderates in line on difficult votes on taxes and regulation in the face of unified Republican opposition. For example, Democrats representing high coal-producing and consuming states and districts will be reluctant to support any cap-and-trade schemes to curb carbon emissions without a broader agreement being reached with the affected interests and at least some Republicans. The same is likely to be true with financial regulation, immigration, tax reform, and efforts to deal with the projected long-term fiscal imbalance.

Obama is likely to stick with his philosophy of inclusiveness even as he manipulates the partisan levers that are a critical resource at the beginning of his presidency. His ambitious progressive agenda is tempered with an instinctive pragmatism. As presidential scholar Fred Greenstein has noted, Obama elevates workability and political feasibility over abstract doctrine in his leadership style. At times this will require playing partisan hard ball but even then with an even temperament that laments its necessity to get some big things done. If the smattering of green sprouts in this spring's economy accurately forecasts a bottoming out of the severe downturn later this year and a gradual recovery, Obama has a good chance of harvesting some important legislative victories in the fall, minimizing the 2010 midterm loss of seats by his party in the House (and possibly gaining the one seat needed in the Senate after Al Franken of Minnesota is seated to make fifty-nine, allowing the Democrats to reach the magic sixty), putting himself and the Democrats in Congress in position to pursue their agenda over six or eight years, and making significant strides toward bolstering their majority status in the country.

Keeping America Safe[*]

Richard "Dick" Cheney

Vice president of the United States, 2001–09; born Lincoln, NE, January 30, 1941, and raised in Casper, WY; B.A. 1965, M.A., 1966, University of Wyoming; Nixon Administration, 1969–74, serving at Cost of Living Council, Office of Economic Opportunity, and within the White House; transition team and Deputy Assistant to President Gerald Ford, 1974; Assistant to President Ford and White House Chief of Staff, 1975–77; U.S. Representative, Wyoming, 1977–1988; chairman, Republican Policy Committee, 1981–87; chairman, House Republican Conference, 1987; House Minority Whip, 1988; U.S. Secretary of Defense, 1989–1993, directing Operation Just Cause in Panama and Operation Desert Storm in the Middle East; chief executive officer (CEO), Halliburton, 1995–2000; awarded the Presidential Medal of Freedom, 1991.

Editor's introduction: Directly following an address on national security by President Obama at the National Archives (where the original Constitution and Bill of Rights are kept), Dick Cheney, the former vice president, spoke at the American Enterprise Institute to defend Bush Administration national security policies and lobby for their continuation. In his speech, he argues for the efficacy and necessity of enhanced interrogation techniques while roundly criticizing the Obama administration for publication of memos relating to Bush-era interrogation programs, among other actions. The release of more information, specifically on what attacks he says were successfully prevented, he maintains, would support his own position. Cheney also lambastes the decision to close the Guantanamo Bay detention facility, contending that it is unsafe to house suspected terrorists within U.S. borders. Having prevented further major terrorist attacks, he asserts, Bush-era policies must be continued.

Dick Cheney's speech: Thank you all very much, and Arthur, thank you for that introduction. It's good to be back at AEI, where we have many friends. Lynne is one of your longtime scholars, and I'm looking forward to spending more time here myself as a returning trustee. What happened was, they were looking for a

---

[*] Delivered on May 21, 2009, at Washington, D.C. Reprinted with permission.

new member of the board of trustees, and they asked me to head up the search committee.

I first came to AEI after serving at the Pentagon, and departed only after a very interesting job offer came along. I had no expectation of returning to public life, but my career worked out a little differently. Those eight years as vice president were quite a journey, and during a time of big events and great decisions, I don't think I missed much.

Being the first vice president who had also served as secretary of defense, naturally my duties tended toward national security. I focused on those challenges day to day, mostly free from the usual political distractions. I had the advantage of being a vice president content with the responsibilities I had, and going about my work with no higher ambition. Today, I'm an even freer man. Your kind invitation brings me here as a private citizen—a career in politics behind me, no elections to win or lose, and no favor to seek.

The responsibilities we carried belong to others now. And though I'm not here to speak for George W. Bush, I am certain that no one wishes the current administration more success in defending the country than we do. We understand the complexities of national security decisions. We understand the pressures that confront a president and his advisers. Above all, we know what is at stake. And though administrations and policies have changed, the stakes for America have not changed.

Right now there is considerable debate in this city about the measures our administration took to defend the American people. Today I want to set forth the strategic thinking behind our policies. I do so as one who was there every day of the Bush Administration—who supported the policies when they were made, and without hesitation would do so again in the same circumstances.

When President Obama makes wise decisions, as I believe he has done in some respects on Afghanistan, and in reversing his plan to release incendiary photos, he deserves our support. And when he faults or mischaracterizes the national security decisions we made in the Bush years, he deserves an answer. The point is not to look backward. Now and for years to come, a lot rides on our president's understanding of the security policies that preceded him. And whatever choices he makes concerning the defense of this country, those choices should not be based on slogans and campaign rhetoric, but on a truthful telling of history.

Our administration always faced its share of criticism, and from some quarters it was always intense. That was especially so in the later years of our term, when the dangers were as serious as ever, but the sense of general alarm after September 11th, 2001, was a fading memory. Part of our responsibility, as we saw it, was not to forget the terrible harm that had been done to America . . . and not to let 9/11 become the prelude to something much bigger and far worse.

That attack itself was, of course, the most devastating strike in a series of terrorist plots carried out against Americans at home and abroad. In 1993, terrorists bombed the World Trade Center, hoping to bring down the towers with a blast from below. The attacks continued in 1995, with the bombing of U.S. facilities in

Riyadh, Saudi Arabia; the killing of servicemen at Khobar Towers in 1996; the attack on our embassies in East Africa in 1998; the murder of American sailors on the USS *Cole* in 2000; and then the hijackings of 9/11, and all the grief and loss we suffered on that day.

Nine-eleven caused everyone to take a serious second look at threats that had been gathering for a while, and enemies whose plans were getting bolder and more sophisticated. Throughout the '90s, America had responded to these attacks, if at all, on an ad hoc basis. The first attack on the World Trade Center was treated as a law enforcement problem, with everything handled after the fact—crime scene, arrests, indictments, convictions, prison sentences, case closed.

That's how it seemed from a law enforcement perspective, at least—but for the terrorists the case was not closed. For them, it was another offensive strike in their ongoing war against the United States. And it turned their minds to even harder strikes with higher casualties. Nine-eleven made necessary a shift of policy, aimed at a clear strategic threat—what the Congress called "an unusual and extraordinary threat to the national security and foreign policy of the United States." From that moment forward, instead of merely preparing to round up the suspects and count up the victims after the next attack, we were determined to prevent attacks in the first place.

We could count on almost universal support back then, because everyone understood the environment we were in. We'd just been hit by a foreign enemy—leaving 3,000 Americans dead, more than we lost at Pearl Harbor. In Manhattan, we were staring at 16 acres of ashes. The Pentagon took a direct hit, and the Capitol or the White House were spared only by the Americans on Flight 93, who died bravely and defiantly.

Everyone expected a follow-on attack, and our job was to stop it. We didn't know what was coming next, but everything we did know in that autumn of 2001 looked bad. This was the world in which al-Qaeda was seeking nuclear technology, and A. Q. Khan was selling nuclear technology on the black market. We had the anthrax attack from an unknown source. We had the training camps of Afghanistan, and dictators like Saddam Hussein with known ties to Mideast terrorists.

These are just a few of the problems we had on our hands. And foremost on our minds was the prospect of the very worst coming to pass—a 9/11 with nuclear weapons.

For me, one of the defining experiences was the morning of 9/11 itself. As you might recall, I was in my office in that first hour, when radar caught sight of an airliner heading toward the White House at 500 miles an hour. That was Flight 77, the one that ended up hitting the Pentagon. With the plane still inbound, Secret Service agents came into my office and said we had to leave, now. A few moments later I found myself in a fortified White House command post somewhere down below.

There in the bunker came the reports and images that so many Americans remember from that day—word of the crash in Pennsylvania, the final phone calls from hijacked planes, the final horror for those who jumped to their death to escape burning alive. In the years since, I've heard occasional speculation that I'm a different man after 9/11. I wouldn't say that. But I'll freely admit that watching a coordinated, devastating attack on our country from an underground bunker at the White House can affect how you view your responsibilities.

To make certain our nation never again faced such a day of horror, we developed a comprehensive strategy, beginning with far greater homeland security to make the United States a harder target. But since wars cannot be won on the defensive, we moved decisively against the terrorists in their hideouts and sanctuaries, and committed to using every asset to take down their networks. We decided, as well, to confront the regimes that sponsored terrorists, and to go after those who provide sanctuary, funding, and weapons to enemies of the United States. We turned special attention to regimes that had the capacity to build weapons of mass destruction, and might transfer such weapons to terrorists.

We did all of these things, and with bipartisan support put all these policies in place. It has resulted in serious blows against enemy operations . . . the take-down of the A. Q. Khan network . . . and the dismantling of Libya's nuclear program. It's required the commitment of many thousands of troops in two theaters of war, with high points and some low points in both Iraq and Afghanistan—and at every turn, the people of our military carried the heaviest burden. Well over seven years into the effort, one thing we know is that the enemy has spent most of this time on the defensive—and every attempt to strike inside the United States has failed.

So we're left to draw one of two conclusions—and here is the great dividing line in our current debate over national security. You can look at the facts and conclude that the comprehensive strategy has worked, and therefore needs to be continued as vigilantly as ever. Or you can look at the same set of facts and conclude that 9/11 was a one-off event—coordinated, devastating, but also unique and not sufficient to justify a sustained wartime effort. Whichever conclusion you arrive at, it will shape your entire view of the last seven years, and of the policies necessary to protect America for years to come.

The key to any strategy is accurate intelligence, and skilled professionals to get that information in time to use it. In seeking to guard this nation against the threat of catastrophic violence, our administration gave intelligence officers the tools and lawful authority they needed to gain vital information. We didn't invent that authority. It is drawn from Article Two of the Constitution. And it was given specificity by the Congress after 9/11, in a Joint Resolution authorizing "all necessary and appropriate force" to protect the American people.

Our government prevented attacks and saved lives through the Terrorist Surveillance Program, which let us intercept calls and track contacts between al-Qaeda operatives and persons inside the United States. The program was top secret, and for good reason, until the editors of the *New York Times* got it and put it on the front page. After 9/11, the *Times* had spent months publishing the pictures and the stories of everyone killed by al-Qaeda on 9/11. Now here was that same newspaper publishing secrets in a way that could only help al-Qaeda. It impressed the Pulitzer committee, but it damn sure didn't serve the interests of our country, or the safety of our people.

In the years after 9/11, our government also understood that the safety of the country required collecting information known only to the worst of the terrorists. And in a few cases, that information could be gained only through tough interrogations.

In top secret meetings about enhanced interrogations, I made my own beliefs clear. I was and remain a strong proponent of our enhanced interrogation program. The interrogations were used on hardened terrorists after other efforts failed. They were legal, essential, justified, successful, and the right thing to do. The intelligence officers who questioned the terrorists can be proud of their work and proud of the results, because they prevented the violent death of thousands, if not hundreds of thousands, of innocent people.

Our successors in office have their own views on all of these matters. By presidential decision, last month we saw the selective release of documents relating to enhanced interrogations. This is held up as a bold exercise in open government, honoring the public's right to know. We're informed, as well, that there was much agonizing over this decision.

Yet somehow, when the soul-searching was done and the veil was lifted on the policies of the Bush administration, the public was given less than half the truth. The released memos were carefully redacted to leave out references to what our government learned through the methods in question. Other memos, laying out specific terrorist plots that were averted, apparently were not even considered for release. For reasons the administration has yet to explain, they believe the public has a right to know the method of the questions, but not the content of the answers.

Over on the left wing of the president's party, there appears to be little curiosity in finding out what was learned from the terrorists. The kind of answers they're after would be heard before a so-called "Truth Commission." Some are even demanding that those who recommended and approved the interrogations be prosecuted, in effect treating political disagreements as a punishable offense, and political opponents as criminals. It's hard to imagine a worse precedent, filled with more possibilities for trouble and abuse, than to have an incoming administration criminalize the policy decisions of its predecessors.

Apart from doing a serious injustice to intelligence operators and lawyers who deserve far better for their devoted service, the danger here is a loss of focus on national security, and what it requires. I would advise the administration to think very carefully about the course ahead. All the zeal that has been directed at interrogations is utterly misplaced. And staying on that path will only lead our government further away from its duty to protect the American people.

One person who by all accounts objected to the release of the interrogation memos was the Director of Central Intelligence, Leon Panetta. He was joined in that view by at least four of his predecessors. I assume they felt this way because they understand the importance of protecting intelligence sources, methods, and personnel. But now that this once top-secret information is out for all to see—including the enemy—let me draw your attention to some points that are routinely overlooked.

It is a fact that only detainees of the highest intelligence value were ever subjected to enhanced interrogation. You've heard endlessly about waterboarding. It happened to three terrorists. One of them was Khalid Sheikh Mohammed—the mastermind of 9/11, who has also boasted about beheading Daniel Pearl.

We had a lot of blind spots after the attacks on our country. We didn't know about al-Qaeda's plans, but Khalid Sheikh Mohammed and a few others did know. And with many thousands of innocent lives potentially in the balance, we didn't think it made sense to let the terrorists answer questions in their own good time, if they answered them at all.

Maybe you've heard that when we captured Khalid Sheikh Mohammed, he said he would talk as soon as he got to New York City and saw his lawyer. But like many critics of interrogations, he clearly misunderstood the business at hand. American personnel were not there to commence an elaborate legal proceeding, but to extract information from him before al-Qaeda could strike again and kill more of our people.

In public discussion of these matters, there has been a strange and sometimes willful attempt to conflate what happened at Abu Ghraib prison with the top-secret program of enhanced interrogations. At Abu Ghraib, a few sadistic prison guards abused inmates in violation of American law, military regulations, and simple decency. For the harm they did, to Iraqi prisoners and to America's cause, they deserved and received Army justice. And it takes a deeply unfair cast of mind to equate the disgraces of Abu Ghraib with the lawful, skillful, and entirely honorable work of CIA personnel trained to deal with a few malevolent men.

Even before the interrogation program began, and throughout its operation, it was closely reviewed to ensure that every method used was in full compliance with the Constitution, statutes, and treaty obligations. On numerous occasions, leading members of Congress, including the current Speaker of the House, were briefed on the program and on the methods.

Yet for all these exacting efforts to do a hard and necessary job and to do it right, we hear from some quarters nothing but feigned outrage based on a false narrative. In my long experience in Washington, few matters have inspired so much contrived indignation and phony moralizing as the interrogation methods applied to a few captured terrorists.

I might add that people who consistently distort the truth in this way are in no position to lecture anyone about "values." Intelligence officers of the United States were not trying to rough up some terrorists simply to avenge the dead of 9/11. We know the difference in this country between justice and vengeance. Intelligence officers were not trying to get terrorists to confess to past killings; they were trying to prevent future killings. From the beginning of the program, there was only one focused and all-important purpose. We sought, and we in fact obtained, specific information on terrorist plans.

Those are the basic facts on enhanced interrogations. And to call this a program of torture is to libel the dedicated professionals who have saved American lives, and to cast terrorists and murderers as innocent victims. What's more, to completely rule out enhanced interrogation methods in the future is unwise in the extreme. It is recklessness cloaked in righteousness and would make the American people less safe.

The administration seems to pride itself on searching for some kind of middle ground in policies addressing terrorism. They may take comfort in hearing disagreement from opposite ends of the spectrum. If liberals are unhappy about some decisions, and conservatives are unhappy about other decisions, then it may seem to them that the President is on the path of sensible compromise. But in the fight against terrorism, there is no middle ground, and half-measures keep you half exposed. You cannot keep just some nuclear-armed terrorists out of the United States, you must keep every nuclear-armed terrorist out of the United States. Triangulation is a political strategy, not a national security strategy. When just a single clue that goes unlearned or one lead that goes unpursued can bring on catastrophe—it's no time for splitting differences. There is never a good time to compromise when the lives and safety of the American people hang in the balance.

Behind the overwrought reaction to enhanced interrogations is a broader misconception about the threats that still face our country. You can sense the problem in the emergence of euphemisms that strive to put an imaginary distance between the American people and the terrorist enemy. Apparently using the term "war" where terrorists are concerned is starting to feel a bit dated. So henceforth we're advised by the administration to think of the fight against terrorists as, quote, "overseas contingency operations." In the event of another terrorist attack on America, the Homeland Security Department assures us it will be ready for this, quote, "man-made disaster"—never mind that the whole department was created for the purpose of protecting Americans from terrorist attack.

And when you hear that there are no more, quote, "enemy combatants," as there were back in the days of that scary war on terror, at first that sounds like progress. The only problem is that the phrase is gone, but the same assortment of killers and would-be mass murderers are still there. And finding some less judgmental or more pleasant-sounding name for terrorists doesn't change what they are—or what they would do if we let them loose.

On his second day in office, President Obama announced that he was closing the detention facility at Guantanamo. This step came with little deliberation and no plan. Now the president says some of these terrorists should be brought to American soil for trial in our court system. Others, he says, will be shipped to third countries. But so far, the United States has had little luck getting other countries to take hardened terrorists. So what happens then? Attorney General Holder and others have admitted that the United States will be compelled to accept a number of the terrorists here, in the homeland, and it has even been suggested U.S. taxpayer dollars will be used to support them. On this one, I find myself in complete agreement with many in the President's own party. Unsure how to explain to their constituents why terrorists might soon be relocating into their states, these Democrats chose instead to strip funding for such a move out of the most recent war supplemental.

The administration has found that it's easy to receive applause in Europe for closing Guantanamo. But it's tricky to come up with an alternative that will serve the interests of justice and America's national security. Keep in mind that these are hardened terrorists picked up overseas since 9/11. The ones that were considered low risk were released a long time ago. And among these, we learned yesterday, many were treated too leniently, because 1 in 7 cut a straight path back to their prior line of work and have conducted murderous attacks in the Middle East. I think the President will find, upon reflection, that to bring the worst of the worst terrorists inside the United States would be cause for great danger and regret in the years to come.

In the category of euphemism, the prizewinning entry would be a recent editorial in a familiar newspaper that referred to terrorists we've captured as, quote, "abducted." Here we have ruthless enemies of this country, stopped in their tracks by brave operatives in the service of America, and a major editorial page makes them sound like they were kidnap victims, picked up at random on their way to the movies.

It's one thing to adopt the euphemisms that suggest we're no longer engaged in a war. These are just words, and in the end it's the policies that matter most. You don't want to call them enemy combatants? Fine. Call them what you want—just don't bring them into the United States. Tired of calling it a war? Use any term you prefer. Just remember, it is a serious step to begin unraveling some of the very policies that have kept our people safe since 9/11.

Another term out there that slipped into the discussion is the notion that American interrogation practices were a "recruitment tool" for the enemy. On this theory, by the tough questioning of killers, we have supposedly fallen short of our own values. This recruitment-tool theory has become something of a mantra lately, including from the President himself. And after a familiar fashion, it excuses the violent and blames America for the evil that others do. It's another version of that same old refrain from the left, "We brought it on ourselves."

It is much closer to the truth that terrorists hate this country precisely because of the values we profess and seek to live by, not by some alleged failure to do so. Nor are terrorists or those who see them as victims exactly the best judges of America's moral standards, one way or the other.

Critics of our policies are given to lecturing on the theme of being consistent with American values. But no moral value held dear by the American people obliges public servants ever to sacrifice innocent lives to spare a captured terrorist from unpleasant things. And when an entire population is targeted by a terror network, nothing is more consistent with American values than to stop them.

As a practical matter, too, terrorists may lack much, but they have never lacked for grievances against the United States. Our belief in freedom of speech and religion, our belief in equal rights for women, our support for Israel, our cultural and political influence in the world—these are the true sources of resentment, all mixed in with the lies and conspiracy theories of the radical clerics. These recruitment tools were in vigorous use throughout the 1990s, and they were sufficient to motivate the 19 recruits who boarded those planes on September 11th, 2001.

The United States of America was a good country before 9/11, just as we are today. List all the things that make us a force for good in the world—for liberty, for human rights, for the rational, peaceful resolution of differences—and what you end up with is a list of the reasons why the terrorists hate America. If fine speech-making, appeals to reason, or pleas for compassion had the power to move them, the terrorists would long ago have abandoned the field. And when they see the American government caught up in arguments about interrogations, or whether foreign terrorists have constitutional rights, they don't stand back in awe of our legal system and wonder whether they had misjudged us all along. Instead the terrorists see just what they were hoping for—our unity gone, our resolve shaken, our leaders distracted. In short, they see weakness and opportunity.

What is equally certain is this: The broad-based strategy set in motion by President Bush obviously had nothing to do with causing the events of 9/11. But the serious way we dealt with terrorists from then on, and all the intelligence we gathered in that time, had everything to do with preventing another 9/11 on our watch. The enhanced interrogations of high-value detainees and the terrorist surveillance program have without question made our country safer. Every senior official who has been briefed on these classified matters knows of specific attacks that were in the planning stages and were stopped by the programs we put in place.

This might explain why President Obama has reserved unto himself the right to order the use of enhanced interrogation should he deem it appropriate. What value remains to that authority is debatable, given that the enemy now knows exactly what interrogation methods to train against and which ones not to worry about. Yet having reserved for himself the authority to order enhanced interrogation after an emergency, you would think that President Obama would be less disdainful of what his predecessor authorized after 9/11. It's almost gone unnoticed that the president has retained the power to order the same methods in the same circumstances. When they talk about interrogations, he and his administration speak as if they have resolved some great moral dilemma in how to extract critical information from terrorists. Instead they have put the decision off, while assigning a presumption of moral superiority to any decision they make in the future.

Releasing the interrogation memos was flatly contrary to the national security interest of the United States. The harm done only begins with top-secret information now in the hands of the terrorists, who have just received a lengthy insert for their training manual. Across the world, governments that have helped us capture terrorists will fear that sensitive joint operations will be compromised. And at the CIA, operatives are left to wonder if they can depend on the White House or Congress to back them up when the going gets tough. Why should any agency employee take on a difficult assignment when, even though they act lawfully and in good faith, years down the road the press and Congress will treat everything they do with suspicion, outright hostility, and second-guessing? Some members of Congress are notorious for demanding they be briefed into the most sensitive intelligence programs. They support them in private, and then head for the hills at the first sign of controversy.

As far as the interrogations are concerned, all that remains an official secret is the information we gained as a result. Some of [the president's] defenders say the unseen memos are inconclusive, which only raises the question why they won't let the American people decide that for themselves. I saw that information as vice president, and I reviewed some of it again at the National Archives last month. I've formally asked that it be declassified so the American people can see the intelligence we obtained, the things we learned, and the consequences for national security. And as you may have heard, last week that request was formally rejected. It's worth recalling that ultimate power of declassification belongs to the president himself. President Obama has used his declassification power to reveal what happened in the interrogation of terrorists. Now let him use that same power to show Americans what did not happen, thanks to the good work of our intelligence officials.

I believe this information will confirm the value of interrogations—and I am not alone. President Obama's own Director of National Intelligence, Admiral Blair, has put it this way: "High-value information came from interrogations in which those methods were used and provided a deeper understanding of the al-Qaeda organization that was attacking this country." End quote. Admiral Blair put that conclusion in writing, only to see it mysteriously deleted in a later version released by the administration—the missing 26 words that tell an inconvenient truth. But they couldn't change the words of George Tenet, the CIA Director under Presidents Clinton and Bush, who bluntly said: "I know that this program has saved lives. I know we've disrupted plots. I know this program alone is worth more than the FBI, the Central Intelligence Agency, and the National Security Agency put together have been able to tell us." End quote. If Americans do get the chance to learn what our country was spared, it'll do more than clarify the urgency and the rightness of enhanced interrogations in the years after 9/11. It may help us to stay focused on dangers that have not gone away. Instead of idly debating which political opponents to prosecute and punish, our attention will return to where it belongs—on the continuing threat of terrorist violence, and on stopping the men who are planning it.

For all the partisan anger that still lingers, our administration will stand up well in history—not despite our actions after 9/11, but because of them. And when I think about all that was to come during our administration and afterward—the recriminations, the second-guessing, the charges of "hubris"—my mind always goes back to that moment.

To put things in perspective, suppose that on the evening of 9/11, President Bush and I had promised that for as long as we held office—which was to be another 2,689 days—there would never be another terrorist attack inside this country. Talk about hubris—it would have seemed a rash and irresponsible thing to say. People would have doubted that we even understood the enormity of what had just happened. Everyone had a very bad feeling about all of this, and felt certain that the Twin Towers, the Pentagon, and Shanksville were only the beginning of the violence.

Of course, we made no such promise. Instead, we promised an all-out effort to protect this country. We said we would marshal all elements of our nation's power to fight this war and to win it. We said we would never forget what had happened on 9/11, even if the day came when many others did forget. We spoke of a war that would "include dramatic strikes, visible on TV, and covert operations, secret even in success." We followed through on all of this, and we stayed true to our word.

To the very end of our administration, we kept al-Qaeda terrorists busy with other problems. We focused on getting their secrets, instead of sharing ours with them. And on our watch, they never hit this country again. After the most lethal and devastating terrorist attack ever, seven and a half years without a repeat is not a record to be rebuked and scorned, much less criminalized. It is a record to be continued until the danger has passed.

Along the way there were some hard calls. No decision of national security was ever made lightly and certainly never made in haste. As in all warfare, there have been costs—none higher than the sacrifices of those killed and wounded in our country's service. And even the most decisive victories can never take away the sorrow of losing so many of our own—all those innocent victims of 9/11 and the heroic souls who died trying to save them.

For all that we've lost in this conflict, the United States has never lost its moral bearings. And when the moral reckoning turns to the men known as high-value terrorists, I can assure you they were neither innocent nor victims. As for those who asked them questions and got answers: they did the right thing, they made our country safer, and a lot of Americans are alive today because of them.

Like so many others who serve America, they are not the kind to insist on a thank-you. But I will always be grateful to each one of them and proud to have served with them for a time in the same cause. They, and so many others, have given honorable service to our country through all the difficulties and all the dangers. I will always admire them and wish them well. And I am confident that this nation will never take their work, their dedication, or their achievements, for granted.

Thank you very much.

Address on Foreign Policy at the Council on Foreign Relations[*]

Hillary Rodham Clinton

U.S. Secretary of State, 2009– ; born Chicago, IL, October 26, 1947; B.A., Wellesley College, 1969; J.D., Yale University, 1973; postgraduate study on children and medicine at Yale Child Study Center, during which staff attorney at Children's Defense Fund and consultant to Carnegie Council on Children; advised House Committee on the Judiciary, 1974; joined faculty of School of Law at University of Arkansas, Fayetteville, 1974; joined Rose Law Firm, 1977, became full partner, 1979; First Lady of Arkansas, 1979–1981, 1983–1992; First Lady of the United States, 1993–2000; chair, Task Force on National Health Care Reform, 1993–94; U.S. senator (D), New York, 2001–09; committees: Budget; Armed Services; Environment and Public Works; Health, Education, Labor and Pensions; Aging; commissioner, Commission on Security and Cooperation in Europe (2001–08); author, It Takes a Village and Other Lessons Children Teach Us *(1996),* An Invitation to the White House: At Home with History *(2000),* Living History *(2004).*

Editor's introduction: Starting with a litany of the challenges facing the global community, Secretary of State Clinton calls for concerted action on the part of all nations, in this speech delivered before the Council on Foreign Relations. She outlines the (many) priorities of the Obama Administration, including averting the spread of nuclear weapons, defeating terrorism, and seeking Middle East peace. We must move away from a multi-polar world toward a multi-partner world, Clinton insists, but also stresses that this emphasis on cooperation does not rule out the use of force. At the same time, drawing a clear distinction between the new administration and the previous one, she disavows a policy of "you're either with us or against us" on the part of the United States in international relations. She outlines the administration's foreign-policy philosophy and tactics and touches on such difficult issues as the nuclear programs of Iran and North Korea.

Hillary Clinton's speech: Thank you very much, Richard, and I am delighted to be here in these new headquarters. I have been often to, I guess, the mother ship in New York City, but it's good to have an outpost of the Council right here down

---

[*] Delivered on July 15, 2009, at Washington, D.C.

the street from the State Department. We get a lot of advice from the Council, so this will mean I won't have as far to go to be told what we should be doing and how we should think about the future.

Richard just gave what could be described as a mini-version of my remarks in talking about the issues that confront us. But I look out at this audience filled with not only many friends and colleagues, but people who have served in prior administrations. And so there is never a time when the in-box is not full.

Shortly before I started at the State Department, a former Secretary of State called me with this advice: Don't try to do too much. And it seemed like a wise admonition, if only it were possible. But the international agenda today is unforgiving: two wars, conflict in the Middle East, ongoing threats of violent extremism and nuclear proliferation, global recession, climate change, hunger and disease, and a widening gap between the rich and the poor. All of these challenges affect America's security and prosperity, and they all threaten global stability and progress.

But they are not reason to despair about the future. The same forces that compound our problems—economic interdependence, open borders, and the speedy movement of information, capital, goods, services and people—are also part of the solution. And with more states facing common challenges, we have the chance, and a profound responsibility, to exercise American leadership to solve problems in concert with others. That is the heart of America's mission in the world today.

Now, some see the rise of other nations and our economic troubles here at home as signs that American power has waned. Others simply don't trust us to lead; they view America as an unaccountable power, too quick to impose its will at the expense of their interests and our principles. But they are wrong.

The question is not whether our nation can or should lead, but how it will lead in the 21st century. Rigid ideologies and old formulas don't apply. We need a new mindset about how America will use its power to safeguard our nation, expand shared prosperity, and help more people in more places live up to their God-given potential.

President Obama has led us to think outside the usual boundaries. He has launched a new era of engagement based on common interests, shared values, and mutual respect. Going forward, capitalizing on America's unique strengths, we must advance those interests through partnership, and promote universal values through the power of our example and the empowerment of people. In this way, we can forge the global consensus required to defeat the threats, manage the dangers, and seize the opportunities of the 21st century. America will always be a world leader as long as we remain true to our ideals and embrace strategies that match the times. So we will exercise American leadership to build partnerships and solve problems that no nation can solve on its own, and we will pursue policies to mobilize more partners and deliver results.

First, though, let me say that while the ideas that shape our foreign policy are critically important, this, for me, is not simply an intellectual exercise. For over 16 years, I've had the chance, the privilege, really, to represent our country overseas as First Lady, as a senator, and now as Secretary of State. I've seen the bellies of starving children, girls sold into human trafficking, men dying of treatable diseases, women denied the right to own property or vote, and young people without schooling or jobs gripped by a sense of futility about their futures.

I've also seen how hope, hard work, and ingenuity can overcome the longest of odds. And for almost 36 years, I have worked as an advocate for children, women and families here at home. I've traveled across our country listening to everyday concerns of our citizens. I've met parents struggling to keep their jobs, pay their mortgages, cover their children's college tuitions, and afford health care.

And all that I have done and seen has convinced me that our foreign policy must produce results for people—the laid-off auto worker in Detroit whose future will depend on global economic recovery; the farmer or small business owner in the developing world whose lack of opportunity can drive political instability and economic stagnation; the families whose loved ones are risking their lives for our country in Iraq and Afghanistan and elsewhere; children in every land who deserve a brighter future. These are the people—hundreds of millions of them here in America and billions around the world—whose lives and experiences, hopes and dreams, must inform the decisions we take and the actions that follow. And these are the people who inspire me and my colleagues and the work that we try to do every day.

In approaching our foreign policy priorities, we have to deal with the urgent, the important, and the long-term all at once. But even as we are forced to multi-task— a very gender-related term—we must have priorities, which President Obama has outlined in speeches from Prague to Cairo, from Moscow to Accra. We want to reverse the spread of nuclear weapons, prevent their use, and build a world free of their threat. We want to isolate and defeat terrorists and counter violent extremists while reaching out to Muslims around the world. We want to encourage and facilitate the efforts of all parties to pursue and achieve a comprehensive peace in the Middle East. We want to seek global economic recovery and growth by strengthening our own economy, advancing a robust development agenda, expanding trade that is free and fair, and boosting investment that creates decent jobs. We want to combat climate change, increase energy security, and lay the foundation for a prosperous clean-energy future. We want to support and encourage democratic governments that protect the rights and deliver results for their people. And we intend to stand up for human rights everywhere.

Liberty, democracy, justice and opportunity underlie our priorities. Some accuse us of using these ideals to justify actions that contradict their very meaning. Others say we are too often condescending and imperialistic, seeking only to expand our power at the expense of others. And yes, these perceptions have fed anti-Americanism, but they do not reflect who we are. No doubt we lost some ground in recent years, but the damage is temporary. It's kind of like my elbow—it's getting better every day.

Whether in Latin America or Lebanon, Iran or Liberia, those who are inspired by democracy, who understand that democracy is about more than just elections—that it must also protect minority rights and press freedom, develop strong, competent and independent judiciaries, legislatures and executive agencies, and commit for democracy to deliver results—these are the people who will find that Americans are their friends, not adversaries. As President Obama made clear last week in Ghana, this Administration will stand for accountable and transparent governance, and support those who work to build democratic institutions wherever they live.

Our approach to foreign policy must reflect the world as it is, not as it used to be. It does not make sense to adapt a 19th century concert of powers, or a 20th century balance of power strategy. We cannot go back to Cold War containment or to unilateralism.

Today, we must acknowledge two inescapable facts that define our world: First, no nation can meet the world's challenges alone. The issues are too complex. Too many players are competing for influence, from rising powers to corporations to criminal cartels; from NGOs to al-Qaida; from state-controlled media to individuals using Twitter.

Second, most nations worry about the same global threats, from non-proliferation to fighting disease to counter-terrorism, but also face very real obstacles—for reasons of history, geography, ideology, and inertia. They face these obstacles and they stand in the way of turning commonality of interest into common action.

So these two facts demand a different global architecture—one in which states have clear incentives to cooperate and live up to their responsibilities, as well as strong disincentives to sit on the sidelines or sow discord and division.

So we will exercise American leadership to overcome what foreign policy experts at places like the Council call "collective action problems" and what I call obstacles to cooperation. For just as no nation can meet these challenges alone, no challenge can be met without America.

And here's how we'll do it: We'll work through existing institutions and reform them. But we'll go further. We'll use our power to convene, our ability to connect countries around the world, and sound foreign policy strategies to create partnerships aimed at solving problems. We'll go beyond states to create opportunities for non-state actors and individuals to contribute to solutions.

We believe this approach will advance our interests by uniting diverse partners around common concerns. It will make it more difficult for others to abdicate their responsibilities or abuse their power, but will offer a place at the table to any nation, group, or citizen willing to shoulder a fair share of the burden. In short, we will lead by inducing greater cooperation among a greater number of actors and reducing competition, tilting the balance away from a multi-polar world and toward a multi-partner world.

Now, we know this approach is not a panacea. We will remain clear-eyed about our purpose. Not everybody in the world wishes us well or shares our values and interests. And some will actively seek to undermine our efforts. In those cases, our partnerships can become power coalitions to constrain or deter those negative actions.

And to these foes and would-be foes, let me say our focus on diplomacy and development is not an alternative to our national security arsenal. Our willingness to talk is not a sign of weakness to be exploited. We will not hesitate to defend our friends, our interests, and above all, our people vigorously and when necessary with the world's strongest military. This is not an option we seek nor is it a threat; it is a promise to all Americans.

Building the architecture of global cooperation requires us to devise the right policies and use the right tools. I speak often of smart power because it is so central to our thinking and our decision-making. It means the intelligent use of all means at our disposal, including our ability to convene and connect. It means our economic and military strength; our capacity for entrepreneurship and innovation; and the ability and credibility of our new President and his team. It also means the application of old-fashioned common sense in policymaking. It's a blend of principle and pragmatism.

Smart power translates into specific policy approaches in five areas. First, we intend to update and create vehicles for cooperation with our partners; second, we will pursue principled engagement with those who disagree with us; third, we will elevate development as a core pillar of American power; fourth, we will integrate civilian and military action in conflict areas; and fifth, we will leverage key sources of American power, including our economic strength and the power of our example.

Our first approach is to build these stronger mechanisms of cooperation with our historic allies, with emerging powers, and with multilateral institutions, and to pursue that cooperation in, as I said, a pragmatic and principled way. We don't see those as in opposition, but as complementary.

We have started by reinvigorating our bedrock alliances, which did fray in recent years. In Europe, that means improved bilateral relationships, a more productive partnership with the European Union, and a revitalized NATO. I believe NATO is the greatest alliance in history. But it was built for the Cold War. The new NATO is a democratic community of nearly a billion people stretching from the Baltics in the East to Alaska in the West. We're working to update its strategic concept so that it is as effective in this century as it was in the last.

At the same time, we are working with our key treaty allies Japan and Korea, Australia, Thailand, and the Philippines and other partners to strengthen our bilateral relationships as well as trans-Pacific institutions. We are both a trans-Atlantic and a trans-Pacific nation.

We will also put special emphasis on encouraging major and emerging global powers—China, India, Russia and Brazil, as well as Turkey, Indonesia, and South Africa—to be full partners in tackling the global agenda. I want to underscore the importance of this task, and my personal commitment to it. These states are vital to achieving solutions to the shared problems and advancing our priorities—nonproliferation, counterterrorism, economic growth, climate change, among others. With these states, we will stand firm on our principles even as we seek common ground.

This week, I will travel to India, where External Affairs Minister Krishna and I will lay out a broad-based agenda that calls for a whole-of-government approach to our bilateral relationship. Later this month, Secretary Geithner and I will jointly lead our new strategic and economic dialogue with China. It will cover not just economic issues, but the range of strategic challenges we face together. In the fall, I will travel to Russia to advance the bi-national presidential commission that Foreign Minister Lavrov and I will co-chair.

The fact of these and other meetings does not guarantee results, but they set in motion processes and relationships that will widen our avenues of cooperation and narrow the areas of disagreement without illusion. We know that progress will not likely come quickly, or without bumps in the road, but we are determined to begin and stay on this path.

Now our global and regional institutions were built for a world that has been transformed, so they too must be transformed and reformed. As the President said following the recent G-8 meeting in Italy, we are seeking institutions that "combine the efficiency and capacity for action with inclusiveness." From the UN to the World Bank, from the IMF to the G-8 and the G-20, from the OAS and the Summit of the Americas to ASEAN and APEC—all of these and other institutions have a role to play, but their continued vitality and relevance depend on their legitimacy and representativeness, and the ability of their members to act swiftly and responsibly when problems arise.

We also will reach out beyond governments, because we believe partnerships with people play a critical role in our 21st century statecraft. President Obama's Cairo speech is a powerful example of communicating directly with people from the bottom up. And we are following up with a comprehensive agenda of educational exchanges, outreach, and entrepreneurial ventures. In every country I visit, I look for opportunities to bolster civil society and engage with citizens, whether at a town hall in Baghdad—a first in that country; or appearing on local popular television shows that reach a wide and young audience; or meeting with democracy activists, war widows, or students.

I have appointed special envoys to focus on a number of specific challenges, including the first Ambassador for Global Women's Issues and an ambassador to build new public-private partnerships and to engage diaspora communities in the United States to increase opportunities in their native lands. And we are working at the State Department to ensure that our government is using the most innovative technologies not only to speak and listen across borders, not only to keep technologies up and going, but to widen opportunities especially for those who are too often left on the margins. We're taking these steps because reaching out directly to people will encourage them to embrace cooperation with us, making our partnerships with their governments and with them stronger and more durable.

We've also begun to adopt a more flexible and pragmatic posture with our partners. We won't agree on every issue. Standing firm on our principles shouldn't prevent us from working together where we can. So we will not tell our partners to take it or leave it, nor will we insist that they're either with us or against us. In today's world, that's global malpractice.

Our diplomacy regarding North Korea is a case in point. We have invested a significant amount of diplomatic resources to achieve Security Council consensus in response to North Korea's provocative actions. I spoke numerous times to my counterparts in Japan, South Korea, Russia and China, drawing out their concerns, making our principles and redlines clear, and seeking a path forward. The short-term results were two unanimous Security Council resolutions with real teeth and consequences for North Korea, and then the follow-on active involvement of China, Russia, and India with us in persuading others to comply with the resolutions. The long-term result, we believe, will be a tougher joint effort toward the complete and verifiable denuclearization of the Korean Peninsula.

Cultivating these partnerships and their full range takes time and patience. It also takes persistence. That doesn't mean procrastinating on urgent issues. Nor is it a justification for delaying efforts that may take years to bear fruit. In one of my favorite observations, Max Weber said, "Politics is the long and slow boring of hard boards. It takes both passion and perspective." Perspective dictates passion and patience. And of course, passion keeps us from not finding excuses to do nothing.

Now I'm well aware that time alone does not heal all wounds; consider the Palestinian-Israeli conflict. That's why we wasted no time in starting an intensive effort on day one to realize the rights of Palestinians and Israelis to live in peace and security in two states, which is in America's interests and the world's. We've been working with the Israelis to deal with the issue of settlements, to ease the living conditions of Palestinians, and create circumstances that can lead to the establishment of a viable Palestinian state. For the last few decades, American administrations have held consistent positions on the settlement issue. And while we expect action from Israel, we recognize that these decisions are politically challenging.

And we know that progress toward peace cannot be the responsibility of the United States—or Israel—alone. Ending the conflict requires action on all sides. The Palestinians have the responsibility to improve and extend the positive actions already taken on security; to act forcefully against incitement; and to refrain from any action that would make meaningful negotiations less likely.

And Arab states have a responsibility to support the Palestinian Authority with words and deeds, to take steps to improve relations with Israel, and to prepare their publics to embrace peace and accept Israel's place in the region. The Saudi peace proposal, supported by more than twenty nations, was a positive step. But we believe that more is needed. So we are asking those who embrace the proposal to take meaningful steps now. Anwar Sadat and King Hussein crossed important thresholds, and their boldness and vision mobilized peace constituencies in Israel and paved the way for lasting agreements. By providing support to the Palestinians and offering an opening, however modest, to the Israelis, the Arab states could have the same impact. So I say to all sides: Sending messages of peace is not enough. You must also act against the cultures of hate, intolerance and disrespect that perpetuate conflict.

Our second policy approach is to lead with diplomacy, even in the cases of adversaries or nations with whom we disagree. We believe that doing so advances our interests and puts us in a better position to lead with our other partners. We cannot be afraid or unwilling to engage. Yet some suggest that this is a sign of naiveté or acquiescence to these countries' repression of their own people. I believe that is wrong. As long as engagement might advance our interests and our values, it is unwise to take it off the table. Negotiations can provide insight into regimes' calculations and the possibility—even if it seems remote—that a regime will eventually alter its behavior in exchange for the benefits of acceptance into the international community. Libya is one such example. Exhausting the option for dialogue is also more likely to make our partners more willing to exert pressure should persuasion fail.

With this in mind, I want to say a few words about Iran. We watched the energy of Iran's election with great admiration, only to be appalled by the manner in which the government used violence to quell the voices of the Iranian people, and then tried to hide its actions by arresting foreign journalists and nationals, and expelling them, and cutting off access to technology. As we and our G-8 partners have made clear, these actions are deplorable and unacceptable.

We know very well what we inherited with Iran, because we deal with that inheritance every day. We know that refusing to deal with the Islamic Republic has not succeeded in altering the Iranian march toward a nuclear weapon, reducing Iranian support for terror, or improving Iran's treatment of its citizens.

Neither the President nor I have any illusions that dialogue with the Islamic Republic will guarantee success of any kind, and the prospects have certainly shifted in the weeks following the election. But we also understand the importance of offering to engage Iran and giving its leaders a clear choice: whether to join the international community as a responsible member or to continue down a path to further isolation.

Direct talks provide the best vehicle for presenting and explaining that choice. That is why we offered Iran's leaders an unmistakable opportunity: Iran does not have a right to nuclear military capacity, and we're determined to prevent that. But it does have a right to civil nuclear power if it reestablishes the confidence of the international community that it will use its programs exclusively for peaceful purposes.

Iran can become a constructive actor in the region if it stops threatening its neighbors and supporting terrorism. It can assume a responsible position in the international community if it fulfills its obligations on human rights. The choice is clear. We remain ready to engage with Iran, but the time for action is now. The opportunity will not remain open indefinitely.

Our third policy approach, and a personal priority for me as Secretary, is to elevate and integrate development as a core pillar of American power. We advance our security, our prosperity, and our values by improving the material conditions of people's lives around the world. These efforts also lay the groundwork for greater global cooperation, by building the capacity of new partners and tackling shared problems from the ground up.

A central purpose of the Quadrennial Diplomacy and Development Review that I announced last week is to explore how to effectively design, fund, and implement development and foreign assistance as part of a broader foreign policy. Let's face it. We have devoted a smaller percentage of our government budget to development than almost any other advanced country. And too little of what we have spent has contributed to genuine and lasting progress. Too much of the money has never reached its intended target, but stayed here in America to pay salaries or fund overhead in contracts. I am committed to more partnerships with NGOs, but I want more of our tax dollars to be used effectively and to deliver tangible results.

As we seek more agile, effective, and creative partnerships for development, we will focus on country-driven solutions, such as those we are launching with Haiti on recovery and sustainable development, and with African states on global hunger. These initiatives must not be designed to help countries scrape by—they are a tool to help countries stand on their own.

Our development agenda will also focus on women as drivers of economic growth and social stability. Women have long comprised the majority of the world's unhealthy, unschooled, and underfed. They are also the bulk of the world's poor. The global recession has had a disproportionate effect on women and girls, which in turn has repercussions for families, communities, and even regions. Until women around the world are accorded their rights—and afforded the opportunities of education, health care, and gainful employment—global progress and prosperity will have its own glass ceiling.

Our fourth approach is to ensure that our civilian and military efforts operate in a coordinated and complementary fashion where we are engaged in conflict. This is the core of our strategy in Afghanistan and Iraq, where we are integrating our efforts with international partners.

In Afghanistan and Pakistan, our goal is to disrupt, dismantle, and ultimately defeat al-Qaida and its extremist allies, and to prevent their return to either country. Yet Americans often ask, why do we ask our young men and women to risk their lives in Afghanistan when al-Qaida's leadership is in neighboring Pakistan? And that question deserves a good answer: We and our allies fight in Afghanistan because the Taliban protects al-Qaida and depends on it for support, sometimes coordinating activities. In other words, to eliminate al-Qaida, we must also fight the Taliban.

Now, we understand that not all those who fight with the Taliban support al-Qaida, or believe in the extremist policies the Taliban pursued when in power. And today we and our Afghan allies stand ready to welcome anyone supporting the Taliban who renounces al-Qaida, lays down their arms, and is willing to participate in the free and open society that is enshrined in the Afghan Constitution.

To achieve our goals, President Obama is sending an additional 17,000 troops and 4,000 military trainers to Afghanistan. Equally important, we are sending hundreds of direct-hire American civilians to lead a new effort to strengthen the Afghan Government, help rebuild the once-vibrant agricultural sector, create jobs, encourage the rule of law, expand opportunities for women, and train the Afghan police. No one should doubt our commitment to Afghanistan and its people. But it is the Afghan people themselves who will determine their own future.

As we proceed, we must not forget that success in Afghanistan also requires close cooperation from neighboring Pakistan, which I will visit this fall. Pakistan is itself under intense pressure from extremist groups. Trilateral cooperation among Afghanistan, Pakistan, and the United States has built confidence and yielded progress on a number of policy fronts. Our national security, as well as the future of Afghanistan, depends on a stable, democratic, and economically viable Pakistan. And we applaud the new Pakistani determination to deal with the militants who threaten their democracy and our shared security.

In Iraq, we are bolstering our diplomacy and development programs while we implement a responsible withdrawal of our troops. Last month our combat troops successfully redeployed from towns and cities. Our principal focus is now shifting from security issues to civilian efforts that promote Iraqi capacity—supporting the work of the Iraqi ministries and aiding in their efforts to achieve national unity. And we are developing a long-term economic and political relationship with Iraq as outlined by the US-Iraq Strategic Framework Agreement. This Agreement forms the basis of our future cooperation with Iraq and the Iraqi people, and I look forward to discussing it and its implementation with Prime Minister Maliki when he comes to Washington next week.

Our fifth approach is to shore up traditional sources of our influence, including economic strength and the power of our example. We renewed our own values by prohibiting torture and beginning to close the Guantanamo Bay detention facility. And we have been straightforward about our own measure of responsibility for problems like drug trafficking in Mexico and global climate change. When I acknowledged the obvious about our role in Mexico's current conflict with narco-traffickers, some were critical. But they're missing the point. Our capacity to take responsibility, and our willingness to change, to do the right thing, are themselves hallmarks of our greatness as a nation and strategic assets that can help us forge coalitions in the service of our interests.

That is certainly true when it comes to key priorities like nonproliferation and climate change. President Obama is committed to the vision of a world without nuclear weapons and a series of concrete steps to reduce the threat and spread of these weapons, including working with the Senate to ratify the follow-on START agreement and the Comprehensive Test Ban Treaty, taking on greater responsibility within the Non Proliferation Treaty Framework and convening the world's leaders here in Washington next year for a nuclear summit. Now we must urge others to take practical steps to advance our shared nonproliferation agenda.

Our Administration is also committed to deep reductions in greenhouse gas emissions, with a plan that will dramatically change the way we produce, consume and conserve energy, and in the process spark an explosion of new investment, and millions of jobs. Now we must urge every other nation to meet its obligations and seize the opportunities of a clean energy future.

We are restoring our economy at home to enhance our strength and capacity abroad, especially at this time of economic turmoil. Now, this is not a traditional priority for a Secretary of State, but I vigorously support American recovery and growth as a pillar of our global leadership. And I am committed to restoring a significant role for the State Department within a whole-of-government approach to international economic policy-making. We will work to ensure that our economic statecraft—trade and investment, debt forgiveness, loan guarantees, technical assistance, decent work practices—support our foreign policy objectives. When coupled with a sound development effort, our economic outreach can give us a better form of globalization, reducing the bitter opposition of recent years and lifting millions more out of poverty.

And finally, I am determined to ensure that the men and women of our Foreign and Civil Service have the resources they need to implement our priorities effectively and safely. That's why I appointed for the first time a Deputy Secretary for Management and Resources. It's why we worked so hard to secure additional funding for State and USAID. It's why we have put ourselves on a path to double foreign assistance over the next few years. And it's why we are implementing a plan to dramatically increase the number of diplomats and development experts.

Just as we would never deny ammunition to American troops headed into battle, we cannot send our civilian personnel into the field underequipped. If we don't invest in diplomacy and development, we will end up paying a lot more for conflicts and their consequences. As Secretary Gates has said, diplomacy is an indispensable instrument of national security, as it has been since Franklin, Jefferson and Adams won foreign support for Washington's army.

Now all of this adds up to a very ambitious agenda. But the world does not afford us the luxury of choosing or waiting. As I said at the outset, we must tackle the urgent, the important and the long-term all at once.

We are both witness to and makers of significant change. We cannot and should not be passive observers. We are determined to channel the currents of change toward a world free of violent extremism, nuclear weapons, global warming, poverty, and abuses of human rights, and above all, a world in which more people in more places can live up to their God-given potential.

The architecture of cooperation we seek to build will advance all these goals, using our power not to dominate or divide but to solve problems. It is the architecture of progress for America and all nations.

More than 230 years ago, Thomas Paine said, "We have it within our power to start the world over again." Today, in a new and very different era, we are called upon to use that power. I believe we have the right strategy, the right priorities, the right policies, we have the right President, and we have the American people, diverse, committed, and open to the future.

Now all we have to do is deliver. Thank you all very much.

2

The Future of Journalism and the Media

What Public Broadcasting Can Learn from Commercial Media, and Vice Versa[*]

Vivian Schiller

President and CEO, National Public Radio (NPR), 2008– ; born Larchmont, NY, September 13, 1961; B.A. in Russian and Soviet studies, Cornell University, 1983, M.A., Russian, Middlebury College, 1984; Russian interpreter, 1985–88; various positions at Turner Broadcasting, starting with production assistant/fixer and moving up to senior vice president of TBS Productions, 1988–1998; senior vice president, CNN Productions, 1998–2002; founder and general manager, Discovery Times Channel, 2002–06; senior vice president and general manager, NYTimes.com, 2006–08.

Editor's introduction: In this speech delivered to the National Press Club, Vivian Schiller, the new CEO of NPR, draws on her background in commercial media to discuss how public and private media can learn from each other. She advises the public media to embrace more bottom-line thinking and a sense of urgency vis-à-vis new media and the economic crisis. She also encourages the sector to focus on its audience through self-promotion and working to expand its reach into minority communities. Regarding what the commercial media could emulate, she names public radio's highly personal relationship with its audience, its brand identity, aspects of its business model, and its robust national network. As to how to improve public radio, she recommends that it expand into other platforms while maintaining its primary loyalty to radio. Among the goals she outlines for public media are greater collaboration, increased newsgathering, multi-platform programming, and more audience involvement.

Vivian Schiller's speech: Thank you, Donna, for that very uplifting introduction. Before I start, I just want to acknowledge a couple of people in the room, aside from Donna. No, I really did appreciate your welcome in all seriousness. And there are some of my colleagues from across Public Broadcasting: Paula Kerger, who's the president and CEO of PBS, Pat Harrison, who is the president and CEO of the Corporation for Public Broadcasting, Antoine Van Agtmael, who, as

* Delivered on March 2, 2009, at Washington, D.C. Reprinted with permission.

you heard, is a member of our board and the head of the NPR Foundation, a very important institution for us, also my colleagues from WAMU. They are the ones that executed and survived that recent pledge drive that Donna referred to.

I have several colleagues here from NPR. And I really appreciate their presence. And lastly, my husband, Phil Frank, who's braved the drive from Bethesda to be here.

After eight weeks on the job—I started January 5th—I may be the newest person in the room to public broadcasting. As Donna mentioned, I've been in commercial media for more than two decades, in TV, both at CNN and at Discovery, and in print and digital media at *The New York Times*.

I've been really fortunate or have always chosen to be part of companies that have a strong public service mission at their center. But nonetheless, they all share the characteristic that they are commercial companies who, at the end of the day, are beholden to shareholders. So this is my first experience, not only in radio, but in a non-commercial organization, a place that funds itself, depending on the day of the week, for either survival or growth but is on its own, beholden to no financial stakeholders.

And just in the short time that I've been on the job, many people have asked me, you know, what do different forms of media have in common, other than, as we heard, a very difficult economy? Who does what better? How is it different? Who has the better model? There's no simple answer to that. But I do have some observations that I'd like to share with you, and that's what I'm going to focus on today.

I have, for the sake of symmetry, sort of five lessons going one way and then five on the other. So I'm going to begin by discussing what, I believe, again based on my eight weeks of experience and observations, that NPR and perhaps public radio and perhaps public broadcasting can learn from commercial media.

Number one is more bottom line thinking. Certainly for a publicly-traded company, the attention of Wall Street can lead to very short-term thinking, which could sometimes lead to very bad decisions. And that is not something that we . . . [inaudible]. But it also leads to a very rigorous, ongoing evaluation of the business and its returns. And I think that is something that certainly we at NPR and across public radio, perhaps across public broadcasting, could do a better job at.

Too much money sometimes is spent on too many programs, on the local and national level, that aren't really effectively reaching an audience. Sometimes we do things because we've always done them without stopping to think, if we were inventing this today, how would we do it differently? And I think that this is something that, again, certainly across public radio, we could learn from our brethren in commercial media.

The second lesson I think is a sense of urgency, some might call it fear. Public radio has never, in my opinion, faced the major disruptive challenges that commercial media have. We certainly are in radio, and we're going to talk about the power of radio a little bit later. But TV and newspapers, I think, have faced in their history much more dramatic, disruptive challenges than radio has. Certainly AM to FM was one, but not on the scale of, you know, radio back in the old days to television, television to broadcast television to cable, et cetera.

And of course now we are all in it together and facing digital media. When I say facing, embracing digital media. But we could become more nimble and innovative in this sense. The third is a focus on audience. Commercial media (you know, and I'll specifically use, the example of television news; most of what I'm talking about has to do with news in journalism) pays a lot of attention to audience ratings, to a fault. Again, too much attention can be a bad thing, when I believe that, as journalists, we should not be so beholden to the 15-second segmentation of how audiences are behaving, that we craft everything down to that level. We need to follow our gut. So being too obsessive can be a detriment to journalism.

On the other hand, I think we could do a much better job of listening to our audience, asking our audience what they think, and serving the audience the kind of programming that they want and they deserve and they expect from us. Again, it's a balance as journalists. There are stories that the audience would never think that we would want, and we're going to give it to them. And that level of serendipity should never be lost. And I think it does go too far in some areas of cable news. But we should pay more attention to the audience.

The fourth lesson that NPR can learn from commercial media is, to do a little bit better job in reaching diverse audiences. At NPR, in terms of NPR programming, in many ways we reach very diverse audiences when it comes to political orientation. That was a delightful surprise to me, just coming from other news organizations. We've all been, you know, both at CNN and *The New York Times*, there are always claims, even if they're unsubstantiated, of bias in one direction or another. But at NPR our audience is remarkably almost perfectly balanced among people who describe themselves as conservative, conservative leaning, liberal, or liberal leaning.

But we are not doing a good enough job in reaching people of color and other diverse groups. I mean, I will point to CNN as doing a very good job. It has grown its African-American audience by 35 percent this year through its programming efforts. And they're doing it not purely as a public service, but because they realize it's good business. Public radio, certainly it is our mission to serve all audiences. We don't do it just because, well, gosh, we think we should, but because we must. In reaching audiences, we must reach a greater diversity of listeners.

And the fifth thing I think that NPR and public radio can learn from commercial media is to not be so shy about shouting from the hilltops what we have. I think we do not do nearly a good enough job promoting and marketing ourselves. You know, I almost get the sense when I have conversations about this that there's a reticence, that there's something a little bit unseemly about saying, "You know what? We do this really well. Our audience appreciates it." We have an astounding audience. In fact, I'm not going to be reticent and you're going to hear me talk a little bit about that audience with no shyness whatsoever in a couple of minutes.

But, you know, promoting and marketing yourself is not just a matter—is not purely self-serving. It's also a service to help the listener. Marketing and advertising exist for a reason; they help people to make informed choices. Obviously people look at advertising as distinct from news reporting, no question about it. But it's part of the service that we should provide. And I think we can do a better job.

I've been doing a number of media interviews. And with John Friedman, who writes the Market Watch column, you know, I went on. I'm generally, by nature, a very sort of hyper-caffeinated person, as those of you who work with me and those of you that live with me know. But in my interview with him, I was going on about, "NPR, we do this," blah, blah, blah. And in his column, he called me a carnival barker, which at first I thought, "Gosh, couldn't he say 'enthusiastic advocate' or something?" But, you know, I decided carnival barker's okay. And if carnival barker's what it takes, then so be it.

Now, I'm going to turn the tables a little bit, and tell you, based on my observations, having just come recently from that world, what I think NPR and public radio have, and, in some cases, public broadcasting has, that commercial media, would kill for.

Number one is our audience. You know, I think the audience factor, which really came home to me when my job was announced—it was [the] beginning of November when the announcement went out. And it got a bit of coverage on NPR obviously, and *The New York Times*, and several other places. And I heard from just about everybody that I'd ever known. I got a lot of voice-mails. And I got over a thousand e-mails from people that I've known through various stages of my career, because I've moved around a little bit.

First of all, it was very nice, of course. And I spent my month off in December answering every one of those e-mails. But as I read through them, something really profound struck me. Which is, they were all the same, in the sense that, the first sentence of every e-mail was something that said, "Oh, congratulations. I'm happy for you," you know, blah, blah, blah. And then the second sentence, and the rest of the e-mail, every single one was an expression of what NPR means to them (and when I say NPR, even people that say NPR don't really know—I mean, they say NPR, but they could be listening to a show from PRI, APM, from their local broadcaster. They really mean public radio. So please understand that I interpret it that way).

And it was always very, very, very personal. It was a show that they planned their commute around, or it was a story that touched them and actually motivated them to action, or it was a reporter or an anchor they have sort of a natural obsession with—whatever it was, it was very intimate. And there was almost a sense in each one of these emailers, that "NPR is mine. It belongs to me."

And I realized what we have that is so extraordinary is a relationship with our audience, and a huge audience (I'll mention that in a minute) that has a relationship with us, not just on an intellectual level, as they certainly do, but on a very emotional level. And that is a powerful thing. I know of no other media company that has sort of that connection in the head and the heart that public radio does.

And by the way, in huge numbers—26 million people tune into some NPR program through, of course, their local station on a weekly level. That is more than the top circulation of the top 50 U.S. newspapers combined. That's a lot of people. *Morning Edition*, just to give you a couple more statistics about what an impact we have—and this is where that carnival barker comes in, so forgive me—*Morning Edition* has a larger audience than any of the network morning shows. The next biggest one is *The Today Show*. And our audience is 45 percent bigger than *Today Show* viewing.

Car Talk is more than twice as much—so, as we say, we're not just serious stuff, so I'm going to compare *Car Talk* to less serious stuff. *Car Talk* is twice as big as the audience for *The Daily Show* and *The Colbert Report* combined. That's pretty powerful. And it's growing. So there's audience.

Brand is the second thing. You know, with the possible exception of *The New York Times*, I really know of no other media company that evokes the kind of brand loyalty that NPR does as an entity. There are certainly forms of media, other branded media, that have larger audiences. Facebook has 175 million active users, which is a mind-blowing number. But I don't think anybody goes, "God, I love Facebook." They love their connection to other people. It's not an affinity for the brand.

You know, in other broadcast media, in the case of television, it's the show. You know, the most successful show in the history of broadcast news is *60 Minutes*. And there's a lot of loyalty to *60 Minutes*. But that has not helped CBS with their other shows, necessarily. People don't think about CBS. They think about *60 Minutes*.

NBC's successful morning and evening shows have loyal audiences . . .[inaudible] I already mentioned. But they're really of no help to the prime-time lineup that has been in fourth place for the last—for years. So the loyalty there is to shows. With us, the loyalty is to the brand, which is very powerful.

People are the third thing. The people in public broadcasting, we are a small army. Actually, we're not even a small army. We're a large army. There are 8,000 people that work in public radio. That's across NPR and all of our stations. If you add public television to that, the total goes up—excuse me, did I say eight million? I meant 8,000. (Eight million? That would be something.) If you add public television to it, that's 23,000 people. Let me tell you something I know by experience. Nobody in public media is there because they think they're going to get rich fast, or even slow. They're all motivated by the mission. If we can all be working together, which is another issue we'll get into later, this is a very, very powerful force, again, unrivaled by anyone else in media.

Fourth is the business model. And I'm going to take a minute on this, because there's been a lot of talk in the media ("talk," I say that figuratively, blogs, what have you, columns in *The New York Times* and elsewhere), about the not-for-profit model, and some think that maybe commercial media should adopt that model, particularly newspapers. First, a lot of the information that's out there, I can tell you, is erroneous. And even where it's not erroneous, I think personally that it is a mistake for newspapers to think that their answer to the issues, the tragic issues that are facing newspapers today, lies in the business model of public radio.

First, let me just explain really, really briefly what our business model is, on a very top-line level. At NPR, sixty percent of our revenue comes from programming, programming fees and membership from the station. We have endowment income—excuse me, we have distributions from our endowment. We have gifts from philanthropists. We have money that comes to us from institutional foundations like the Ford Foundation. And all of those together equal another—what?—twenty-five, twenty-six percent, a little bit more than that.

We have underwriting and sponsorship. In the commercial world, we call that advertising, although—it is advertising. It's got certain rules around it that make it a little bit different, both on radio and online. And lastly, we do have some funding through the Corporation for Public Broadcasting. For NPR, that is less than one percent directly from the CPB, which is funded by the government. Stations who fund us are funded a level, about thirteen and fourteen percent.

So if you take those apart, what's there that can help commercial media? I think frankly, not much of any of them. Endowments, first of all, are not a silver bullet. We are fortunate to have an endowment that is anchored by a very large gift from Joan Kroc, for which we are very grateful. But an institution like *The New York Times*, for example, according to my own back-of-the-envelope calculation (I'm not a financier), I would think that that would have to be in the range of $5 billion dollars or more.

Donations, sure. If newspapers want to experiment with sort of tip jars on their websites, I think that's fine. I see no reason why there's a problem with that. But I don't believe it's really going to move the needle. Newspapers are now, as you know, looking at reinstituting the paywall on their sites after some of them took it down. I have a personal connection to this, which is that when I went to *New York Times*, I actually was the person who ended Times Select. And now they're looking at putting parts of it back. But, you know, it's all right. You know, hard times call for difficult measures.

And then there's government funding, you know, whether it comes through CPB or others. I don't believe that for news organizations, that is a path they should take for reasons of independence. You know, for us, it's a little bit different. The CPB money supports the platform. Originally, it supported the creation of the platform. We will potentially be seeking further funding for the stations, for the platform, but not for journalistic coverage. And so I want to be very clear about that.

So moving off the business model, the question is, is there something in there that commercial media can learn from public radio? Yes, certainly they can learn. But I don't think it's the answer.

And finally, the fifth element of what I think NPR has that commercial media would love to have, and perhaps the most important of all, is our national local system. This is really the secret sauce of public radio, and I think for public television in a similar way.

I could tell you in every place that I've ever been, we would have killed to have—or, excuse me, I shouldn't say that. We would have been very happy to have the kind of, you know, in the case of public radio, a national newsgathering power-house with 17 bureaus, in this country and around the world, supplying national/international news, and affiliations with local entities in every single city, state, and campus in America. This is a tremendously powerful asset. And it is tremendously powerful for us if we can figure out a way to work better together. I'll get back to that in a second.

So given all these lessons going either way, what do these lessons tell us in terms of the future of NPR, which is, of course, what I represent? And I'm going to leave commercial people alone and let them solve their own problems for the time being. And that is, if we take this incredibly powerful brand that I've talked about and the audience that is public radio, and we add into this stew the kind of bottom-line orientation, the good part of the bottom-line orientation from commercial media, and the urgency or the fear that this is an opportunity right now in these economically difficult times, like never before, and a moment that may not last, and we apply into this the fact that we are the national and local system that we are today, to me that is an incredibly powerful thing. And frankly it brings me and many of my colleagues at NPR (we spend a lot of time talking about this) to the inevitable conclusion that we must branch out into other platforms.

Now, let me just be really clear. This is not a repudiation of radio, not at all. Let me say that again. Radio is the heart and soul of our organization. It is where most of our audience is. And frankly, having been, now having worked in every single one, now including radio, of the so-called legacy media, I can tell you that I think in many ways, radio is the most resilient because of the way people use radio. You can't use radio in the way that you use other forms of media. So it is complementary to other platforms. We will continue to invest in it. It will continue to be the center.

So I want to make sure that that is really clear. But at our core, we are a content company whose increasingly rare strength, frankly, in the world of journalism is the quality of our original worldwide news, information, and cultural program-ming. And it is our responsibility, I believe, to deliver that to the audience however they choose to consume it, not the way we want them to consume it, but how they want us to deliver it—yeah, okay, you got that. Any way. This comes back to the whole audience thing.

You know, I look back, because I'm new and I don't have the history from the beginning of public broadcasting, I look back at the Public Broadcasting Act of 1967 to try to sort of understand, well, why was public broadcasting created in the first place? And when you read all the reasons, it really makes a lot of sense. Because we were filling a void that at the time was truly a void in terms of quality programming on television and elsewhere. And we remain, of course, the only source of free quality programming.

But I was looking at it and thinking about, well, what does it have to say? Or, if we were writing it today, what might it say that would give us some guidance of where we need to go?

So I'm going to try this line out on you, okay? All right? So here's the line. Tell me what you think afterwards. We must consider new ways to build a great network for knowledge, not just a broadcast system, but one that employs every means of sending and storing information that the individual can use. That's the line. Sounds very digital, doesn't it? Sound like somebody that's worked in digital media, comes out of Silicon Valley.

I didn't write that line. That was Lyndon Baines Johnson. Actually it was Bill Moyers, writing for LBJ. But he spoke the words. And it was part of the original Public Broadcasting Act. I don't have to tell you, it sort of knocked my socks off when I saw it. It's almost like they were anticipating the Internet before Al Gore invented it. But what they did was anticipate, I believe, everything: the need for us to reach out to our audience in every platform that exists.

So what do we need to do with this? Running out of time, so I'm going to move quickly through them. Number one, we must collaborate as a system on our journalism. We don't collaborate all that well. When we do, it works great. But there's a lot of room for improvement. I'm talking about NPR with public radio stations, with public television, with other not-for-profits outside the system. There are wonderful homegrown new public media entities that are springing up like ProPublica and Ground Report and other innovators. Maybe even with newspapers—we need to band together. Because those 23,000 people are really a powerful force.

Number two, we need to step up our newsgathering. This is not a time, while we're cutting elsewhere, that we can shrink from our responsibility. The audience tells us they want their public radio stations to cover their communities the way NPR covers the world. We need to help the stations that don't have the resources to cover their communities. And we will. We particularly need to strengthen on a local and national level an investigative journalism. Who, on a local and state level, will hold public officials accountable in a world where local newspapers are dying? We're quickly seeing this year many communities that have no local newspapers. And frankly, investigative journalism is what newspapers do best. We need to step into that void.

We must become a network on every platform—websites, mobile, and any way people choose to use us. Every station, every public radio station should have the support from NPR and others to become as indispensable online or on their iPhone or whatever it might be as they are in radio. And we need to figure out a way to count it and tell everyone what a powerful audience we have.

And lastly, we need to bring our audience into the dialogue. We have those passionate people who care so much and feel like they own NPR. They're a pretty extraordinary demographic. I know the same is true for public television. They have things to say. We can bring them into this process. We should become, not what we are today in our traditional media, one to many, but the many to many, many to many in terms of station to station, citizen to station, station to citizen, citizen to NPR. We should become a true network in the little "n" sense of the worl.

People think they own us anyway. So let's bring them into the conversation. NPR's role in this in terms of this kind of expansion is to enable, to help galvanize these changes. We do not want to control. We do not want to dominate. We do not want to bypass our message to audiences on the local level. We don't want to put local public radio websites out of business. We actually want to put ourselves out of business in the sense that we will have morphed into a constellation of sites on the local level, fed with national and international news, the services that we can provide, and become the kind of powerhouse on the digital level that we are in radio.

It's part of our mission. Bill Moyers, I mean LBJ, said it himself. We have challenges to overcome. One is technology, although frankly, I think that's the easiest part. The second challenge is the economy. I think it works for us on some levels and that we are going to feel a renewed sense of urgency, but it works against us, in digital media, where the revenue models are nascent, to say the least. And we have the challenge that I mentioned earlier, which is, we're not great at working together.

But we have the urgency now. And I believe that this is going to be our unique opportunity to rally together and serve the American public in ways that we do so well. So we have these challenges. We must overcome them. We will overcome them. We must embrace change, and we need to tell everybody about it. That's all I have to say. Thank you.

Keynote Address to the "News Literacy: Setting a National Agenda" Conference[*]

Arthur Ochs Sulzberger, Jr.

Publisher, The New York Times, *1992– ; born Mount Kisco, NY, September 22, 1951; B.A., Tufts University, 1974; reporter,* Raleigh Times, *1974–76; London correspondent, Associated Press, 1976–78;* The New York Times *positions: Washington bureau correspondent, 1978–1981, Metro reporter and editor, 1981–83, various business positions, 1983–87, assistant publisher, 1987–88, deputy publisher, 1989–1992.*

Editor's introduction: Prior to this keynote address, delivered at the State University of New York at Stony Brook, *New York Times* CEO Arthur Sulzberger, Jr., presented a ten-minute video created for a 2005 Google conference that featured various *Times* writers and editors discussing the paper's authority, judgment, and trustworthiness. In his speech, Sulzberger sounds a similarly positive note about journalism's future despite the industry's well-known challenges, observing that actual physical newspapers remain prominent and profitable. In order to ensure that it continues to provide quality journalism, he says, the *Times* plans to increase its on-line revenue. He goes on to describe the Times Company's past efforts to generate on-line dollars, including its ill-fated Times Select project, which charged users for access to the work of *Times* columnists. Sulzberger insists that different forms of news, as well as their various delivery platforms, can co-exist with one another. He also stresses the overall importance of journalism, with its emphasis on verification over assertion, accuracy over sensation.

Arthur Sulzberger, Jr.'s speech: Thank you and good evening.

It is a delight to be with you this evening and to see so many long-time friends and colleagues. We come together at a time of extraordinary change and challenge to what many would call a profession, but I suspect most of us feel is a calling.

Journalism—whether published in newspapers or magazines, broadcast on television or on the radio; or consumed online or on a mobile device—is under

---

[*] Delivered on March 12, 2009, at Stony Brook, NY. Reprinted with permission.

enormous stress, both from the permanent shifts set off by the Internet and from the cyclical forces unleashed by this current severe economic downturn.

But something even more fundamental is going on around us and it's at the heart of this conference and our common desire to carry the banner for news literacy far and wide. Journalism is being transfigured by the new information ecosystem and its very definition is changing. Given the volcanic explosion of Web sites, search engines and social networking channels, how could it not?

In some ways, journalism is expanding and offering us great opportunity. In other ways, it is contracting, resulting in a wave of self-doubt among practitioners of our craft and confusion among our consumers.

So let me go back in time for a moment.

Four years ago, I was asked to speak at Google's Zeitgeist conference. My colleagues and I brainstormed about that speech and decided that a lot of the engineers in the room—many of whom had the very best educations that our system can offer—really didn't know what journalism was.

Remember, this was the era when some thought that blog networks were going to replace the kind of journalism that we practice at *The Times*. So we created a video, letting our own people explain what they do to the hundreds of digerati that were in the room that day.

I want to again use this video to ground my remarks in fundamental principles, ones that all of us here tonight feel are so critical to maintaining the unfettered flow of reliable facts and knowledge that sustains our democracy.

That was 2005, which in retrospect looks like the good old days. While we have improved our tools and our commitment to providing world-class news and information anywhere in the world remains strong, the business model is under tremendous strain.

High-quality journalism—covering City Hall or Iraq—is getting harder and harder to pay for. Traditional revenue streams are, in many cases, anemic and getting weaker. Due to the combination of secular and cyclical pressures I mentioned earlier, the immediate future looks, at minimum, grim.

As Paul Krugman, *The Times*'s Nobel Prize–winning economic columnist remarked recently about the financial hurricane: "If this goes on much longer, I think I might give it all up, move to the U.S. Virgin Islands, and start a Ponzi scheme."

Now I am not here to wax poetical about the past. It was, in its way, much overrated (unless you're reflecting on the glory days of working as a reporter in the Washington bureau of *The New York Times*, under the skilled leadership of Bill Kovach, a great boss, who was here earlier today).

Nor am I here to bemoan our fate. Quite honestly, I am tired of reading about the death of . . . take your pick: journalism, newspapers, engaged readers. Even *The Times* today was wondering out loud on the front page as to where newspapers were heading, et tu brute. My view is that what we offer, in all its iterations, is quite valuable and our profession will endure.

In a recent signed editorial in *The Times*, Eduardo Porter cited another Nobel Prize–winning economist, Amartya Sen, who said that China's horrific Great Leap Forward could not have happened in India because newspapers would have closely chronicled the suffering of the people.

Closer to home, each of us can cite an example of some public or private sector boondoggle that was upended because an inquisitive journalist was paying attention. Whether delivered in print or online, in a blog or a video, quality journalism will always have immense social utility. As Bill Keller, our executive editor, noted two years ago, journalistic organizations are "an institutional bulwark against powerful forces that would tame or silence us."

While Wikipedia and online aggregators serve their purpose, serious news gathering operations are more necessary than ever as the public and private decision-makers and the concerned public gather the news and information needed to more thoughtfully progress into a most uncertain future.

And finally, I am not here to tell you I have the answers to our current dilemma—attracting more revenue, be it by charging for an online article reporting on the day's activities in the Middle East the way iTunes charges for U2's latest hit single, or examining new journalistic organizational structures, such as moving from a traditional profit-making model to a not-for-profit entity whose funding is secure in the hands of, say, Bernie Madoff.

One of the many reasons why such a solution is so elusive is that what works for *The New York Times* is not going to work for *Newsday* or *The LA Times*; what works for NYTimes.com is not going to be a solution for *Politico, Salon* or *Slate*. As I will discuss shortly, each site has a different relationship to the Internet and has to be evaluated on a case-by-case basis.

In our heart of hearts, we all wish there would be the equivalent of the deus ex machina moment when the gods descend and provide us with a perfect business model for the new media. Alas, Mount Olympus has been quiet for quite a while, and real life tends to be a bit messier and less predictable.

As an aging devotee of Outward Bound adventures, I prefer to think of this as a challenging river trip. We know where we are and we know where we are heading. What we do not know is exactly what's around each bend. What is needed isn't certainty, but rather flexibility, aligned with courage, stamina and expertise—all of which will be critical to the success and safety of our journey.

What is of even greater import is our adherence to core values: maintaining loyalty to those bedrock beliefs that have sustained quality journalism through so many economic and political cycles.

At a recent NYU Media Talk, the irrepressible David Carr remarked that "News has always been the killer app."

In a pithy way, he expresses a deeply-held feeling. It reminds us that quality news matters and that how people will get this quality journalism will continue to evolve. At The New York Times Company, we state this journalistic value proposition, or what we call our Core Purpose, just a bit more formally (what a surprise):

"To enhance society by creating, collecting and distributing high-quality news and information."

And on Monday, David's media column caused quite a stir. He raised a lot of questions about the original sin of providing free content online and what we can do to either put the genie back in the bottle or create an alternate economic model that rescues newspapers.

And this returns us to the biggest issue before all of us tonight and tomorrow: what do we need to do to earn enough revenue to maintain robust newsrooms and uphold the rights and privileges granted to us by our Constitution?

It's obvious, but let me say it anyway: For many of us, our long-term financial success will be determined by how quickly our digital revenue growth outpaces the downturn in our print revenues.

At The New York Times Company, we are focusing on three key levers to achieve this breakthrough moment: attracting more users, deepening their engagement and then earning revenue from their usage. To do all this will require making bets on how this new medium will evolve and making investments in that vision.

This is certainly not an easy task. Our insights into human behavior and technological evolution may guide us. Two main contributors to *The Times*'s online success are here tonight: Jon Landman—to whom I am indebted for being invited—and Vivian Schiller. Both will tell you with great pride and enthusiasm that we have been busy creating a new form of Web journalism that is both informative and compelling. At least they had better be telling you that.

For instance, if you came to NYTimes.com at noon on January 20, you would have seen:

- Live video of President Obama's Inaugural address;
- An interactive graphic comparing President Obama's words with the language of past inaugural addresses;
- A distinctive patchwork display of photos from readers;
- Useful maps of inaugural sites in Washington, D.C.;
- A wholly original reimagining of the journalistic chestnut, the "voices" story, in the form of an ever-morphing chart displaying people's hopes for what the new president might accomplish;
- Moment-by-moment blogging;
- and our usual riveting reporting and analysis.

Taken as a whole, the experience was immediate, personal and compelling. And you didn't have to struggle to leave the Mall.

Engagement is the name of the game. Serious news sites must create a new, more organic, more personal relationship with their readers. While there has been a "Letter to the Editor" forum in newspapers since the late 19th century, journalism's relationship with our readers has been one-sided.

We need to be able to respond to our audiences' demand for interactivity, community, multimedia, news and information on an increasingly wide range of topics.

We have to respond to their desire to do something with the content we make. Our readers want to share it, or blog it, or comment on it, or tweet it. They want to use our journalism as raw material for what they make. This can be a very good thing because it does enhance our audiences' involvement with our sites, but it also takes us back to issues of authority and what is and is not "Real Journalism."

And, we want them to feel that they are part of a vital, ongoing conversation and that there is something missing in their lives when they stay away for too long.

Our strategy must be rooted in the fundamental premise that we must be *of* the Internet, not merely *on* it, requiring all of us to move from publishing our content on the Web to becoming full Web publishers.

For years, we hoped that financial success would just come from making our products more accessible, informative and entertaining. The idea was simple: work harder, be more creative and thoughtful, and the revenues will return in force. Regrettably, there were larger, more complex forces at work and we are now confronting some hard truths:

- Let us start with the fact that a deep, cyclical downturn has dramatically affected key areas of commerce, including the real estate, employment, automotive and retail industries, the lifeblood of American newspapers and local television.
- The Internet has proved to be a far superior advertising platform for listings. The classified businesses are disappearing from newspapers and are unlikely to migrate in any significant way to news Web sites.
- Selected display categories are also subject to secular shifts as users move from print to digital consumption. Beyond that, marketers are growing skeptical of the ability of display ads on any platform to capture the consumer's attention in a fragmented media landscape.
- And, Internet businesses have proven incapable of replicating the economics of print. Few people have been willing to pay for online news. Advertising rates for online inventory are relatively low. And news Web sites are poorly organized to take advantage of the contextual advertising model that dominates the Internet.

With this in mind, there are now all kinds of solutions and tactics being offered up to allow online news sites to adapt financially to the changing conditions, but it is a little bit like the banking crisis. We know there is an answer out there somewhere, but we are not sure what it will turn out to be.

So the immediate response of journalism organizations, including ours, to all this economic and technological disruption is to make substantial expense reductions. These have included closing production facilities, creating new methods of distribution, reducing the size of our newspapers and layoffs.

Remember what Bill Schmidt, *The Times*'s deputy managing editor, was saying about the expense of keeping reporters in Iraq? Now, with the sad state of news media finances, there has been a substantial reduction in coverage of that critically important area of the world. Afghanistan will undoubtedly also receive short shrift from the world's newsrooms because of cost.

As I noted earlier, the demand continues, but we are still left in the paradoxical position of having a product that an *increasing* number of people use, but which has *decreasing* revenues and profitability. This, coupled with radically different user experiences, argues for new goals and initiatives.

We need a thorough and *realistic* assessment of the audience scale necessary to achieve our respective economic ambitions or consider alternative business models.

We must engage in a deep and realistic examination of the value we add for marketers, of the services that we offer today to support that value and of the new services we will need to offer in the future. We must invest in creating the skills and competencies to accomplish these things.

We also need to pursue a set of industry initiatives that support quality news, the protection of intellectual property, the value of quality content in the advertising marketplace and, speaking of this conference, news literacy.

Taken together, this is about re-conceptualization and more thoughtful execution. It is about being bold and willing to think about all the available options and imagine a future that seems within our grasp. It is about constant reinvention and taking full advantage of the Web, an amazing laboratory for entrepreneurs, technologists and, of course, journalists.

NYTimes.com has already experimented with different strategies for collecting revenue.

- In the mid-90s we collected fees from our international users, but we then changed course and opened up the site to our worldwide audience on July 14, 1997—Bastille Day, a most fitting metaphor for tearing the online walls down.

- A little less then a decade later, we launched our TimesSelect experiment, which for a modest fee provided exclusive access to Op-Ed and news columnists on NYTimes.com, easy and in-depth access to *The Times*'s online archives, early access to select articles on the site, as well as other exciting features.

- After two years, as the Web evolved, it became necessary to change our priorities and our focus. While TimesSelect generated more than 200,000 subscriptions and around $10 million, we decided to end this initiative. We realized that the exploding world of search meant that the ad revenues resulting from our increased traffic—created by offering this content for free—would grow faster than the subscription model.

Today, in the face of the economic downturn, we have renewed our analysis of how paid content can augment our core advertising business. The trick, of course, is to garner incremental revenue from the user without significantly cannibalizing the high-rate ad pages that now account for a very significant amount of money.

Unlike many local news Web sites that still depend mostly on declining classified ad revenues, NYTimes.com has a very large national display revenue stream.

As we develop new pay-for-content ideas, we must carefully balance our ability to generate meaningful dollars from both sources.

Most of our thinking revolves around the fact that we have almost uniquely achieved substantial scale throughout the world and have become part and parcel of the global discourse. This achievement has significant journalistic and financial ramifications and we do not want to take any step that significantly reduces our presence on the Web.

Other prominent news-gathering sites may be less interested in scale and that might give them the flexibility to pursue an even more aggressive paid-content strategy. What we have learned over the last decade and a half is that the Web has very few generally accepted rules for financial success, and they are inevitably overturned by the next digital cycle and next breakthrough algorithm.

Some of you may be wondering: Does all this activity portend the end of print?

Of course not. It is still a popular and profitable medium.

There are more than 830,000 readers who have subscribed to *The New York Times* for two years or more, up from 650,000 just over 2 years ago.

And just today, the Center for Media Research released a study, which revealed that:

- 83 percent of Americans say print newspapers are relevant.
- 53 percent subscribe to a newspaper, and
- 55 percent say newspapers are their primary source of news, over national TV, local TV and "news aggregators."

This is good news: print and digital can co-exist in the marketplace. But, as we have learned over the past 15 years, we need to become even better at integrating our print and Web properties. They offer two very different products and two distinct value propositions. Our challenge is to integrate both while embracing the unique strengths of each medium.

As we think about all these economic issues, we have to keep in mind why we are here tonight. Your conference on news literacy sends a strong message that the journalistic and academic professions must do all that we can to keep our audiences, especially the younger generations, well-informed.

In last Sunday's Week in Review, there was an excellent article by Kate Zernike, "Generation OMG," which discussed how the children of this generation are responding to all the recent upheaval and how growing up during the Great Depression provides some useful parallels.

We can help ameliorate some of the ensuing discomfort by ensuring that our children not only follow the news, but understand what is happening. They need the tools to make sense of what is taking place around them. They hear their parents and friends relentlessly talking about a weak global economy, brutal conflicts in Iraq, Afghanistan, Pakistan and the increasing threat of nuclear proliferation. (By the way, you should read *The Inheritance*, a new book by our Washington correspondent, David Sanger, which offers some very insightful comments on some of these topics.)

This is all very scary stuff. Our children need Real Journalism.

They need reassurance that the world is not coming to an end and that history teaches us that humankind is quite resilient, especially during periods of crises and controversy.

They need to know that we have persevered during World Wars, a Great Depression and the Cold War and we have the wherewithal to overcome what we face today.

Your conference and other initiatives such as the News Literacy Project will help us teach this invaluable lesson and The New York Times Company is very proud to be part of these efforts. I commend and applaud your efforts.

Together we can create a future where quality journalism thrives, where it lives organically alongside the many new forms of user-generated content, amid the chaotic and swirling global conversation taking place on the Web.

Together we can ensure that citizens, especially our young people, understand the cornerstone attributes that make quality journalism important in their lives, such as verification rather than assertion, accuracy as opposed to speed and sensation, transparency and the idea of correcting one's mistakes. In short, many of the things my colleagues talked about in my short film.

And together, we can take these messages to our young people so they will understand how different kinds of information in this wonderfully diverse, multi-platform world can, do and will exist together.

Thank you for inviting me.

Testimony on the Future of Journalism before the U.S. Senate[*]

David Simon

Creator, show runner, executive producer, head writer, The Wire *HBO television series, 1999–2008; born Washington, D.C., 1960; graduated from the University of Maryland, 1983; police reporter,* Baltimore Sun, *1983–1995; writer and producer,* Homicide: Life on the Street *television series, 1995–99; author,* Homicide: A Year on the Killing Streets, *1991;* The Corner: A Year in the Life of an Inner-City Neighborhood, *with Ed Burns, 1997.*

Editor's introduction: In testimony delivered before the U.S. Senate Committee on Commerce, Science and Transportation, David Simon casts a plague on the houses of both old and new media, calling blogs parasites and accusing old media of butchering itself in the name of profit long before the Internet destroyed its business model. He insists that newspapers will have to charge for on-line content and argues that Wall Street-approved models will not serve in a field where a public trust is at issue, nor should media companies accept government support for the same reason. He describes as "intriguing" a model in which newspaper companies might be granted nonprofit status or in which local newspapers might be handed over to existing nonprofit organizations.

Mr. Simon's speech: Thank you, Senator.

I'd also like to say I'm proud to be following Mr. Coll, whose work with the *Post* and *The New Yorker,* and in his books, represents the highest standards of craft. I endorse the last 7 minutes of testimony.

My name's David Simon, and I used to be a newspaperman in Baltimore. What I say will likely conflict with what representatives of the newspaper industry will claim, and I can imagine little agreement with those who speak for new media.

From the captains of the newspaper industry, you may hear a certain martyrology, a claim that they were heroically serving democracy, only to be undone by a cataclysmic shift in technology. From those speaking on behalf of new media, Web blogs, and that which goes by the name of Twitter, you will be treated to

---

[*] Delivered on May 6, 2009, at Washington, D.C.

assurances that American journalism has a perfectly fine future online and that a great democratization is taking place.

Well, a plague on both their houses. High-end journalism is dying in America. And unless a new economic model is achieved, it will not be reborn on the Web or anywhere else. The Internet is a marvelous tool, and clearly it is the information delivery system of our future. But, thus far, it does not deliver much first-generation reporting. Instead, it leaches that reporting from mainstream news publications, whereupon aggregating Web sites and bloggers contribute little more than repetition, commentary, and froth. Meanwhile, readers acquire news from aggregators and abandon its point of origin; namely, the newspapers themselves. In short, the parasite is slowly killing the host.

It's nice to get stuff for free, of course, and it's nice that more people can have their say in new media. And, while some [in] our Internet community [are] rampantly ideological, ridiculously inaccurate, and occasionally juvenile, some of it's also quite good, even original.

Understand, I'm not making a Luddite argument against the Internet and all that it offers, but you do not, in my city, run into bloggers or so-called citizen journalists at city hall or in the courthouse hallways or at the bars where police officers gather. You don't see them consistently nurturing and then pressing others—pressing sources. You don't see them holding institutions accountable on a daily basis. Why? Because high-end journalism is a profession. It requires daily full-time commitment by trained men and women who return to the same beats, day in and day out. Reporting was the hardest and, in some ways, most gratifying job I ever had. I'm offended to think that anyone anywhere believes American monoliths as insulated, self-preserving, and self-justifying as police departments, school systems, legislatures, and chief executives, can be held to gathered facts by amateurs, presenting the task—pursuing the task without compensation, training, or, for that matter, sufficient standing to make public officials even care who it is they're lying to or who they're withholding information from.

Indeed, the very phrase "citizen journalist" strikes my ears Orwellian. A good—a neighbor who is a good listener and cares about people is a good neighbor. He is not in any sense a citizen social worker. Just as a neighbor with a garden hose and good intentions is not a citizen firefighter. To say so is a heedless insult to trained social workers and firefighters.

Well, so much for new media, but what about old media? While anyone listening carefully may have noted that—I'm sorry. Cut that part. While anyone listening carefully may have noted that I was brought out of my reporting in 1995, that's well before the Internet began to threaten the industry, before Craigslist and department store consolidation gutted the ad base, before any of the current economic conditions applied. In fact, when newspaper chains began cutting personnel and content, the industry was one of the most profitable yet discovered by Wall Street.

We know now, because bankruptcy has opened the books, that the *Baltimore Sun* was eliminating its afternoon edition and trimming nearly 100 reporters and editors in an era when the paper was achieving 37-percent profits. Such shortsighted arrogance rivals that of Detroit in the 1970s, when automakers offered up Chevy Vegas and Pacers and Gremlins without the slightest worry that mediocrity would be challenged by better-made cars from Germany or Japan. In short, my industry butchered itself, and we do so at the behest of Wall Street, in the same unfettered, free-market logic that has proven so disastrous for so many American industries. Indeed, the original sin of American newspapering lies in going to Wall Street in the first place.

When locally based family-owned newspapers like the *Sun* were consolidated into publicly owned newspaper chains, an essential dynamic, an essential trust, between journalism and the community served by that journalism was betrayed.

Economically, the disconnect is now obvious. What did newspaper executives in Los Angeles or Chicago care whether readers in Baltimore have a better newspaper, especially when you can make more money putting out a mediocre paper than a worthy one? Where family ownership might have been content with 10 or 15 percent profit, the chains demanded double that and more, and the cutting began long before the threat of new technology was ever sensed.

Editorially, the newspaper chains also brought an ugly disconnect into the newsroom and, by extension, to the community. A few years after the A.S. Abell family sold the *Sun* to *Times Mirror*, fresh editors arrived from out of town to take over the reins of the paper. They looked upon Baltimore, not as an essential terrain to be covered with consistency, to be explained in all its complexity, year in and year out, for readers who had and would live their whole lives in Baltimore. Why would they? They had arrived from somewhere else, and they—if they won a prize or two, they would be moving on to bigger and better opportunities within the chain.

So, well before the arrival of the Internet, as veteran reporters and homegrown editors took buyouts, news beats were dropped, and less and less was covered with rigor or complexity. In a city in which half the adult black males are without consistent work, the poverty and social services beat was abandoned. In a region where unions are imploding and the working class eviscerated, where the bankruptcy of a huge steel manufacturer meant thousands lost medical benefits and pensions, there was no longer a labor reporter. And though it's one of the most violent cities in America, the Baltimore criminal courts went uncovered for more than a year.

Meanwhile, the out-of-town editors used manpower to pursue a handful of special projects, Pulitzer-sniffing as one does. The self-gratification of my profession does not come, you see, from covering a city, and covering it well, from explaining an increasingly complex and interconnected world to citizens, from holding basic institutions accountable; it comes from someone handing you a plaque and taking your picture.

And so, buyout after buyout, from the first staff reduction in 1992 to the latest round last week in which nearly a third of the remaining newsroom was fired, the newspaper that might have mattered enough to charge online for content simply disappeared. Where 500 men and women once covered central Maryland, there are now 140.

I don't know if it's too late already for American newspapering, but if there's to be a renewal of the industry, a few things are certain and obvious. First, the industry is going to have to find a way to charge for online content. Yes, I've heard the postmodern rallying cry that information wants to be free. But information isn't. It costs money to send reporters to London, to Fallujah, to Capitol Hill, and to send photographers with them, to keep them there day after day. It costs money to hire the best investigators and writers, and then back them up with the best editors. And how anyone can believe that the industry can fund this kind of expense by giving its product away online to aggregators and bloggers is a source of endless fascination to me. A freshman marketing major in any community college can tell you that if you don't have a product for which you can charge people, you don't actually have a product.

Second, Wall Street and free-market lodging, having been a destructive force in journalism over the last few decades, is now not suddenly the answer. Raw, unencumbered capitalism is never the answer when a public trust or public mission is at issue.

Similarly, there can be no serious consideration of public funding for newspapers. High-end journalism can and should bite any hand that tries to feed it, and it should bite a governing hand most viciously.

Moreover, it's the right of every American to despise his local newspaper for being too liberal or too conservative, for covering X and not covering Y, for spelling your name wrong when you do something notable, and for spelling it correctly when you do something dishonorable. As love-hate relationships go, it's a pretty intricate one, and an exchange of public money would prove unacceptable to all.

But, a nonprofit model intrigues, especially if that model allows for locally-based ownership and control of news organizations. Anything the government can do in the way of creating nonprofit status for newspapers should be seriously pursued. And further, anything that can be done to create financial or tax-based incentives for bankrupt or near-bankrupt newspaper chains to transfer or donate unprofitable publications to locally-based nonprofits should also be considered.

Lastly, I would urge Congress to consider relaxing certain antitrust prohibitions so that the *Washington Post,* the *New York Times,* and various [other] newspapers can openly discuss protecting copyright from aggregators and plan an industry-wide transition to a paid online subscriber base. Whatever money comes will prove essential to the task of hiring back some of the talent, commitment, and institutional memory that has been squandered.

Absent this basic and belated acknowledgment that content matters—in fact, content is all—I don't think anything can be done to save high-end professional journalism.

Journalism's Many Crises[*]

Todd Gitlin

Professor of journalism and sociology, Columbia University, 2002– ; born New York, NY, January 6, 1943; B.A., cum laude, mathematics, Harvard University, 1963; M.A., political science, University of Michigan, 1966; Ph.D., sociology, University of California, Berkeley, 1977; lecturer, New College, San Jose State University, 1970–76; lecturer, Board of Community Studies, University of California, Santa Cruz, 1974–77; lecturer, Department of Sociology, University of California, Berkeley, 1978; assistant professor of sociology and director, Mass Communications Program, University of California, Berkeley, 1978–1983; associate professor of sociology and director, Mass Communications Program, University of California, Berkeley, 1983–87; professor of sociology and director, Mass Communications Program, University of California, Berkeley, 1987–1994; chair in American Civilization, École des Hautes Études en Sciences Sociales, Paris, 1994–95; professor of culture, journalism, and sociology, New York University, 1995–2002; author, Uptown: Poor Whites in Chicago, *with Nanci Hollander, 1970;* Busy Being Born, *1974;* The Whole World is Watching: Mass Media in the Making and Unmaking of the New Left, *1980;* Inside Prime Time, *1983;* The Sixties: Years of Hope, Days of Rage, *1987;* The Murder of Albert Einstein, *1992;* The Twilight of Common Dreams: Why America Is Wracked by Culture Wars, *1995;* Sacrifice, *1999;* Media Unlimited: How the Torrent of Images and Sounds Overwhelms Our Lives, *2002;* Letters to a Young Activist, *2003;* The Intellectuals and the Flag, and Other Essays on Liberal Social Thought after September 11, *2006;* The Bulldozer and the Big Tent: Blind Republicans, Lame Democrats, and the Recovery of American Ideals, *2007; contributor to various periodicals (including* The New York Times, Los Angeles Times, *and* The Nation*), online magazines, and scholarly journals; editor,* Campfires of the Resistance: Poetry from the Movement, *1971;* Watching Television, *1987.*

Editor's introduction: Written for the conference "Journalism in Crisis," at the University of Westminster in London, but delivered via Skype from his Columbia University office, Todd Gitlin's talk identifies several crises, not only fiscal but also ethical and cultural, that face American journalism. Declining circulation and

* Delivered on May 19, 2009, at London, U.K. Reprinted with permission.

advertising revenue, as well as mounting debt and unprofitable Web sites, bedevil newspapers along with a cultural shift to diffused attention. Gitlin describes where newspaper Web sites, television, radio, and commentary blogs fit into this new media landscape. He argues that journalism suffers from a crisis of authority that stems partly from the failure to rigorously investigate authority, for example, in the run-up to both the Iraq War and the recent financial crisis. Finally, he discusses possible ways to address the crisis in public-policy terms.

Todd Gitlin's speech: The word "crisis" is overused, as are the anodyne "problem" or "issue." (As in the highly flexible, "I have issues.") Ordinary troubles become inflated into "crises" because crises sound somehow more dignified or electrifying. A problem sounds possibly serious, if hypothetically soluble, but a crisis sounds, as well, critical.

Yet the overuse might lead us to bend over backwards and fall into euphemism—calling a grave matter "a little difficult," for example, as is common, for some reason, in American discourse today. There are crises. History proceeds by convulsions, not only increments—or rather, increments build up into crises, and before one knows it, the landscape has changed, one is living in a different world, and the world before it changed is barely conceivable and certainly unrecoverable. It was a foreign country; they did things differently there.

In the case of the murky future of journalism, it is fair to speak of crisis— crises, actually. The landscape has changed, is changing, will change—radically. Just because the industry is crying wolf does not mean that the wolf is not nearby. In the story, when the real wolf showed up, no one was ready.

Four wolves have arrived at the door of American journalism simultaneously while a fifth has already been lurking for some time. One is the precipitous decline in the circulation of newspapers. The second is the decline in advertising revenue, which, combined with the first, has badly damaged the profitability of newspapers. The third, contributing to the first, is the diffusion of attention. The fourth is the more elusive crisis of authority. The fifth, a perennial—so much so as to be perhaps a condition more than a crisis—is journalism's inability or unwillingness to penetrate the veil of obfuscation behind which power conducts its risky business.

CIRCULATION AND REVIEW

The surplus of crises has commentators scrambling for metaphors, even mixed ones. The Project for Excellence in Journalism put it this way in a recent report: "The newspaper industry exited a harrowing 2008 and entered 2009 in something perilously close to free fall. Perhaps some parachutes will deploy, and maybe some tree limbs will cushion the descent, but for a third consecutive year the bottom is not in sight." The newspaper industry in the United States is afflicted with a grave and deepening sense that it is moribund, that the journalistic world they knew is vanishing; that it is melting away not just within their lifetimes but before their eyes.

The numbers virtually shout out that this is not paranoia. Overall, newspaper circulation has dropped 13.5 percent for the dailies and 17.3 percent for the Sunday editions since 2001; almost 5 percent just in 2008. In what some are calling the Great Recession, advertising revenue is down—23 percent over the last two years —even as paper costs are up. Nearly one out of every five journalists working for newspapers in 2001 is now gone. Foreign bureaus have been shuttered—all those of the *Boston Globe*, for example, New England's major paper. I recently met the *Chicago Tribune*'s South Asia correspondent, responsible for India, Pakistan, and Afghanistan, with five years of experience there. Having been recalled to work on the Metro desk in Chicago, she resigned.

There is, in particular, the advent of competition for classified advertising, long the newspapers' financial mainstay, but now available free online. In the recession, display advertising is way down. Newspapers overall lost 83 percent of their stock value last year. You can buy a share of stock in the McClatchy papers, which used to be one of the highest-quality chains, for less than the cost of a single copy of the paper. The Tribune Company, which owns the *Los Angeles Times* and several other major papers, has filed for bankruptcy. So have the papers in Minneapolis and Philadelphia. The afternoon papers in Denver and Seattle have closed, and in Detroit, weekday home delivery for both dailies takes place on Thursdays and Fridays only; Monday through Wednesday, only a smaller edition is sold at newsstands.

Overall, newspapers remain profitable, in the low to mid teens, but several corporate chains took on enormous piles of debt when they made acquisitions in recent years (The Tribune: $13 billion in acquiring the Times Mirror Corp). Chain ownership of local newspapers by corporations that trade on the stock exchange undermined them. With expectations of declining profits in the future, investors pursued what is cynically called a "harvest strategy"—bidding up their stock market value in expectation that profits would have to be harvested quickly, before the bottom fell out of their financial value. Profitability, they reasoned, would come from cost-cutting, which meant cutting back the practice of journalism. The chains cut back on coverage in order to try to compensate for the loss of advertising revenue. This has not won back readers. One prominent television commentator recently said: "*The New York Times* has 60 people in its Baghdad bureau. As far as I can tell, the *Times* doesn't have that many subscribers under the age of forty." He was joking, of course. Of course.

Here are some excerpts from another study, from 2008, by the Project for Excellence in Journalism:

> Meet the American daily newspaper of 2008.
>
> It has fewer pages than three years ago, the paper stock is thinner, and the stories are shorter. There is less foreign and national news, less space devoted to science, the arts, features and a range of specialized subjects. Business coverage is either packaged in an increasingly thin stand-alone section or collapsed into another part of the paper. The crossword puzzle has shrunk, the TV listings and stock tables may have disap-

peared, but coverage of some local issues has strengthened and investigative reporting remains highly valued.

The newsroom staff producing the paper is also smaller, younger, more tech-savvy, and more oriented to serving the demands of both print and the Web. The staff also is under greater pressure, has less institutional memory, less knowledge of the community, of how to gather news and the history of individual beats. There are fewer editors to catch mistakes.

And still revenue plunges, if not so much because circulation is shrinking than because business acumen did. Obviously newspaper companies have made many poor business decisions in recent years, from taking on mountainous debt to establishing a precedent of free internet access. When poor business decisions are chronic and widespread, you have to conclude that the companies have entered a twilight where anxiety has gotten the better of understanding. How stable even the *New York Times* can remain, given its own precipitous stock decline in the last five years, is unclear. Its two-tier stock arrangement, designed to preserve control within the Sulzberger family, may not insulate it enough if losses continue to mount. The Chandler family of Los Angeles, reduced to squabbling, ended its own reign there, and Dow-Jones' Bancroft family sold out to Rupert Murdoch a year and a half ago. The Washington Post Company seemed to have dodged the bullet by buying the testing company Kaplan, re-annointing itself an "education and media company," and letting the tail wag the dog—Kaplan accounts for more than half of company revenue. But if that expedient has saved the paper, it is a more meager paper. A longtime foreign correspondent who took a buyout a few years ago told me that when he visited the newsroom recently, the old globe that pinpointed the Post's foreign bureaus was gone—it would have looked too embarrassing.

To limit the discussion to the last decade or so both overstates the precipitous danger and understates the magnitude of a secular crisis—which is probably a protracted crisis in the way in which people know—or believe they know—the world. In the US, newspaper circulation has been declining, per capita, at a constant rate since 1960. The young are not reading the papers. While they say they "look" at the papers online, it is not clear how much looking they do. We may well be living amidst a sea change in how we encounter the world, how we take in its traces and make sense of them, a change comparable to the shift from oral to written culture among the Greeks and the shift to printing with movable type in 15th and 16th century Europe.

This shift has been in play, accelerating, disrupting theories of linear progress, or progress through linearity, for almost two centuries—from photography through film and television to the Internet, in the rise of screens and the relative decline of sequential text.

It isn't my purpose here to try to sum up what might be gained and lost in such a transition—surely both sides of the ledger are active. Nor is it my purpose to lock onto some hard-and-fast black-and-white theory of utter, utter change in sensibility. The newspaper was always a tool for simultaneity (you don't so much read a paper as swim around in it, McLuhan was fond of saying) at least as much as a tool for cognitive sequence. What if the sensibility that is now consolidating itself—with the Internet, mobile phones, GPS, Facebook and Twitter and so on —the media for the Daily Me, for point-to-point and many-to-many transmission —what if all this portends an irreversible sea-change in the very conditions of successful business? The question is not answerable. But that is exactly the point. To navigate a business in such choppy seas is no task for the faint-hearted.

THE CLAMOR FOR ATTENTION

Attention has been migrating from slower access to faster; from concentration to multitasking; from the textual to the visual and the auditory, and toward multi-media combinations. Multitasking alters cognitive patterns. Attention attenuates. Advertisers have for decades talked about the need to "break through the clutter," the clutter consisting, amusingly, of everyone else's attempts to break through the clutter.

Now, media and not just messages clutter. Measured by the criterion of how people spend their time, the central activity of our civilization is connection to media. At work, at home, on the street, in the car, in elevators and malls, commuting or waiting, we spend much of our day in a torrent of images and sounds, navigating through it, filtering it, desirous of it and through it—sometimes immersed, sometimes floating, sometimes wading, sometimes choosing, sometimes engulfed. Success goes to the media, portals, and sites that attract attention.

Accordingly, not only has print circulation plunged, but the amount of time spent with newspapers is also declining. According to the Pew Research Center for the People and the Press in 2006, while "the total time that people spend with the news is largely unchanged from a decade ago," still "the time people devote to reading newspapers is down from an average of 19 minutes to 15 minutes, partially because fewer are reading papers and partially because those who do spend a bit less time at it." Just under one-fifth of Americans between the ages of 18 and 34 claim to look at a daily newspaper—which is not to say how much of it they read. The average American newspaper reader is 55 years old.

Of course significant numbers of readers are accessing—which is not to say reading—newspapers online, but the amount of time they seem to spend there is bifurcated. In roughly half of the top 30 newspaper sites, readership is steady or falling. Still, "of the top 5 online newspapers—ranked by unique users—[the] three [national papers] reported growth in the average time spent per person: NYTimes.com, USAToday.com, and the Wall Street Journal Online." One thing is clear: whatever the readership online, it is not profitable.

As for national television news, the median age of evening news viewers is 61. The average age at Rupert Murdoch's Fox News is over 65. The average age of all network TV viewers just crossed 50. The median age in the United States is 38. Cable news audiences spiked up during the 2008 campaign, but then subsided. Even local news, the home of "If it bleeds, it leads," has seen viewership decline.

MEDIA SATURATION

The undermining of newspapers is the product of many converging factors, which I would summarize under the heading, "media saturation." Media saturation is the product of compound, feverish competition for the attention of persons that is capable of being monetized—and it works. There is, of course, the rise of the Internet. There is the increased time Americans spend working and commuting, which is that much less time for newspapers.

It is true that newspaper websites are gaining readers, or visitors. Unique viewers are estimated to "add 8.4 percent to the average newspaper's readership, making up most, but not all, of the audience decline." Still, even online ads fell last year, by 0.4 percent, and add up to less than 10 percent of newspaper revenue.

As for public television, the situation is equivalent. Public funding amounts to roughly half of the budget of the nightly *NewsHour*, corporations donate the other half in exchange for vanity quasi-commercials. But in the age of "maximizing shareholder value" over the past few decades, corporate support has declined. Foundations have taken up some of the slack, but their own endowments have taken a beating, and they've cut their grants too. Public radio is a bright spot, with 13 percent of Americans saying they regularly get most of their news from National Public Radio (NPR). These are disproportionately the college-educated and older.

THE "OPINION" BLOG

Now, the rise of opinion blogs and sites gives reason to think that political discourse is far from dead—even, perhaps, more absorbing, at least for the young, than the old regime of newspapers and television. The 2008 political campaign generated unusual interest from young people, who told pollsters they "get their news" from the internet (although it's far from clear that their claims can be taken at face value). But it is worth considering that very little of the hard nuts-and-bolts work of reporting is done by internet sites. Almost all current-events blogs collect news from newspaper sites or the handful of internet sites that commission actual reporting (as opposed to commentary, informed or not). The blogs do amalgamate and "connect dots," and the connecting of dots is a necessary function of a journalism that enables people to intervene in governance.

An example from a website, Talking Point Memo (TPM), with which I'm associated: In 2006, seven United States attorneys were dismissed in midterm by George W. Bush's Department of Justice. These dismissals were made known locally. They were unusual. Local reports were amalgamated at the national level by a de facto collaboration of TPM readers who posted such stories, in effect improvising a national newsroom. TPM reporters conducted their own investigations. A pattern emerged: the US attorneys had been fired in order to prevent investigations of Republican politicians or because they refused to initiate investigations that would damage Democrats. Congressional hearings ensued. The upshot was that nine high-level officials resigned, including the Attorney General, Alberto Gonzales. Eventually, the Justice Department Inspector General declared that the process used to fire the first seven attorneys and two others dismissed around the same time was "arbitrary," "fundamentally flawed," and "raised doubts about the integrity of Department prosecution decisions." A necessary condition for this rectification was that an assortment of scattered facts was collected into a larger, more penetrating story. This is a prototype of the practice of journalism.

Very few online sites practice the unearthing of facts. For the most part, they opinionate—which is a useful but parasitic activity. It may consolidate opinion among those who feel the need to have opinions; it may bolster feeling; it may mobilize people into political action. But the circulation of news bits originally gathered by newspapers and other dead-tree journalistic endeavors does not preserve reportorial jobs. It does nothing for the economic viability of the mainline press. It speaks to networks of readers who cluster around the opinion sites purposively. They do not stumble upon the big news having looked into the paper because of an interest in sports, comics, or crossword puzzles.

JOURNALISTIC CAREERS?

The revenue that sustains the online sites comes almost exclusively from advertising. Subscriptions, in general, do not work (*The Wall Street Journal* is the great exception in the US). Precious few full-time reporters make a living from the Internet. Most blogs and other news sites are written by people who make their living in other ways, or are working for vanity owners willing to lose money (for a while), or are promoting their freelance careers. Increasingly, Internet journalists will be forced to make their livings with "day-job" careers—like professors.

What this means for journalists starting out is that expectations for journalistic careers are in the process of shifting. It is foolhardy to expect to make a career climbing a single ladder in a journalistic establishment now. Many of our own students at the Columbia Journalism School seem to understand that from the start. As a result, we may recruit more adventurous students—in my view, not a bad thing, though the danger is that adventurousness comes with a steep price of ill-preparation.

WHAT'S THE BUSINESS MODEL FOR SERIOUS REPORTING?

The question that remains, the question that makes serious journalists tremble in the US, is: who is going to pay for serious reporting? For the sorts of investigations that went on last year, for example, into the background of the surprise Republican nominee for Vice President, Governor Sarah Palin of Alaska. Planes to Alaska from the lower 48 states were suddenly choked with reporters from mainstream media. What with the cost of flying nowadays, how many online sites, even the handful of nonprofits supported by public interest foundations, could afford to send a reporter, even if they had the will, drawn in part by the scent of family scandal? A couple of new foundation-supported nonprofit news sites are just starting up to do original, especially investigative, reporting, a development greatly to be welcomed. Voiceofsandiego.org has won attention, with a staff of 11 including 6 reporters and a photographer. Minnesota's MinnPost.com has a staff twice the size. In Paris, mediapart.fr hopes to sustain itself with a few tens of thousands of paid subscribers. Such enterprises seem to be well launched. What they will amount to is anyone's guess.

AUTHORITY

Arguably the erosion of trust is journalism's deepest trouble as well as the one longest in the making. Seen from the public's vantage point, there is a crisis of authority. Do we believe what we read? Should we? What does it mean if we don't? Surveys establish that newspapers have been losing public confidence, as have television networks and local broadcasters as well. Overall, CNN is no more trusted than Fox News. The local paper is not viewed much differently than the *New York Times*. According to one recent study, fewer than one in five Americans say they can believe "all or most" media reporting, down from more than 27 percent—a rather low figure in itself—five years ago. From the news organization's point of view, there is a crisis of credibility, and attendant anxiety. If the public doubts that objective journalism is possible, on what basis can journalists claim professional status? On what does their standing rest? In what sense do they matter in the life of the society? Should they fasten themselves to the mast of objectivity or free themselves altogether from its strictures—and in the latter case, how should they proceed?

Journalism's legitimacy crisis has two overlapping sources: ideological disaffection from right and left, and generalized distrust. Between them, they register something of a cultural sea change. The authority of American journalism has, for a century or so, rested on its claim to objectivity and a popular belief that that claim is justified. These claims are weakening. Americans remain suspicious of political life in the first place. "The pursuit of happiness" is understood as first of all a private pursuit. As Daniel Bell once wrote, America's "sociological foundation was the denial of the primacy of politics for everyday life." Private life deserved to be protected from the State—the American Constitution was founded on that promise. Perhaps the great genius of the newspaper was not simply in the invention of reporting but in the paper's ability to serve as the great aggregator, so that something of a public sliver or even a polygon if not a sphere was created by the sum of all papers, as incidental readers accumulated into functional publics.

Fragmentation has derailed that model. Insofar as newspapers and television news are forfeiting their authority now, and people who do want more than a smattering of news are increasingly congregating around talk radio, cable television, and online sites that match their ideological preconceptions, we are entering unknown cultural territory.

What happens when postmodern suspicion becomes generalized? Pessimists think that the society's ability to adapt to real-world change is impaired. Optimists, who tend to be younger, think that journalistic refashioning and collaboration can produce a model of "distributed knowledge" convertible into the foundation of a positive political transformation. Whether or not we are haltingly working our way toward a productive "revaluation of values" in journalism, I have no idea.

DEFERENCE

No survey of the journalistic landscape, even one this superficial, can omit the journalistic failings that are generated not by particularly poor business decisions, not by technologically assisted fragmentation and media supersaturation, but by the abiding, classic and characteristic sin of journalism: deference to authorities.

We have seen in recent years two devastating failures to report the world—devastating not simply in their abject professional failures but in that they made for frictionless glides into catastrophe. The first was in the run-up to the Iraq war, when the major media tossed away skepticism in favor of cheerleading on the question of Bush's commitment to the existence of a Qaida-Saddam alliance and on the question of WMD. Official mea culpas in the *New York Times* and *Washington Post* only acknowledged after the fact how the reporting was sexed up, how "the intelligence and facts were being fixed around the policy," because journalists did not hesitate to defer to government officials whose cornering of the national security market and mastery of the manipulation of the objectivity fetish went unchallenged.

More recently, we have the run-up to the financial crisis, where (as a study in the current issue of the *Columbia Journalism Review* establishes) the overwhelming majority of articles in the ostensibly critical-minded financial press looked upon the housing-credit bubble as a miraculous achievement of nature. In this case, the authorities deferred to were the bankers, deregulators, and financial analysts whose stake in the bubble was sizable and whose mastery of arcana, and/or ability to obscure the proliferation of nonsensical gambles in the name of unrestrained market rationality, was held to be definitive.

Given these grave failures of journalism even when it was operating at greater strength not so long ago, one might say that rampant distrust is a reasonable and even a good thing. Walter Lippmann famously wrote in *Public Opinion* 85 years ago that journalism was an instrument of public purpose, an effort "to bring to light the hidden facts, to set them into relation with each other, and make a picture of reality on which men can act." The press' failure to connect dots, to piece together the facts and meaning of developments in their profusion, broke the crucial link in the chain, the one that Lippmann summarized in the operative words: "on which men can act."

So even a forthright and broad-gauged address to the crises of circulation, revenue, attention and authority will not restart any Golden Age. It would be foolish to expect it. It is not as though journalism is the only rotten pillar of global society. Journalism cannot be relied on when breakdowns in public trust and intelligence are severe, as long as the political system benefits from institutional myopia, and great fortunes thrive on public ignorance.

RESOLUTIONS

It always warms the heart and calms the mind to follow a discussion of crises with an unveiling of resolutions. The sequence has a pleasing cadence, even when it has to strain for justification. The present case is one of those occasions when talk of resolution is—to say the least—premature.

One reason is circumstantial. The coincidence of crises makes an exit strategy scarcer. How much of the travail of 2008 can be ascribed to the Great Recession, and how much is structural, a function of Internet competition, declining attention, and declining authority all at once? The Project on Excellence's conclusion is that "roughly half of the downturn in the last year was cyclical, that is, related to the economic downturn. But the cyclical problems are almost certain to worsen in 2009 and make managing the structural problems all the more difficult."

Notice the reference to "managing the structural problems." They cannot be solved, they can only be managed. The unavoidable likelihood, pending a bolt from the blue, is that the demand for journalism will continue to decline and that no business model can compensate for its declining marketability. No meeting of newspaper people is complete these days without a call—some anguished, some confident—for a "new business model" that would apply to the online "paper." The call has been issued over the course of years now. It might be premature to say so, but one might suspect that it has not been found because there is none to be found.

The repute of journalism as a force for enlightenment rested heavily on the assembling of what was, in a sense, an accidental public. Even in times of high circulation, the readership of newspapers came through two fairly distinct channels. There was an amalgamation of citizens charged, or charging themselves, with the task of knowing their world better in order to govern themselves. These readers were frequently partisan. In the 19th century, they had their own newspapers. Even in the 20th century, with the promotion of the ideal of objectivity, they were often interested parties. This amalgam was supplemented by a wide array of readers who were drawn to the newspapers to consult features, recipes, comics, sports reports, and movie schedules, and who, having been drawn there, grazed past news of the wider world and became passingly familiar with the actions of governments and other prime movers.

The fact that large numbers, even majorities of the population, were drawn to the news became a resource for reformers of all stripes. Public opinion—which was a phantom, as Walter Lippmann argued—was there to be mobilized because the public assembled itself around the breakfast tables and on railroad cars, reading the papers. With the decline of the newspaper comes the decline of the unitary public as a force capable of being mobilized.

This doesn't mean that the new media dispensation is a bulldozer set against democracy. The success of the Obama campaign last year in turning the Internet into a force for mobilization makes that plain. Still, the new administration groans under the weight of its obligations, and whether it can sustain that mobilization remains to be seen. Meanwhile, the diminishment of news continues, and much as we are in the business of stripping away our illusions, there is no way this can be good. As the sociologist Paul Starr has recently argued, the coverage that suffers most as newspaper costs are cut is the local- and state-level coverage for which there is the least independent demand. In the chronically corrupt state of New Jersey, for example, there were 50 reporters assigned to cover the state capital twenty years ago; now, 15 remain. The major national newspapers will survive in some fashion, I don't doubt (much). But the middle levels are crumbling.

Proposals to shore up newspapers, to rescue them from the consequences of their horrendous business decisions, tend to point to two possible sources. Both, in turn, rest on public policy.

One way to go is financial support for nonprofit foundations, charities, the likes of which own newspapers in a few cities, and are, selectively, supporting reporting through nonprofit websites like ProPublica.org and Voiceofsandiego.org. Of course, the very existence of nonprofit foundations rests on tax policies that advantage their creation. So in the end, it is public policy and only public policy that will determine what kind of journalism survives.

A few weeks ago, at Senate hearings, Steve Coll, a former managing editor of the *Washington Post*, proposed that Congress make it easier for news organizations to refound themselves on nonprofit bases and moreover to subsidize reporting now being shut down. Many proposals are circulating: tax subsidies for newspaper subscriptions; new advantages to nonprofit newspaper owners. If there were a national endowment that poured money into serious reporting via local boards dominated by professional (platform-neutral) journalists, it could do a great deal to wall off the journalists from the smothering embrace of the state.

Or the unregulated, laissez-vous-faire market. Even in the US, we're rapidly running out of alternatives to public finance. Perhaps it can still be said that the experience of the BBC demonstrates that financing can be heavily insulated from control. The US, lacking the license fee, has more trouble. Still, even in the US, it's time to move to the next level and entertain a grown-up debate among concrete ideas.

Can a public board give representation to a range of voices, including nominees by Congress, thereby improving the odds that decent reporting survives the ineptitude of newspaper publishers? I don't know. Are the BBC and Channel 4 models for hands-off subsidy? I don't know that either.

What I do know is that journalism is too important to be left to business interests. If there were any doubt as to what newspapers at their best can accomplish for the public good, you need look no further than the British parliamentary scandal. If there were any doubt that the best American newspaper is worried about the coverage that newsroom shrinkage is preventing, take this headline, from page 3 of the *New York Times* of May 21st: "Death Row Foes See Newsroom Cuts as Blow."

Leaving it to the myopic, inept, greedy, unlucky, and floundering managers of the nation's newspapers to rescue journalism on their own would be like leaving it to the investment wizards at the American International Group (AIG), Citibank, and Goldman Sachs, to create a workable, just global credit system on the strength of their good will, their hard-earned knowledge, and their fidelity to the public good.

A crisis is a terrible thing to waste, as Rahm Emanuel said. I hope my next talk can be called "Building New Foundations from Garbage".

3

The Energy Crisis

Achieving Energy Security and Addressing Climate Change*

James Mulva

Chairman, president, and chief executive officer (CEO), ConocoPhillips, 2004– ; born Green Bay, WI, June 19, 1946; B.B.A., 1968, M.B.A., 1969, University of Texas; U.S. Navy officer, 1969–1973; Phillips Petroleum Company: various positions including vice president and treasurer, 1973–1990; chief financial officer (CFO), 1990–94; senior vice president, 1993; president and chief operating officer (COO), 1994–99, chairman and CEO, 1999–2002; president and CEO, ConocoPhillips, 2002–04.

Editor's introduction: In this address, presented at a National Press Club luncheon, James Mulva insists that the movement toward a green energy policy must coincide with immediate energy needs. He advocates a national energy policy rather than the piecemeal approach he claims has been taken so far. Mulva outlines four principles the policy should incorporate: supply diversity (including greater U.S. production of fossil fuels), energy efficiency, technological innovation (funded partly by government incentives), and environmental stewardship. Describing the U.S. Climate Action Partnership, of which his company is a member, he restates its call for a national framework to reverse the growth of greenhouse emissions. He also defends the energy industry against accusations of unfair profit-taking.

James Mulva's speech: Thank you, Sylvia, for those nice words. Ladies and gentlemen, as a visitor to Washington, I feel a keen sense of history in the air. On Pennsylvania Avenue, workers are putting final touches on the grandstands for next week's inauguration. In just seven days, our new President will take office. President-elect Obama is personally very impressive. His confidence and calmness are reassuring. The transition process has been smooth. And talented people are joining his staff and his Cabinet.

Meanwhile, though, on Main Street across America, the public recognizes that we face staggering challenges that really cannot be deferred, among them the global economic slowdown, the U.S. recession and job losses, the financial and credit crises. They're affecting everyone. And the world's geopolitical hotspots

---

* Delivered on January 13, 2009, at Washington, D.C. Reprinted with permission.

continue to smolder. We must meet these challenges head-on, so there is a thirst for new leadership. I know I speak for everyone here in saying that we all want success for the new President and his Administration. We all want to see our problems successfully addressed and overcome.

The question is, how should we go about it? A year or even six months ago, with gasoline prices triple what they are today, energy security was on the A-list of the vital issues facing the Administration, Congress, and the worldwide public. So was climate change. Now, they have taken somewhat of a back seat, replaced by the new challenges that we're facing.

But complex issues are often very much interrelated. For example, by restricting energy development at home, we export dollars for imports, which means we also export jobs, the trade balance worsens, the dollar weakens, and government tax revenues fall. Also, what may be considered minor geopolitical events in oil-producing regions become more urgent strategic threats.

One of the solutions that President-elect Obama has suggestion is the creation of a green energy economy. This is intended to help address energy security, climate change, and job creation. We agree that we must reduce the environmental footprint of energy production and consumption. But we must also be realistic about the cost of green energy, also about its true potential and how long it will take for commercial-scale supply contributions.

At the same time, we must be realistic about society's needs. Our economy requires readily available energy today, not just the promise of it ten or twenty years from now. This energy must be reasonably and competitively priced when compared to energy costs in other countries. And finally, we must avoid inadvertently creating unattainable public expectations. An energy transition will not occur overnight at little cost and with no inconvenience.

So how can we reconcile these realities with the concept of a green energy economy? We should start with the basics by enacting a balanced national energy policy. Now, you may be surprised to learn that the U.S. does not already have one. There have been a number of constructive energy bills passed by Congress over the years. But when taken collectively, they did not ultimately solve the country's energy dilemma. The problem is that none of these bills dealt comprehensively with all the issues surrounding energy uses and sources. They never encompassed all forms of energy. They never took the opportunity to incent and inspire increased supply. They also never sought to reduce demand by encouraging greater energy efficiency.

Instead, they chose winners and losers. They focused on the supply sources that seemed to be most popular at that point in time. They ignored or even penalized other potential sources. For example, today's popular and politically appealing choice is alternatives and renewable energy. But what about all the other sources that actually make up the bulk of our supplies? Given our past history, it should be clear that we need a different approach. We need a comprehensive policy that incorporates four principles.

And the first is broad supply diversity, and the second greater energy efficiency. Third is technological innovation, and fourth, sound environmental stewardship, including addressing climate change. I'll explain starting with supply diversity.

We need more energy in all forms. ConocoPhillips strongly supports development of alternative and renewable sources like solar, wind, geothermal, biofuels, and others. But there is, to borrow a well-known phrase, an inconvenient truth. We also need more fossil fuels—oil, natural gas, and coal—as well as more nuclear power. Alternative energy cannot come online fast enough at the scale required to replace these sources, not for decades to come.

So the U.S. must encourage more domestic oil and natural gas development. It could easily do so by opening for exploration some of the promising areas that are now off-limits. The public overwhelmingly agrees. Although the 27-year-old offshore drilling moratorium has expired, there are still needless restrictions. And some in Congress even want to re-impose the ban. This would be, in our opinion, a mistake of historic proportions. The central and western Gulf of Mexico today yield 25 percent of domestic production of oil and natural gas. This keeps hundreds of billions of dollars at home that would otherwise go for imports.

There also may be substantial potential for oil and gas resources in eastern Gulf of Mexico and off the Atlantic and Pacific coasts. But it's time for us to find out just what may be there. A comprehensive energy policy should also encourage development of non-traditional fossil fuels such as oil sands, oil shale, and natural gas hydrates. These sources are abundant and are located within our borders or very nearby.

For example, Canada's oil sands are one of the world's largest hydrocarbon deposits. They hold more than eight times current U.S. reserves. And available volumes could grow with new technology. The U.S. is the logical market for this oil. It already flows to refineries in the Midwest for processing. This creates jobs, generates income tax revenue, and increases regional fuel supplies.

But there are some who want to stop this oil from coming here. They object to the carbon intensity and the impact of development. Canada and its citizens have already weighed the pros and cons. They are devising environmental standards that will account for the resulting greenhouse gas emissions. So the oil sands will be developed. Either we bring this oil here to the U.S. from a secure and friendly source, or watch it go to other countries instead.

Now the second tenet of a comprehensive policy must be improving our energy efficiency. Since the 1970s, the United States has doubled its economic output per unit of energy consumed. That's great progress, but we can still do far much more. The public is driving less, so gasoline demand is down. There is also greater awareness of the need for energy efficiency at home and at work. Now, government could inspire further improvement through public education and by enacting broader efficiency standards.

Third, the new policy should promote innovation by encouraging research and development. Industry is making substantial investments already. Government can encourage further private investment by granting incentives. We also need public investment in technologies that realistically can't be funded by industry, such as those that require very long lead times or highly advanced science. Examples would include natural gas hydrates, nuclear fusion fuel cells. We would benefit, too, also from greater support in our educational system, particularly in the scientific and engineering disciplines. Otherwise, we anticipate a shortage of industry technical personnel in the future.

And fourth, we must achieve these priorities while serving as good environmental stewards. As part of this, our industry must invest in cleaner forms of energy. For example, ConocoPhillips is one of North America's leading producers of clean burning natural gas. We also blend ethanol into our gasoline. We produce renewable diesel fuel from surplus animal fats and vegetable oils. And we are researching next-generation biofuels. We are developing new materials for the lithium ion batteries that will be used in electric cars. And we're also considering investments in other energy sources.

To summarize, we believe that as the U.S. pursues a green energy economy, its policies should encourage development of all forms of energy. They should promote energy efficiency, technical innovation, and environmental protection. Oil and natural gas have a vital role to play in this energy equation. They will continue as our leading energy sources for the foreseeable future. They will help bridge the gap from today until alternative, and renewable energy become more fully available.

By producing more energy here at home, we would strengthen our national industrial base and help with respect to leading the economic recovery. We would create jobs, generate government tax and royalty revenue, and help relieve the trade deficit. Conventional fossil fuels can also be relatively green themselves. Natural gas is abundantly available today. Hopefully gas from hydrates will prove viable in the future.

A stronger domestic energy industry would also be an even more effective technology incubator. For example, our company has developed a proprietary technology to turn coal into cleaner burning gas. We are researching biofuels that would utilize existing infrastructure such as refineries, pipelines, and marketing outlets. This approach would make new biofuels less expensive and less destructive to our way of transportation distribution and life.

In addition, the industry's expertise lends itself to the development of carbon capture and storage capability. We have a lot of technology and applicable experience that can relate to such a function. This could become one of the key solutions to greenhouse gas emissions.

Now, this brings me to climate change, which is another interrelated issue. We believe that the public will not allow new energy development unless resulting carbon impact is addressed. Conversely, the public will not favor reductions in carbon emissions if, as a result, energy prices are forced upward too much or too fast. Both issues must be addressed, therefore, together.

Now, ConocoPhillips, as Sylvia indicated, belongs to the U.S. Climate Action Partnership. This is a coalition of businesses and environmental groups that share a vital belief. We believe that time is not on our side in terms of climate change, that each year the U.S. delays controlling its emissions, the greater the future risk. So USCAP is calling for a mandatory national framework to slow, stop, and then reverse the growth of greenhouse gas emissions. In the absence of this framework, ConocoPhillips, like many other companies, is voluntarily managing our emissions. We are improving the efficiency of our facilities [and] our refineries. We have a climate change plan that calls for new control processes and technologies; it also calls for identifying potential investment opportunities in low- or zero-carbon businesses. Additionally, we also are pretty active traders of carbon in Europe and Canada.

But voluntary efforts are not going to be enough. And neither is the current patchwork of state initiatives. They very widely create overlaps and inefficiencies. Instead, we need a single, consistent national program. In two days, USCAP will release its comprehensive climate policy recommendations. They should convey a—well, these recommendations were hammered out during about two years of hard work, analysis, debate, and compromise. They should convey a high degree of credibility and merit because of the broad and diverse membership of USCAP. It includes manufacturers of products from cars to medical devices to pharmaceuticals. There are energy producers and electric utilities. There are companies engaged in mining, financial services, and consulting. There are prominent environmental organizations.

In short, there's a broad representation of business and industry and of the environmental community. So the consensus recommendations are neither a one-sided, pro-industry approach nor a solely pro-environmental approach. They are balanced. They can and should serve as a guide to Congress as it creates climate policy. I will not preempt USCAP by providing specific details, but I can tell you that the recommendations are substantive and will be widely communicated to Congress, the Obama Administration, and to the public.

There's one final area in which the energy industry must do more. And that is addressing our place in society. You know, obviously, society needs energy, and it powers nearly all economic activity. That's not going to change even as the sources evolve over time. There will always be entities that supply energy, and energy will always have some cost associated with it. Unfortunately, our industry has been tarred by misperceptions on energy prices and profits. It's always tempting to blame us whenever energy prices rise.

However, prices respond to world supply and demand, which should be pretty clear at this point in time. Some of the public understands this and so does the media. Unfortunately, too many in government choose to ignore the facts. They ignore that U.S. policy contributes to supply challenges, and thus, from time to time, price increases. There also is a lack of recognition of the scope, scale, and size of the projects necessary to bring on additional supplies. Easy-to-find energy has already been found and developed. It's the more difficult that is ahead of us. And lack of knowledge of the development time that major projects require: Many things that we do are not six or twelve month efforts. They're three, four, and most likely, five and six year projects, and sometimes take ten years to develop. Investment decisions must be made and billions of dollars spent years in advance of the project startup.

As for the record profits of the past few years, they have now deflated. Few people know that since the year 2000, oil industry returns on investment only kept up with the average of the S&P 500. They had lagged behind for many years. But the concern over the absolute size of profits has inspired a fixation on taxing the industry. Our effective tax rate is already twice that of manufacturing companies in general.

An example, the recent financial bailout contained new tax provisions that impact only the oil industry. We are relieved at President-elect Obama's recent statement that a windfall profits tax is no longer on his agenda. We further urge that future legislation not single out the oil and natural gas sector alone to pay for alternative energy, or for reducing carbon emissions. This is vital because we must retain adequate financial capability. We need to continue to make multi-billion dollars of new investments, provide new jobs, develop new technology, and find the oil and natural gas that our country needs. Our industry should be recognized for what it is: We are an asset that is essential to the national security and economic health of our country.

So I conclude. As we look forward to the coming week, I want to stress once again that ConocoPhillips is ready, willing, and eager to work with the new Administration. We join in congratulating President-elect Obama on his historic achievement in winning the presidency. And we offer our support for his efforts to address the country's challenges. We understand the current intense focus on economic recovery, but we also urge Congress and the incoming Administration to remember the economic importance of sound energy and climate policies. They are key to our long-term prosperity and the well-being of our country. We need comprehensive, well-thought-out policies, and we need them soon.

Natural Gas and the Jackrabbit*

Jesse H. Ausubel

Director, Program for the Human Environment, Rockefeller University, 1993– ; vice president, programs, Alfred P. Sloan Foundation, 2009– ; born New York, NY, September 27, 1951; A.B., Harvard College, 1974, M.I.A. and M.B.A., resource economics, operations research, Columbia University, 1977, Ph.D. (Hon. Causa), Dalhousie University, 2009; fellow, Climate Research Board, National Academy of Sciences, 1977–79; research scholar, Resources and Environment, International Institute for Applied Systems Analysis, 1979–1981; study director, National Research Council Board on Atmospheric Sciences and Climate, 1981–83; director of Studies, National Academy of Engineering, 1983–89; fellow, Science and Public Policy, Rockefeller University, 1989–1993; program director, Alfred P. Sloan Foundation, 1994–2009.

Editor's introduction: In this speech, presented to the PowerSouth Energy Cooperative, which provides wholesale power in Alabama and Florida, Jesse H. Ausubel makes a case for methane as a viable form of green energy instead of so-called "renewable" sources. Ausubel advises against irrational exuberance about the potential for change due to temporary financial upheavals and describes long-term trends in energy use as defined by decarbonization. Methane, he maintains, is the best source for providing electrical power, and he urges the development of methane-fueled zero-emissions power plants, or ZEPPs. He claims that the whole notion of "fossil" fuels is erroneous, and that massive stores of energy from methane may come from within the Earth. Ausubel further insists that in fact renewables are quite damaging to the environment and are largely inefficient.

Jesse Ausubel's speech: Thanks to Chairman Gary Smith and the PowerSouth Energy Cooperative for the opportunity to speak about the energy business viewed through a green lens. In the end my green lens will focus on natural gas, methane, not so-called renewables. My task is to explain why methane is green and destiny, and why renewables are neither green nor destiny.

---

* Delivered on January 22, 2008, at Sandestin, Florida. Reprinted with permission.

First, let me comment on a current temptation. The sudden crash of the US and world economies during 2008 tempts us to have faith in revolutionary change. For energy systems, we should resist the belief that in a short time everything can be different. Very stable trends characterize the energy system. In fact, the stable trends finally appear to go unscathed through economic depressions, wars, and, for better or worse, fashions in public policy.

Let me begin with an extreme example of public policy, the central planning that followed a famous revolution, the Bolshevik Revolution of 1917 in Russia's. The Russian Revolution and later World War II literally drove Russians back into the woods to collect their fuel. Yet, these extreme political and economic shocks were later entirely absorbed. A "business as usual" extrapolation of market substitution using logistic curves for the period 1890–1915 predicts market shares of primary fuels in the USSR in 1950 very nicely. By 1950 one sees no visible effect on the energy system of World War I, the Bolshevik Revolution, the Great Depression, or World War II. Wood was disappearing right on schedule, coal peaking, oil growing, and soon gas would be soaring, and nuclear penetrating.

I would say the energy system had arrived at its genetic destiny. Along the way, the leaders of Russia and its adversaries had made the population miserable. Yet, the so-called leaders and planners made no lasting effect on the USSR energy system.

America's experience in energy systems differs little from Soviet Russia. Consider for the US the change of four variables—population, affluence, consumer behavior, and technological efficiency—that together cause emissions of sulfur dioxide and carbon dioxide. Charting the changes of combinations of these variables against growing affluence between 1900 and 2007 reveals the effect of intervals of economic depression and recession. For sulfur, in the Depression of 1930–1935 the system backtracked and then resumed its trajectories, barely affected. The chaotic fluctuations during the post-war recession of 1945–1952 were similarly soon absorbed. For sulfur, the system worked its way through a 100-year program of growing and then declining emissions. Richer was first dirtier, but then richer became cleaner, in a great arc economists call a Kuznets curve, for the American economist Simon Kuznets.

What differs between sulfur and carbon is the duration of the life or product cycle. For carbon, completing the arc—the Kuznets curve—will take three hundred rather than the one hundred years sulfur took. Carbon will weigh in the energy system for another 75 years or so.

Returning to the regressive effects of economic turmoil, a zoom into the carbon dioxide emission story during the Depression in shows the effects in detail. The system darts this way and that before regaining its long-run orientation. We observe the jack rabbit behavior of a system in a depression. To summarize, periods of depression and other forms of shock such as war do not revolutionize an energy system, though they do release lots of hot air from politicians and pundits.

Here let me introduce the most important trend in the environment for the energy business, namely decarbonization. Hydrocarbons are of course a mix of hydrogen (H) and carbon (C). Each combines with oxygen to release energy, with the hydrogen converted to water (H_2O), and the carbon mostly converted to carbon dioxide, CO_2, which is food for plants but also a greenhouse gas that now worries a lot of people. On average, when one removes the water, biomass fuels such as wood, hay, and oats have a ratio of about 40 C to 4 H. Charcoal is essentially pure C. Coal comes in many shades but typically has about 8 C for each 4 H. Popular liquid products, like gasoline and jet fuel, average about 2 C for each 4 H. Methane, CH_4, burns only 1 carbon for each 4 hydrogen atoms, 1/40th the ratio of wood.

Twenty-five years ago, my colleagues Cesare Marchetti, Nebjosa Nakicenovic, and Arnulf Gruebler and I put all the hydrocarbons humans used each year for the past two centuries in a hypothetical gigamixer and plotted the history of fuel in terms of the ratio of C to H. To our surprise we found a monotonic trend, namely the ascent of hydrogen. We named the trend decarbonization for the concomitant descent of carbon.

The history of hydrocarbons is an evolutionary progression from biomass to coal to oil to natural gas and on to hydrogen, eventually derived from non-fossil fuels in order to keep the primary mix clean of carbon. Carbon loses market share to hydrogen as horses lose to cars or typewriters lose to word processors. The slow process to get from 90 percent C to 90 percent H in the fuel mix should take about 300 years and pass the 90 percent mark about 2085. Let's say 2100 so as not to appear overconfident.

Some decades have lagged and some accelerated but the inexorable decline of carbon seems clear. Times make the man. The patron of my university, John D. Rockefeller, surfed on this long wave by standardizing oil. Al Gore surfed the wave to a Nobel Peace Prize. Over the past 20 years decarbonization has entered the vernacular, and a New York money manager even has a decarbonization mutual fund. Successful people and companies ride the wave of history and arrogate fame and money. I hope people hearing or reading this speech do so.

A variation of decarbonization as a competition between carbon and hydrogen shows the kilos of carbon per unit of energy, thus integrating fuel switching with increases in efficiency, that is, technical progress, for example better motors. The global kilos of carbon per joule of energy slide inexorably downward. The variation of carbon per GDP further integrates energy with consumer behavior, that is, whether consumers favor energy with their marginal dollar. The US is not an exception to the world trend. The US will soon celebrate its centennial of falling carbon per dollar.

One naturally asks why long-term decarbonization lines always point down for C and up for H. The explanation is that the overall evolution of the energy system is driven by the increasing spatial density of energy consumption at the level of the end user, that is, the energy consumed per square meter, for example, in a city. Finally, fuels must conform to what the end user will accept, and constraints become more stringent as spatial density of consumption rises.

The spatial density of consumption in vertical cities like Shanghai is soaring. Such rich, dense cities accept happily only electricity and gases, now methane and later hydrogen. These are the fuels that reach consumers easily through pervasive infrastructure grids, right to the burner tip in your kitchen.

Ultimately the behavior of the end user drives the system. When the end user wants electricity and hydrogen, the primary energy sources that can produce on the needed scale while meeting the ever more stringent constraints that attend growth will eventually and inexorably win. Economies of scale are a juggernaut over the long run.

One contributor to economies of scale is the heat value of the fuel per kilo. Replacing brown coal with methane raises the energy per ton of fuel as it decarbonizes. Thirteen railroad cars of biomass such as switchgrass equal about one railcar of coal and half a car of oil. Economies of scale match best with technologies that grow smaller even as they grow more powerful, as computer chips, electric motors, and power plants all have done. Miniaturization matters because it multiplies the potential market, as laptops show compared to mainframe computers. Moreover, miniaturization is green. It shrinks our footprint.

Miniaturization also matters because, notwithstanding the present depression, over the long-run energy use will keep rising. One reason is that computer chips could well go into 1000 objects per capita, or 10 trillion objects worldwide, as China and India log into the game. By the way, some studies suggest the total energy system demand of a cell phone is not unlike a refrigerator, because the telecom system must flood the skies with waves and always be on. PowerSouth managers probably know exactly how its customers have increased demand by filling homes, hotels, and offices with wifi and flat screens even as lamps and appliances became more efficient.

What is the most promising way for the energy system to meet fluctuating and then again rising consumer demand amidst green fears? For electricity, the obvious and destined route is methane, and PowerSouth is about halfway there. Methane is inherently good for reasons now well established, but it can be even better.

The next big trick is to take rocket engines and turn them into power plants. One might, say, take a cruise missile or even the space shuttle and turn it upside down and operate it for a few hundred thousand hours. While methane consumption grows, humanity will not permit itself to dispose of much of its carbon in the air. So, engineers and managers must also capture the emissions and make a methane-fueled Zero Emission Power Plant or ZEPP.

Operating on methane, a ZEPP puts out electricity and carbon dioxide that can easily be sequestered. From an engineering point of view, the key is air separation or abundant cheap oxygen so that the fuel can be burned neatly with the O_2 and leave streams only of CO_2 and water. While in principle any fuel could be an input to such a machine, the theme of clean-up on the front end favors methane. Coal is a minestrone with sulfur, mercury, cadmium, and other headaches. Why buy rocks that will leave piles of these elements that will likely cause a plant site to become a regulated toxic waste dump, when one can purchase methane that is already almost purely C and H? Chemical engineers appreciate the benefits of fine feedstock.

ZEPP technology is exemplified by the Kimberlina plant of a company called Clean Energy Systems in Bakersfield, California, which already has operated for 4 years a prototype ZEPP of 20 MW, which I visited myself. Some day the Kimberlina plant may become an environmental world heritage site for its contribution to decarbonization. Operating at high temperatures and pressures, the plant, or rocket one might say, is delightfully compact.

Clean Energy Systems is also working on a 200 MW generator, whose dimensions are even more striking. Think of a 200 MW generator or turbine as a mobile home and the power park as half a dozen trailers. The "All in" efficiency of the ZEPP including compressed CO_2 as a by-product should be about 50 percent. The CO_2 can be sequestered underground in a saline formation or used lucratively for enhanced oil recovery or enhanced gas recovery.

Pushing the envelope on pressure and temperature, Japanese colleagues at Tokyo Electric Power Company calculate that a ZEPP a few decades hence could reach 70 percent efficiency, green indeed compared to the 30 percent of today's coal plants. Doubling the efficiency of power plants attracts me as a way to spare carbon emission. My dream is a 5 GW ZEPP, super fast, operating at high temperatures and high pressures and thus super compact. A single machine the size of a locomotive would more than double PowerSouth capacity and fit comfortably within the existing infrastructure!

Where will the methane come from? Here let me introduce a heresy. I reject the notion of "fossil" fuels, which implies that all or most oils and natural gases derive from the buried and chemically transformed remains of once-living cells. Think of Earth instead as a steaming plum pudding, outgassing since forever. Primordial, non-biological carbon comes in the first place from the meteorites that helped form Earth and other planetary bodies. Abiogenic carbon clearly abounds on such planetary bodies as Titan, which enjoyed no Carboniferous or Jurassic eras with giant ferns and dinosaurs. Now astronomers sniff outgassing methane on Mars, too.

Water also abounds inside Earth, perhaps ten times as much as in the oceans. Suppose the carbon is upwelling from the core and mantle of the planet and then, through a range of interactions with hydrogen and oxygen at high temperatures and pressures, enters the crust from below as a carbon-bearing fluid such as methane, butane, or propane. Continual loss of the very light hydrogen brings it closer to what we call petroleum or even coal. Emissions from volcanoes and earthquakes give further evidence of very deep hydrocarbons eager to outgas.

The fossil theory relies on the long unquestioned belief that life can exist only at the surface of Earth. In one of the most exciting scientific developments of recent years, science has now established the existence of a huge, deep, hot biosphere of microbes flourishing within Earth's crust, down to the deepest levels we drill. In fact, humanity has never drilled deeper than life. Mud from the deepest holes of 30,000 and 40,000 feet bears life. These deep microbes can best be explained by diffuse methane welling from the depths on which methane-loving bugs thrive. Oil, too, is very desirable to microbes.

So, the alternate concept is that the deep hot biosphere adds its products to the upwelling hydrocarbons. The bioproducts have caused us to uphold the belief that the so-called fossil fuels are the stored energy of the Sun. I believe much, maybe most, of the oil and gas is not the stored energy of the Sun but primordial hydrocarbons from deep in Earth. And they keep refilling oil and gas reservoirs from below, as reported in fields deep under the Gulf of Mexico. Alternate theories of the origins of gas, oil, and coal may well revolutionize Earth sciences over the next two to three decades, and lift estimates of resource abundance. Methane may more truly be an inexhaustible and even renewable fuel, generated continually deep in Earth, than forests, which humanity managed to eliminate from much of North Africa, for example, for about 2000 years..

New theory will also help reveal methane resources in little-explored places, such as the continental margins, where the sea floor slopes from a few hundred meters deep to a few thousand. Now frequent discoveries of communities of life that live around cold seeps of methane on continental margins suggest that margins have lots of fracture zones where gas upwells. Methane seeps are plentiful on the slopes of PowerSouth's service area in the Gulf of Mexico, near the potentially giant Jack Field touted in September 2006.

A more embracing theory of the margins in which outgassing methane occurs all along their extent creates not only startling life on the margins but vast ribbons of opportunity for offshore exploration. Israel just proved the opportunity by finding deep carbon 16 thousand feet beneath 5 thousand feet of water on its continental margin. The abundance of deep carbon, especially accessible offshore, and its possible explanation, is a big story for the energy industry. The big news from Brazil is not the few gallons of alcohol from sugar cane that provide less than 10 percent of that nation's primary energy, but the plans of Petrobras to expand offshore natural gas extraction from astonishingly rich and surprising superdeep wells from 7 million cubic meters per day in 2013 to 40 million per day in 2020.

Working in the oceans brings immense responsibility. The oceans are beautiful beyond imagination, as the discoveries of the Census of Marine Life research program repeatedly show. But we have already squandered many riches of the oceans, and we do not want to squander or harm more. The energy industries, including PowerSouth, should become leading stewards of marine life, supporting creation of protected areas, research, and monitoring, while operating perfectly where society does permit operation. Florida and other states in the Gulf Region can see the example of operators in places such as Norway, where gas extraction activities from subsea structures minimally impact the environment.

Returning to the land, shale formations such as the Barnett and Marcellus also harbor vast amounts of methane. The recent documentation of the US reserves of about 2000 tcf, comparable or larger than the fabled Russian reserves, should limit methane price volatility, a widely cited objection to the growth of methane's market share.

Methane is compact, but uranium is 10,000 to 100,000 times more so. Small is beautiful, and nuclear is very small. It is, after all, atomic power. While the competition will take another century or so, finally nuclear energy remains the overwhelming favorite to produce the hydrogen and electricity that Alabama and Florida, not to mention Bangalore and Shanghai, will demand. The important point is nuclear's environmental superiority to so-called renewables.

The reason, as hinted already, is that efficiency must be reckoned in space as well as energy and carbon. The essence of green is "No New Structures!", or at least few new visible ones, in the Gulf of Mexico or South Alabama. I repeat that, like computers and the Internet, the energy system to be deeply green should become more powerful and smaller. During the 20th century, electric generators grew from 10 to 1 million kW, scaling up an astonishing 100,000 times. Yet a power station today differs little in the space it occupies from that of 50 or 100 years ago.

What about the so-called renewable forms of energy? They may be renewable, but calculating spatial density proves they are not green. The best way to understand the scale of destruction that hydro, biomass, wind, and solar promise is to denominate each in watts per square meter that the source could produce.

In a well-watered area like the Southeast, a square kilometer produces enough hydroelectricity for about a dozen Americans, while severely damaging life in its rivers. In any case, one needs catchment areas of hundreds of thousands of square kilometers to provide gigawatts of electricity, and no such areas remain in the Southeast.

The Southeast abounds in productive forest, but PowerSouth would need to harvest from every acre of three typical Alabama counties to provide kilowatts equal to those generated by a single 1000 MW nuclear power plant on a square kilometer or two.

Shifting from logs to corn, a biomass power plant requires about 2500 sq km of prime Iowa farmland to equal the output of a single 1000 MW nuclear power plant on few hectares. PowerSouth would need to farm every acre of Covington County to generate the kilowatts you would get from a nuclear power plant.

Windmills to equal the same nuclear plant cover almost 800 square km in a very favorable climate.

Photovoltaics require less but still a carpet of 150 sq km to match the nuclear plant.

The spatial ratio for a Toyota rather than a large power plant is equally discouraging. A car requires a pasture of a hectare or two to run on biofuels, unwise as the world's vehicle population heads toward 1 billion.

Biofuels, wind, solar, and other so-called renewables massacre habitat. I want to spare land for nature, not burn, shave, or toast it.

No economies of scale adhere to any of the solar and renewable sources, including by the way the sources of ocean energy, such as tides, waves, and the thermal gradient, which also suffer from combinations of dilution and intermittency. If customers need another megawatt, suppliers must site and build yet another windmill, another structure. Supplying more customers or more demanding customers requires matching increases in infrastructure, indeed likely even larger areas, as energy suppliers will probably have used the most fertile, most wavy, windiest, sunniest, and wettest sites first.

Moreover, bridging the cloudy and dark as well as calm and gusty weather takes storage batteries and their heavy metals. The photovoltaics raise nasty problems of hazardous materials. Burning crops inflates the price of food. Wind farms irritate with low-frequency noise and thumps, blight landscapes, and whack birds and bats.

And, solar and renewables in every form require large and complex machinery to produce many megawatts. Per average megawatt electric, a natural-gas combined cycle plant uses 3.3 million tons steel and 27 cubic m concrete, while a typical wind energy system requires construction inputs of 460 million tons of steel and 870 cubic meters of concrete per average megawatt electric, about 130 and 30 times as much. The wind industry is a very heavy industry, as the sight of some of Earth's largest trucks transporting turbines shows.

Renewable energies also invoke high risk as sources of supply in a changing climate. Clouds may cover the deserts investors covered with photovoltaics. Rain may no longer fall where we built dams and planted biomass for fuel. The wind may no longer blow where we build windmills. Maybe PowerSouth should put its Iowa windmills on railcars, as Ronald Reagan wanted to put Peacekeeper intercontinental ballistic missiles on railcars rather than in silos.

And finally, without vastly improved storage, the windmills and photovoltaics are supernumeraries for the coal, methane, and uranium plants that operate reliably round the clock day after day.

Lots of politicians, consumers, and even investors live in an era of mass delusion about solar and other renewables, which will become an embarrassing collection of stranded assets. But let's use our intelligence and resources to build what will work on the large scale that matters for decarbonization rather than to fight irrationality. Humans are not rational after all, and the environment for the energy business never will be.

What about efficiency? On efficiency, I maintain the engineer's view that improvements are embedded in the lines of development of any machine or process. In spite of market failures and other obstacles, increases in efficiency are documented for everything from aircraft and autos to air conditioners and ammonia production. We will be busy squeezing out inefficiency for at least another millennium. The overall thermodynamic efficiency of our energy system, measured from the woodchopper to the hot soup on the dinner table, advanced from only perhaps 1 percent in 1000 to 5 percent in 2000. Cars, most reviled, are perhaps 15 percent efficient, while homes viewed as machines may be only 3–5 percent efficient. The difficulty is, no one has found a way to sustain improvements in efficiency beyond the 1–2 percent/year that seem built into most processes. A big problem seems to be user's time budgets. People discard efficiency strategies like car-pooling if they conflict by even a few minutes with convenience.

While social and other engineers have not discovered durable ways to multiply the rate of increase of energy efficiency, the year 2008 reminded households and enterprises broadly of the virtues of thrift. Thrift and frugality have not been prominent values in world society in recent decades. Indeed, one may attribute the present economic crisis to a worldwide pandemic of Debt Culture. Fortunately, PowerSouth, rooted in rural economy in the best sense, did not join the Debt Culture. For the US, debt soared to three times Gross Domestic Product, as individuals, households, companies of all sizes, and governments at all levels basically decided they could print money a go-go. The adjustment will likely create jackrabbit behavior in the energy system, as Stalin or the Great Depression did, but does not change the fundamentals, like the destiny of natural gas. But it may make finding capital for pipelines and ZEPPs harder.

Now let me return to strategies and fate. Despite public impressions about renewables or coal, in fact during the last decade most orders for new US power plants were gas. Befitting its high rank in decarbonization and benefiting from low prices, gas will become dominant in the next 10–20 years. In the end, the system wins. Don't forget the System; it won't forget you.

So, what is left for strategy, of businessmen or politicians? Their challenge is to minimize waste and unproductive debt, to be on the right side of fate. Waste in the US energy play comes, for example, from the failure to separate natural gas from oil. As an environmentalist, each time I hear "oil & gas" talked about like inseparable twins, I hear missed opportunity. Oil and gas are very different fuels. I spend most of my time with Greens of various kinds, and I believe many Greens would accept drilling for natural gas, whether off-shore Florida or in upstate New York, if natural gas is the exclusive target, if it is not a cover for drilling for more oil and the problems that come with oil.

Politicians could help, or could recognize reality and ratify and legitimize it, by forming state and national energy policy directly about natural gas and not "oil & gas" or "fossil energy." The rights of way for pipelines are the sorts of problems that the political system must and should address. So are liquefied natural gas (LNG) terminals; LNG adds flexibility to the system. So are safety of transport and storage of gas, and underground sequestration of CO_2. Oil will remain a big product for another thirty or forty years, but oil is not a growth industry, whereas enormous need and room exist for growth in thoroughbred natural gas.

Keep in mind that natural gas can penetrate oil's stronghold, the market for mobility. CH_4 can provide both the gigawatts to charge batteries and other forms of electrified transport and the hydrogen to power fuel cells. Americans might be surprised how civil the energy discussion would become if a Natural Gas First policy were decisively promoted.

Let me now summarize. Very stable trends, particularly those of decarbonization and miniaturization, appear finally to go unscathed through economic depressions, wars, and central planning. Fortunately, these trends are green, or perhaps they persist as trends precisely because they are green, that is, they meet constraints of the system associated with increasing spatial density of energy consumption.

Renewables may be renewable but they are not green. Failing to benefit from economies of scale, they offer few watts per square meter and demand more space and volume from nature than the system finally will permit.

Planning, strategy, and R&D should essentially support the invariants in the system. Symmetrically, one should avoid the wasteful, painful excursions around the long-term trends organized by Lenin and Stalin, or the US coal and renewable interests, whom I lump together. For a trillion-dollar industry like energy, jackrabbit search strategies are very costly. For PowerSouth, the strategic green prescription is simple: with due attention to environment and safety, favor methane and compact new machines that use methane efficiently.

From Rhetoric to Reality*

U.S. and Global Energy Security

Shirley Ann Jackson

President, Rensselaer Polytechnic Institute (RPI), 1999– ; member, President's Council of Advisors on Science and Technology, 2009– ; born Washington, D.C., August 5, 1946; S.B., 1968, Ph.D., 1973, Massachusetts Institute of Technology (MIT); researcher, AT&T Bell Laboratories, 1976–1995; professor, Rutgers University, 1991–95; chairwoman, US Nuclear Regulatory Commission, 1995–99.

Editor's introduction: In this speech, delivered at the Johns Hopkins University School of Advanced International Studies, Shirley Ann Jackson addresses what she calls "the linked vulnerabilities of energy security and global climate change." Dr. Jackson sets a frightening stage of climate problems already threatening human life as well as a shift in power and influence internationally from energy users to energy suppliers. She outlines principles for getting "from the extant to the green" and discusses such potentialities as a smart electrical grid and mechanisms to develop and implement new technologies like the Advanced Research Projects Agency for Energy (or ARPA-E). She describes the challenges of increased nuclear power and offers technical possibilities for making it safer and more proliferation-proof. Finally, she warns of a "quiet crisis" of fewer students of science, engineering, and related fields.

Shirley Ann Jackson's speech: Good afternoon. Thank you for inviting me to speak at this distinguished forum.

I will speak, today, on our need to lay the appropriate framework for tackling the linked vulnerabilities of energy security and global climate change. The extreme urgency of these twin challenges requires that the framework be fully comprehensive and consistent. It must address interlinked aspects including policy and regulation, infrastructure, markets, research, technological innovation, and human capital—each leveraging each. A less comprehensive approach will prove incoher-

---

* Delivered on February 5, 2009, at Baltimore, MD. Reprinted with permission.

ent, *ad seriatum*, and, ultimately, ineffective—as has happened so often in prior attempts.

To begin, I suggest that we change our language—that we move beyond the term "energy independence" and use, instead, "Energy Security." Independence implies that we are able to "go it alone," fully supplying our own needs. The term appeals, perhaps, to an aspect of the American psyche—but, it is an unfortunate misnomer. There *is* no energy independence. Of the approximately 190 countries in the world, not one is energy independent—nor likely to be any time soon. Energy Security, on the other hand, suggests the imperatives inherent in the interlinking of national security, global security, and climate security.

CONTEXT

We must understand the complex context within which to frame an effective approach.

We are at a time of exceptional uncertainty and enormous change, when our nation and the entire world face challenges perhaps greater, and more intricate, than ever before.

An unprecedented series of financial market events and their ensuing economic impacts-that are echoed in markets and economies around the globe—have forced us to relinquish past assumptions and former remedies. The geopolitical and geostrategic consequences are still evolving, and the outcomes are not yet clear.

World economic growth is predicted to slide below 3 percent—after an extraordinary run of boom years, in which global gross domestic product (GDP) rose as high as 5 percent, year after year.

We are unsure of our own economy. With extreme credit tightening, the cost of credit is escalating—if it is available. We have burgeoning bankruptcies, foreclosures, layoffs, job loss, bank instability, sinking corporate profits, and an additional national deficit that may reach over $1 trillion, as the full costs of a bailout of financial institutions and economic stimulus are felt.

Nor are we alone. China is implementing a stimulus package of its own, to boost commerce and employ thousands, as the ranks of unemployed migrants from rural areas to cities continue to grow—leading to fears of social unrest. Great Britain is staving off new rounds of bank failure and is dealing, as well, with swelling unemployment and protectionist sentiment. With Russia's oil- and gas-driven economic boom softening, now that the price of oil has fallen to $40 a barrel, once-unquestioned domestic approval ratings of Prime Minister Vladimir Putin are weakening too.

National alignments are changing, as global power, based on the geography of energy and other natural resources, shifts. New player nations, such as Russia, Brazil, India, and China hold new sway in the international sphere. Consider that almost half the world's lithium—used in Blackberrys and sought by automakers for lithium-ion batteries for electric cars—is in Bolivia.

CLIMATE CHANGE

I returned, earlier this week, from the annual meeting of the World Economic Forum. Although its primary focus was on global economic recovery, there was an underlying acknowledgement that, with the planet absorbing more heat than it is emitting, unplanned climate change remains a core challenge that must be addressed globally, holistically, and now. Likewise, there is the growing understanding that climate change and energy security are linked vulnerabilities, which must be addressed immediately—and together.

You may have read about vast "brown clouds" that are sweeping from the Arabian Peninsula, across India and parts of China, to the Yellow Sea. The noxious clouds are a mix of automobile exhaust, coal-fired power plant emissions, chemical industry effluents, and particulate matter from slash-and-burn agriculture, and dung and wood cooking fires. The clouds are blotting Asian skies, reducing sunlight, decreasing crop yields, altering weather patterns, and fouling the lungs of millions. These are critical problems. Climate change does not wait.

In 1850, atmospheric carbon dioxide stood at roughly 280 parts per million. Today, the figure is 385 parts per million. If the concentration of carbon dioxide in the atmosphere reaches 450 parts per million, researchers say that rising seas will threaten coastal areas and reduce rainfall by 10 percent—about as much as the 1930s Dust Bowl drought. Carbon dioxide accounts for about half of the climate warming effect. The other half consists of chlorofluorocarbons, methane, and pollutants such as soot. A National Academy of Sciences study indicates that because of complex interactions between the atmosphere and the oceans, the effects of climate change may last for centuries, even if we succeed in cutting heat-trapping greenhouse gas emissions.

There is growing understanding that we have reached the point of consequences—cascading consequences; that global climate change has very real economic, internal stability, national security, and foreign policy implications that must be acknowledged and dealt with.

Already, melting Arctic ice has opened the once non-navigable Northwest Passage. Ironically, the increased access makes extraction of undersea oil and gas deposits more commercially viable, raising the potential for international conflict over energy resources. In fact, Canada has increased its military presence there.

Desertification in Africa is heightening tensions between nomadic and farming peoples, setting the stage both for starvation and possible genocide.

In low-lying coastal areas—Bangladesh, as an example—millions may be forced to relocate to higher ground. India is constructing a wall along its 2,500 mile border with Bangladesh. Where instability, violence, and extremism fester, climatic changes exacerbate tensions and threaten geopolitical alliances.

On the broader energy front, uncertainty of energy supply, amplified demand, unpredictable price swings, and the impact of climate change have been major drivers of a global energy system restructuring. This restructuring continues, even in the present recessionary environment, and includes new forces, new players, and new alignments.

- New energy markets are developing worldwide, providing opportunity and options for new players.
- Supplier countries and their national oil companies are changing the terms of reference for traditional energy behemoths, especially with regard to oil and gas supply.
- Oil-generated wealth and central banks in developing countries are changing who plays in global financial markets.
- Nations are realigning, shifting old alliances.
- Corporations are realigning their priorities, changing how they do business, and making investments—obviously, to secure market opportunity and to assure energy supply, but also, to improve energy efficiency and reduce their carbon footprint.
- Strategies for climate change mitigation and new markets, also, are driving new trading schemes and investments in new sources and new technologies.

New energy markets have emerged because worldwide energy consumption is being driven by population growth, developing economies, improving living standards, and new energy-dependent technologies. The growth in energy consumption in China, while slowing with the economic downturn, will continue, because China's urban areas seek to create 25 million jobs annually to absorb new job seekers and population migration to urban centers. China is expected to add at least 50,000 megawatts of electrical generating capacity each year—roughly the equivalent of the entire electrical grid of England. Indeed, the lion's share of the Chinese stimulus package will go to such infrastructure.

The original "seven sisters"—western companies that controlled Middle East oil after World War II—are losing prominence to a new set of seven. Saudi Aramco, Russia's Gazprom, China's CNPC, NIOC of Iran, Venezuela's PDVSA, Brazil's Petrobras, and Petronas of Malaysia control almost a third of the world's oil and gas production, and more than a third of its total reserves.

The old "seven sisters," which became four after mergers in the 1990s—Chevron, Exxon-Mobil, BP, and Royal Dutch Shell—produce about 10 percent of the world's oil and gas, and hold just 3 percent of reserves. The International Energy Agency estimates that 90 percent of new production supplies, over the next four decades, will come from developing countries—a big shift from the past. This is leading supply countries, and their national oil companies, to change production-sharing contract terms with "traditional" international oil and gas companies, and to seek greater ownership of assets and a greater share of revenues.

The emergence of the "sisters" from oil-rich countries has been the basis for the creation of Sovereign Wealth Funds (SWF). These are nation-owned entities that have used, primarily, oil revenues to accumulate and manage national funds for investment objectives. Worldwide, it is estimated that some $3 trillion has been assembled in SWFs, especially out of the Middle East. Before the recent downturn, this was projected to reach $7.5 to $11 trillion by 2013. These substantial funds, and their sovereign support, offer both challenges and opportunities for governments and corporations, and are changing behaviors between and among these entities. A number of countries are using accumulated sovereign reserves to stimulate their own economies to survive the global economic recession.

The fact that many of the new "sisters" are state-owned, and that growth in the oil and gas industry rests in their hands, is restructuring national and international alliances, and will impact them for decades to come.

Consider that Russia has used its oil and gas abundance to lock up deals with European countries, even as there is concern that Russia may use its dominant energy position as a political tool.

For example: Gasunie, the Dutch National gas company, has taken a stake (9 percent) in the controversial Nord Stream Pipeline Project. The pipeline, controlled by Gazprom (the Russian gas monopoly), would carry gas directly from Russia under the Baltic Sea to Germany—bypassing Poland, Belarus, Ukraine, and the Baltic States. Some countries (the Baltic States in particular) have objected to the pipeline on the basis of environmental concerns. For others, such as Poland, it means a revenue loss (from transit fees). For still others, it can affect supply (Ukraine).

Although the deal is on track, Gasunie authorities say the global credit crisis is pushing up financing costs, and Russian Prime Minister Vladimir Putin, last week, threatened to scrap the project altogether because of delays caused by EU lawmakers, who have called for a new study of the pipeline's environmental impact. The deal, also, gives Gazprom the option to acquire, from Gasunie, a 9 percent stake in the Balgzand-Bacton pipeline, connecting the Netherlands and the U.K. This would give Gazprom a stake in a British supply pipeline for the first time.

Such moves reflect energy supply concerns in EU countries, which import 80 percent of their oil and gas. EU concerns about Russian geopolitical uses of oil and gas appeared to be borne out when Russia cut off European gas supplies through Ukraine in January because of a Ukraine-Russian contract dispute involving Gazprom's supply of gas to Ukraine. The dispute was resolved, and shortly thereafter, the Russian ambassador to the EU suggested a Gazprom-Ukrainian-EU consortium to oversee the supply of gas to Europe.

The invasion of Georgia by Russia last summer raised questions about the security of oil and gas pipelines through that former Soviet republic. The pipelines begin in Azerbaijan, passing through Georgia en route to ports on the Black Sea and the Mediterranean Sea, where tankers ship the crude, primarily to Western Europe. The pipelines supply about 1 percent of the world's daily oil needs and are owned, in part, by BP, which shut down one line during the fighting as a precaution. Although the lines were not damaged, the invasion, and the location of a Russian fleet off the Georgian coastline, successfully demonstrated that Russia could easily seize their control and emphasized Russia's growing influence in the region, and over Europe.

These realities have led the EU to develop strategies for redundancy of supply, and for new and renewable sources of energy and energy efficiency, both to assure supply through diversification, and to mitigate climate change.

We face a future of bracing adjustment to this changing world.

As we shape our national energy goals and strategies, we must understand and account for the restructuring of the global energy system, its impact on markets, and on international alignments.

Last week, President Barack Obama directed the Transportation Department to establish higher automobile and light truck fuel efficiency standards for model year 2011, and directed the EPA to review the denial of the California waiver request to make emissions standards more stringent than Federal limits. With these (and other) steps, the President made it clear that his administration will address the urgency of energy security and climate change via a linked approach, and in the process, build the "new energy economy."

In a very difficult economic climate, some may ask: "Can we afford to do this?" We cannot afford not to do this. Consider a single element of our dilemma—our dependence on imported oil. Although our consumption has fallen temporarily, it remains above 19 million barrels of oil per day, and we produce just over 5 million. Moreover, the need for energy to fuel economies and to improve living standards—globally—has not gone away. The urgency of climate change is ever-present. The interlinked challenges of energy security and climate change are a global economic security issue, and, for the U.S., a national security issue as well.

STIMULUS PACKAGE AND ENERGY

Calling his economic recovery plan a "down payment" on a new energy economy, the President pledged to put Americans to work on clean energy investments, building a new electricity grid with more than 3,000 miles of transmission lines, and retrofitting federal buildings and some 2.5 million homes for more energy efficiency. The plan includes new mass transit options, and would double our capacity to generate alternative energy over the next three years.

The $819 billion stimulus package—the American Recovery and Reinvestment Act—passed last week by the U.S. House of Representatives, calls, in addition, for investment in digital infrastructure that holds potential for future industries—very much in the way the 1950s investments in interstate roads and highways facilitated the growth of automakers and national retail chains.

Broader energy and climate change legislation is expected later this spring.

Now that we are moving—now that national leadership is committed to action—we must focus on pathways that will lead us from the extant to the green, from rhetoric to reality.

Individual steps have been taken—by states, by regions, by companies, by citizens. Several sector—specific plans have been proposed. What is required is to bring people together across sectors for coalescence around clear goals. But there must be a framework for discussion and action—leading to a comprehensive energy security roadmap. Such a framework should be guided by five key principles:

- First—redundancy of supply and diversity of source. This entails maximizing domestic production and ensuring reliable sources for necessary energy imports. This provides protection against supply disruption events, such as natural disasters or geopolitical instability, and a hedge against price volatility.

- Second—providing for energy conservation and environmental sustainability, with calculation of full lifecycle costs, including the environmental impact of every proposal, program, and product. The sustainability equation must include the carbon cost of source development, from production through use and disposal, and must account for unintended consequences.

- Third—linking optimum source to specific sector of use, thinking strategically about how each sector—electricity generation, residential and commercial heating/cooling, construction, transportation, etc.—is linked to source, for efficiency, cost effectiveness, sustainability, and reliability. We must consider how one sector impacts another—e.g. electricity generation and transmission versus transportation. This principle suggests that we ask not only where conversion from fossil fuels is possible, but where it is possible first. While ground transportation may run acceptably on electricity, airlines, at least today, clearly, cannot. Source for sector of use suggests that we may want to reserve a portion of our fossil fuel to the airline industry, which supports about 33 million jobs internationally, accounts for 7.5 percent of the global domestic product, and is essential to the global economy. If a decision is taken to promote plug-in hybrid vehicles, the resulting greater dependency on electricity, the power plant fuel, and the capacity to generate that electricity must be taken into account, as well as grid capacity and a nationwide network of electric power "charging stations."

- Fourth—investment in sound infrastructure for energy generation, transmission, and distribution, including the necessary regulatory and operational protocols to ensure the safe, secure, and reliable performance of refineries, power plants, the electrical grid, and other facilities.

- Fifth—the development of appropriate supporting policies for well-functioning energy markets, with safeguards against market manipulation. This requires transparent pricing and price signals. An example relates to the carbon content of fuels, processes, and commercial and consumer goods. Proposals have focused on reducing carbon content or carbon dioxide production from point sources through financial incentives—primarily through a cap-and-trade system for carbon dioxide, in which allowances would be sold and the amount of allowance would ratchet down annually. Others espouse a carbon tax to induce reduction of carbon dioxide emissions. The feasibility of either approach will depend upon consistent definition and measurement of the true carbon content of products and processes.

The pathways that follow require policy and regulatory framework, early steps, new technology, research and development, and human capital development.

PATHWAY: POLICY AND REGULATION FRAMEWORK

We must focus on developing cross-sector policy, and regulatory pathways that are consistent across federal, state, regional, and local levels, and that incent all sectors—business and industry, academe, financial, labor, government—in a common direction, so that they do not work at cross purposes.

More immediately, as the U.S. Senate debates the economic recovery package, we will want a consistent, cross-agency policy framework to assure that "shovel-ready" infrastructure projects coincide with future energy security goals.

An example is provided by the work of the U.S. Council on Competitiveness. I serve as University Vice Chairman of the U.S. Council on Competitiveness, and I co-chair its Energy Security, Sustainability, and Innovation (ESIS) initiative, along with James W. Owens, Chairman and Chief Executive Officer, Caterpillar Inc., and D. Michael Langford, National President, Utility Workers Union of America (AFL-CIO). Last fall, the Council released a comprehensive energy security action agenda for the first 100 Days of the new Administration and Congress.

ELECTRICAL GRID

The Council's Plan calls for beginning a National Electrical Transmission Super-highway by engaging state regulatory authorities in streamlining the current regulation/oversight patchwork for transmission within states, and between states, for better interoperability standards for the national grid. This "smart grid" must be able to integrate multiple intermittent and distributed alternative energy sources—wind, solar, biomass, etc., and smart appliances—anywhere, at any time, through a simple "plug-and-play" interface. "Smart grid" challenges include energy storage and active load management to balance renewable source intermittency, advanced control systems for "plug-and-play" operation, and for integrating new technologies responsive to high-level system control, and efficient 24/7 operation, with guaranteed stability and power quality.

Policies for "real-time pricing" is one way to induce "demand response," making the system more responsive to power scarcity, thus more secure. With "real-time pricing," customers pay the current wholesale price of electricity, which can vary from less than 1 cent to almost $1 per kilowatt-hour, providing incentive for customers to use price-sensitive switches. These devices switch off power-using appliances when the price rises above a certain level. Rensselaer economists hope to estimate the dollar value of the benefits of increased demand response, and incorporate predicted demand response into the decisions that the system operator makes to control for costly overcompensations to power scarcity.

The current system is wasteful when it turns on enough power plants to compensate for a complete lack of, say, wind power, because there is almost always some wind power, and there is always some reserve generation capacity on stand-by. Rensselaer researchers hope to develop procedures that optimally account for the likely contribution from intermittent sources, instead of assuming there will be none-procedures to assist in deciding how much fossil-fuel-burning generation to turn on, minimizing the expected cost of power generation.

At Rensselaer, researchers, also, are simulating the effects of different carbon dioxide emission reduction policies on emissions, costs, prices, profits, fuel use, reliability, price volatility, and economic efficiency in the electric power sector.

PATHWAY: EARLY STEPS

The Council's 100-day Action Plan asks that the new Administration and Congress take several immediate steps—some already in the works. It asks that:

- There be a Mandate that Federal procurement—for goods, services, new construction, and facilities retrofits—lead the market toward higher energy efficiency standards, with concomitant reduction of carbon load. Such leadership by example, and by requirement, will encourage the private sector in this direction. President Obama already has moved in this direction.
- That energy source subsidies be equalized to encourage the development and sustainable utilization of all energy sources, and create incentives for, the discovery and deployment of new energy sources.
- That we establish a national "clean energy" bank, modeled on the U.S. Export-Import Bank and the Overseas Private Investment Corporation (OPIC), to provide long-term financing for private sector investment in sustainable energy solutions.

PATHWAY: TECHNOLOGY

ARPA-E

A proposed structural mechanism to develop and implement new technologies is the Advanced Research Projects Agency for Energy (or ARPA-E) created in August 2007 by the America Competes Act, to sponsor "creative, out-of-the-box, transformational," high-risk, high-payoff energy research and development.

Its mission is to reduce dependence on energy imports, lower energy-related emissions, and improve energy efficiency in all sectors. A corollary mission is to ensure that the U.S. retains its technological lead in the development and deployment of advanced energy technologies.

ARPA-E has a complex "customer" base within the federal government, and among state and local governments, which have oversight and regulatory authority for many energy efficiency standards.

Important questions remain concerning its structure and function. How will ARPA-E fit into existing government structures? To whom will it report? How will it be staffed? At what level will it be funded—both in its start-up phase and as it ramps up to full operation? What oversight mechanisms will be used to ensure that the research and development (R&D) that receives funding is tied directly to ARPA-E objectives? Each of these questions deserves careful consideration if ARPA-E is to succeed.

Concerning specific technology pathways, I could talk extensively about technological developments in traditional energy resources used in better ways, including gas, oil, smaller safer cars, and smart lighting and smart displays technologies that involve light-emitting diodes (LEDs) and organic light-emitting diodes (OLEDs). I could describe new renewable energy sources, such as hydrogen fuel cells, photovoltaic technologies, nano-materials and compound semiconductor materials for use in renewables, and developments in wind, solar, safer nuclear power plant design, bio-energy including algae and jatropha oil cultivation, and bio-chemical solar energy. Many are in research phases at the Rensselaer Center for Future Energy Systems, a collaborative effort with Cornell University and Brookhaven National Laboratory. With the understanding that any exclusion is in consideration of our time, I offer only a few examples from work at Rensselaer.

DISTRIBUTED GENERATION TEST GRID

The first example demonstrates that pathways to policy and pathways to technology often intersect.

Distributed Generation (DG) is expected to play an important role in enabling the pursuit and attainment of Renewable Portfolio Standards (RPS), which require states to generate electricity from renewable resources. Distributed generation refers to a small-scale electric generation facility located at or near customer sites (usually industrial), often interconnected to the utility for reliability and power redundancy.

Rensselaer researchers are studying these fundamentally different power sources and the power electronic circuits and controls of these complex and dynamic systems. They are creating a test bed that will simulate the grid and allow the interconnection of sources—such as wind, solar, combined heat and power (CHP), fuel cell, etc.—and loads (equipment, motors, LEDs) to create a platform for extended distributed grid study. They also are studying the stability and dynamic behavior of a utility distribution grid with small inertia, and investigating power quality interactions in inverter-based Distributed Generation. The focus is to develop and test new control features that meet industry safety standards.

In this context, alternating-current simulation has the potential to improve power system operation, policy decision-making, and decisions about what kinds of power plants and transmission equipment should be built.

NUCLEAR TECHNOLOGY

Nuclear power, perhaps, has a unique role in atmospherically benign energy-source technologies. Nuclear power plants emit only negligible amounts of greenhouse gases. They can supply the baseline loads of electricity to power large metropolitan centers. They can be kept online at constant (rather than intermittent) levels of reliability, relatively independent of shifts in weather, and are competitive with coal and gas fired electricity generation today.

No other source of energy has this unique combination of features.

Nuclear power presents unique challenges, as well—related to safety, security, proliferation, and the disposal of waste.

As the challenges of energy security and climate change have gained urgency, we have witnessed a resurgence of interest in nuclear power. In multiple countries operators have renewed nuclear power plants' licenses, extending plant lifetimes. In Asia, nuclear construction has picked up pace. Strong interest in new nuclear design has been expressed on nearly every continent, among countries that already have nuclear power, and among newcomers as well.

Although safety remains a widespread concern, public opinion is strengthening that nuclear power plants can be operated at high levels of safety performance—dependent upon strong safety standards, robust safety culture among operators, and the oversight of a credible, independent regulator. Security improvements have emerged, particularly in the aftermath of September 11th, 2001, which prompted intensive re-evaluations—across every industrial sector—to address vulnerabilities to technologically sophisticated terrorist attacks.

However, the linked challenges of nuclear proliferation and waste disposal remain. No country yet has completed a facility for the deep geological disposal of high-level nuclear waste. Progress on the U.S. geological disposal facility at Yucca Mountain, Nevada, has been slowed by political concerns. The only other geological waste disposal facility under construction is in Olkiluoto, Finland. Neither is likely to be completed before 2020.

A key consideration is how to increase the security associated with nuclear fuel production, its use, and with the storage and monitoring of spent nuclear fuel, and decrease proliferation risk. A primary barrier for would-be nuclear proliferators is the difficulty of obtaining the fissile nuclear material suitable for nuclear weapons use: that is, the technological difficulty of producing weapons-grade uranium through enrichment, or of separating plutonium through the reprocessing of spent nuclear fuel. Although both enrichment and reprocessing may have legitimate civilian uses, and both are permitted activities for signatories of the 1970 Treaty on the Non-Proliferation of Nuclear Weapons, as more countries focus on nuclear power as a solution to energy security and climate change, international concern for corresponding risks continues to build.

Though not every country needs to produce and/or reprocess its own nuclear fuel, those that make the sizable investment in nuclear power will want assurance that nuclear fuel will be readily available—without being subject to geopolitical changes of nuclear fuel supplier countries.

There are two primary avenues for addressing this challenge. The first—an institutional and political solution—would be the creation of new international arrangements for nuclear fuel production to provide user countries with the necessary assurance of the supply of nuclear fuel. Another would be the formation of a public-private partnership between one or more international or regional organizations or companies, each governed by an agreement of its members, both to ensure the supply of nuclear fuel to bona fide users, and to strictly monitor any proliferation-sensitive operations under international safeguards. Either would reduce, if not eliminate, the motivation for each nuclear power user country to have a complete fuel cycle.

The second avenue is technological—support for research and development on innovative nuclear fuel cycles with enhanced proliferation resistance. Pathways for innovation include: pursuit of a thorium fuel cycle; steps to make the conventional uranium enrichment and fuel reprocessing operations more transparent to monitoring; modular reactor cores designed to operate for the full reactor lifetime without refueling; and reprocessing approaches that do not separate out pure plutonium (i.e., so that the transuranic elements are kept together for re-use in new fuel elements, and highly radioactive waste is correspondingly minimized). None of these technological innovations are intended to produce "proliferation-proof" nuclear fuel cycles. But they can fortify barriers against proliferation, making what is already a technologically complex challenge (the production of weapons-grade nuclear material) even less accessible to would-be proliferators.

The future of nuclear power rests with how the interlinked challenges of fuel cycle closure, nuclear waste disposal, and nuclear proliferation can be addressed.

Both policy and technology have more far-reaching implications than they are given credit for. As the United States works toward global climate change agreements—the post–Kyoto protocol negotiations scheduled for the end of this year in Copenhagen—our policy and technology pathways acquire foreign policy and financial market implications. U.S. policy developments have the potential to become more broadly applied as global standards, and can help establish the United States as an environmental leader in achieving international cooperation and agreement. Technological innovations become available through commercial markets to other countries, increasing the distribution of energy efficiencies, environmentally benign technologies, and sustainable sources, while contributing to U.S. economic strength.

PATHWAY: RESEARCH AND DEVELOPMENT

Research and development is so basic, yet investment has declined over time. This is another of the Council's Action Plan steps. It asks that we ramp up investment in energy research, development, and commercialization, by at least tripling the current federal investment in basic and applied energy research and development, as well as other measures to facilitate test-beds and commercial pilots.

PATHWAY: HUMAN CAPITAL DEVELOPMENT

The Quiet Crisis and a Green Energy Workforce

Policy and regulations, first steps, technology, and research and development are essential innovation pathways to energy security and climate change mitigation. But robust innovation of every kind relies entirely upon a single resource-human capital. To move our nation, our world, our environment from rhetoric to reality, from the extant to the green, we must put more focus on, and effort into, fostering a green energy workforce.

As a university president and a theoretical physicist, I have deep concerns that our national innovation capacity is in jeopardy. Converging forces, building over more than a decade, have created what I have dubbed the "Quiet Crisis." These forces are eroding the production of the scientists, mathematicians, engineers, and technologists—the advanced professionals whom we must have for the robust innovation and for effective policy formation—that will address our energy security challenges.

The scientists and engineers who came of age in the post-Sputnik era are beginning to retire. At the same time, we are no longer producing sufficient numbers of new graduates to replace them. This looming talent gap already is evident in many parts of the energy sector, especially in the nuclear and oil and gas industries.

Only about a third of American students, for example, take a physics course in high school. When 6,000 incoming American college freshmen were tested, it was found that they knew about half of what their Chinese counterparts, who take physics courses from 8th grade through the 12th grade, knew. Both groups, however, scored equally poorly on a test of scientific reasoning, in which they considered scientific hypotheses and proposed a solution using deductive reasoning.

We continue to attract talented international scientists, engineers, and graduate and undergraduate students, but we do not encourage enough of them to come, or hold onto those whom we do attract, as much as we did in the past. Other nations are investing in their own education and research enterprises, offering new opportunities for their scientists and engineers to study and to work at home. The "flattening" world means that they, also, can find employment elsewhere, not necessarily in the United States.

Our demographics have shifted. The "new majority" in the United States now comprises young women and the racial and ethnic groups which, traditionally, have been severely underrepresented in our advanced science and engineering schools. It is these "nontraditional" young people to whom we, also, must look for our future scientists and engineers.

This "Quiet Crisis" is "quiet" because the true impact unfolds gradually over time—it takes two decades to educate a biomolecular researcher or a nuclear engineer. It is a "crisis" because our national technological innovation capacity rests solely upon such talent.

Addressing the Quiet Crisis—identifying the talent in all of our young people, and interesting them in the marvels of science and engineering, the wonders of discovery and innovation—is a beginning. But with the urgency of energy security and climate change, we must redouble our efforts and do more.

There is no time to lose.

Because of its urgency, human capital development, too, is incorporated in the First 100 Days Action Plan of the Council on Competitiveness, which asks that we mobilize an energy workforce by creating a "Clean Energy Workforce Readiness Program" and support advanced study by creating competitive, portable undergraduate and graduate fellowships for study in energy-related disciplines. This is a necessary part of maintaining and enhancing our national capacity for innovation by developing our own talent, including the underrepresented majority—women and underrepresented minorities—while continuing to attract and retain exquisite talent from abroad.

The new President's education agenda includes making mathematics and science education a national priority. The plan includes recruiting mathematics and science degree graduates to the teaching profession, and finding and supporting ways to help these teachers learn from professionals in the field. The plan is to ensure that all children have access to a strong science curriculum at all grade levels. The stimulus package contains approximately $140 billion for schools. In the near term, the funds will build and renovate classrooms, and keep hundreds of thousands of teachers from being laid off. The package also includes money for long-term reforms, including teacher bonuses tied to student performance, charter school facilities, and state data systems. This spending is in the stimulus plan approved last week in the House, but it is not in the Senate version.

One key to progress is to engage more women and minority graduate students in pursuing teaching at the highest levels. The lack of these groups as role models to demonstrate career paths in the STEM fields is yet another reason we lose students from these disciplines at the university and graduate school levels.

While a new generation of young people is in middle and high school, and undertaking advanced study in college and graduate school, we must find ways to re-educate and re-train the current workforce to energy related industries. All institutions—from trade schools and community colleges to major research universities—will want to examine their offerings to make possible re-education and training in these areas.

CONCLUSION

Tackling the multifaceted aspects of national and global energy security requires the broadest, most comprehensive of frameworks. The array of policies that guide our actions, and the regulations that will implement programs, likewise must be comprehensive, transparent, and consistent. Making a real difference will entail vigorous innovation, and that rests upon a robust green energy workforce.

There are historians who contend that the 20th century actually began in 1914, with cataclysmic world war, the end of monarchies and empires, redrawing of the maps of Europe and the Middle East, first attempts at international cooperation, and, also, with technological advances that vastly bettered daily life.

We stand at a similar point today—at what is, perhaps, the true beginning of the 21st century—amid great change and great challenge. How we tackle national and global energy security, how we heal our planet's climate, how we seize economic opportunities inherent in these challenges, how we conserve fossil fuels and innovate sustainable energy sources, how we manage the interactions between and among nations—how all of these play out over the next decades—will determine our relationship to the planet, our dealings with each other as humans, our history and our future.

Thank you.

Remarks at the Aspen Environment Forum[*]

Lisa P. Jackson

Administrator, Environmental Protection Agency (EPA), 2009– ; born Philadelphia, PA, February 8, 1962, early life in New Orleans, LA; B.S., Tulane University; M.S., Princeton University; various positions, EPA, 1990–2006; assistant commissioner for compliance and enforcement, then assistant commissioner for land use management, then commissioner, New Jersey Department of Environmental Protection, 2002–06; commissioner, New Jersey Department of Environmental Protection, then chief of staff to New Jersey Governor Jon Corzine, 2006–08.

Editor's introduction: In her keynote address at the Aspen Environment Forum at the Sundeck Restaurant, Environmental Protection Agency (EPA) Administrator Lisa P. Jackson warns that it is imperative to make major changes to address global warming and reiterates President Obama's pledge to double clean energy use in three years and to cut more than 80 percent of harmful greenhouse gas emissions by 2050. She points out that environmental concerns are closely tied to those of public health, education, and the economy, and argues that "if you think climate protection challenges economic growth, wait and see what climate change has in store."

Lisa P. Jackson's speech: This is a time for big ideas.

We're here tonight as Republicans and Democrats, as scientists, government officials, educators, venture capitalists, environmental advocates, and business leaders. We're here to talk about clean energy and the environment.

But we're also talking about international affairs, inner city poverty, food supplies, transportation, government policy, and economic possibilities.

We've come to this mountaintop to share our visions of the promised land.

We've come here to share our big ideas.

And we've come here at a crossroads in our country's history.

As a nation, we face the most serious economic downturn since the Great Depression.

---

[*] Delivered on March 25, 2009, at Aspen, CO.

Every American is anxious about what that means—not just for their future but for the next generation as well.

At the same time that we face this economic crisis, there isn't a moment to lose in protecting the public health and confronting the rapid advance of climate change.

This is not an academic discussion anymore. We don't have the luxury of a far-off day of reckoning.

The world's leading scientists predict notable, if not drastic, changes within our lifetimes if we don't get started right away.

Those changes pose very real threats to our economic stability. They jeopardize the public health. And they raise serious concerns about our national security.

For those reasons and more, we are embarking immediately on an aggressive environmental agenda.

The President has committed to double our clean energy use in the next three years. And he has set an ambitious goal of cutting more than 80 percent of harmful greenhouse gas emissions by the year 2050.

Now, let me say: I am a mother of two young boys. Any parents here know that makes me an active American consumer.

I also want my sons to go to college and get jobs when they get older.

So both the short- and long-term strength of the economy are not only professional but personal concerns of mine.

I know what it's like for people who are struggling to make ends meet, especially in these times.

The last thing EPA wants to do—and the last place we want to position the environmental movement or the climate change debate—is somehow standing in the way of the nation's economic recovery.

Thankfully, we have in President Obama a leader who has rejected the false choice between a green economy and a green environment.

President Obama and many others have stood up to say that our economic future and our environmental future are inextricably linked. They, of course, are right.

We also recognize connections to other key issues.

In health care, the people that get sick at two and three times the average rate because of pollution in their neighborhoods are the same people that predominantly seek treatment in emergency rooms.

That drives up costs for everyone and slows down much needed reform.

Or in education, when children repeatedly miss school with asthma, allergies, or complications from exposure to mercury and lead, they suffer in their educational outcomes as well as their long-term economic potential.

Not to mention the toll it takes on working parents that have to stay home to tend to their children. These are setbacks we can't afford in this or any economy.

The way out of these challenges is through a clean energy transition, through a reduction of harmful emissions in our air, and through the creation of millions of green jobs across the country.

This is a time for big ideas.

I'm proud to be here as part of an administration that is taking action on big ideas—starting with the American Recovery and Reinvestment Act.

One newspaper wrote that, standing alone, the clean energy measures in the stimulus plan represented "the biggest energy bill in history."

On Tuesday, the President met in Washington with researchers and entrepreneurs to explain how we're using stimulus funds to create 300,000 green jobs and double our supply of renewable energy.

For the long term, the President proposed a 10-year, $150 billion dollar investment in clean energy.

For EPA, the stimulus means more than $7 billion invested in "shovel-ready" projects that protect human health and safeguard the environment—things like refurbished water infrastructure, cleanup of Brownfield and Superfund sites, projects to cut emissions in diesel engines, and repair work on leaking underground storage tanks that are polluting land and groundwater supplies.

Along with the ARRA, the President also proposed in his first budget the highest level of funding support that EPA has seen in our 39-year history.

Let's be clear: that means we have the highest level of expectation that we have seen in our 39-year history, too.

You'd better believe I've got some big ideas.

We are also at a critical moment of world leadership. Around the globe, other nations are looking to us for action.

We just saw a great example of that at the global environment summit in Nairobi.

For years, our official policy has been to oppose any binding international standards on mercury levels. Last month, we agreed to join in the effort to lower the levels of mercury worldwide.

Once we changed that policy and committed our support, other countries like China and India came right to the table.

They were perfectly willing to follow our lead, but completely unwilling to act without us.

That is the power we have to make a difference, to be the standard-bearer and have a truly global impact.

The world is waiting for our big ideas.

Right now, we have greater opportunities to protect public health and the environment than ever before—and EPA wants to play a leading role.

That's why, when I've spoken to reporters, industry leaders, community members, or other stakeholders, I've tried to send a very clear, consistent message. It's one of the messages that I'm here to give you, and that I hope you will join with me in carrying it.

And it's that EPA is back on the job. That's just a catchy slogan if we don't make it into real, tangible change.

That's why we've been hard at work.

We've already announced plans to review the California waiver on auto emissions and proposed standards for nationwide greenhouse gas reporting. And those standards are carefully tailored to get us the information we need without hurting small businesses.

We're focusing resources on monitoring toxic air pollution around certain schools, to ensure that our nation's children are not exposed to harmful toxins in the place where they go to learn.

Most recently, we submitted to the White House a proposed endangerment finding on carbon and other heat-trapping pollutants.

We have tried to make clear—as has the President and his staff—that the best solution is to work with Congress to pass comprehensive legislation that would include a nationwide cap and trade system. In constructing the system we have to make sure that we reward innovation and discourage pollution, make investments that create jobs, invest in renewable energy that encourages energy independence.

It's important to remember that as we propose the endangerment finding, we don't want to create a regulatory thicket that costs both government and businesses untold expenses in enforcement and compliance.

We're not looking—as some alarmists have claimed—to run rampant and regulate every Dunkin' Donuts and every cow.

This is not a step towards a doomsday scenario that shuts down the American economy. This is a step towards proactive solutions. This is a step towards innovation, investment and implementation of technologies that reduce harmful emissions.

It is a step towards green jobs, cleaner air, and a better future for our children.

We want every stakeholder at the table so that we can get our whole country moving forward on this important work.

For those concerned that this poses a threat to our economy, I'm asking you in particular to help us develop and put in place new solutions.

Share with us your big ideas.

Because if you think climate protection challenges economic growth, wait and see what climate change has in store.

We have long since passed the tipping point. One way or another, we have to bring our emissions down.

I'm asking everyone to take part in shaping that outcome.

I look forward to hearing all of your big ideas.

Our challenge now is to take these big ideas and turn them into sustained action.

Even the best ideas aren't enough if we don't roll up our sleeves and push forward every single day.

When I was in New Jersey, I worked with the residents of the Ramapough Mountain community in Upper Ringwood.

Their community is a small cluster of neighborhoods set on top of the Ringwood Superfund site.

Ringwood had been used for years as disposal grounds for lead-based paint sludge.

It was the suspected cause of chronic illnesses for the people who called the area home. Many of them battled with asthma, cancer, and other diseases.

In 1994, after years of cleanup, Ringwood was removed from the Superfund site list. But the problems there persisted. After a long period of continued work, and the tremendous engagement of the Ramapough community, it was re-designated a Superfund site in 2006.

The good news is that the cleanup is moving forward today.

The bad news is that it didn't happen before the harm had been done. Not before children had gotten sick. Not before families and businesses had decided to move out of the area. Not before parklands and drinking water had been polluted.

The story of that site and those people are vivid reminders that a big idea isn't all that it takes.

Environmental protection is about human protection. It's about community protection and family protection.

It's about safeguarding public health in the places where people live, work, play and learn.

That's not something we can put off for some other day.

I can't think of a higher calling than coming back to the EPA at this important moment.

I'm honored to have the chance to work with all of you to address the urgent, ongoing and—in many cases—long overdue issues we face.

We have the support. We have the momentum we need. Let's make the most of it.

Thank you again, and I look forward to working with all of you.

4

The Auto Industry: The Bailout and Beyond

Testimony on the State of the Domestic Automobile Industry before the U.S. Senate[*]

Ron Gettelfinger

President, United Automobile, Aerospace & Agricultural Implement Workers of America (UAW), 2002– ; born De Pauw, IN, August 1, 1944; graduated from Indiana University, 1976; chassis line repairman, Ford Motor Company, starting in 1964; various union positions including plant chairman in 1978; president of local union 862, 1984–1992; director of UAW Region 3, 1992–98; vice president, UAW, 1998–2002.

Editor's introduction: In the following remarks, UAW President Ron Gettelfinger, this time on the same side of the table as auto executives, requests that $25 billion in public money be provided as emergency bridge loans to the Big Three automakers. He attributes dismal auto sales to the credit and financial crises and argues against any bankruptcy proceedings, believing that they would result in massive job losses and have dire consequences for retired autoworkers and the economy as a whole. Gettelfinger also disputes claims that rich union contracts are to blame for the downfall of the American auto industry.

Ron Gettelfinger's speech: Mr. Chairman, my name is Ron Gettelfinger. I am President of the International Union, United Automobile, Aerospace & Agricultural Implement Workers of America (UAW). The UAW represents one million active and retired members, many of whom work for or receive retirement benefits from the Detroit-based auto companies and auto parts suppliers across the United States. We welcome the opportunity to appear before this Committee to present our views on the state of the domestic automobile industry: Part II.

The UAW believes the situation at GM, Ford and Chrysler is extremely dire. As is evident from the materials which have been submitted by the companies in response to the letter from Speaker Pelosi and Majority Leader Reid, it is imperative that the federal government act this month to provide an emergency bridge loan to the domestic auto companies. Without such assistance, GM could run out of funds by the end of the year, and Chrysler soon thereafter. These companies

---

[*] Delivered on December 4, 2008, at Washington, D.C.

would then be forced to liquidate, ceasing all business operations. The collapse of these companies would inevitably drag down numerous auto parts suppliers, which in turn could lead to the collapse of Ford.

The UAW appreciates the desire of Congress, as expressed in the letter from Speaker Pelosi and Majority Leader Reid, to ensure that any assistance from the federal government is conditioned on strict accountability by the companies and a demonstration that they can be viable businesses in the future. We fully support both of these key principles.

Specifically, the UAW supports conditioning any emergency bridge loan on strict accountability measures, including:

- tough limits on executive compensation, prohibiting golden parachutes and other abuses, and making it clear that top executives must share in any sacrifices;
- a prohibition on dividend payments by the companies;
- giving the federal government an equity stake in the companies so that taxpayers are protected; and
- establishing an Advisory Board to oversee the operations of the companies to ensure that all funds from the emergency bridge loan are spent in the United States, that the companies are pursuing viable restructuring plans, and that the companies are meeting requirements to produce advanced, more fuel-efficient vehicles.

We are prepared to work with members of this committee to incorporate other accountability requirements that may be appropriate.

In addition, the UAW supports conditioning any emergency bridge loan on the companies pursuing restructuring plans that will ensure the viability of their operations in the coming years. For such restructuring plans to succeed, we recognize that all stakeholders—equity and bondholders, suppliers, dealers, workers and retirees, and management—must come to the table and share in the sacrifices that will be needed.

The UAW and the workers and retirees we represent are prepared to do our part to ensure that the companies can continue as viable operations. As indicated in our previous testimony, workers and retirees have already stepped forward and made enormous sacrifices.

- In 2005 the UAW reopened its contract mid-term and accepted cuts in wages for active workers and health care benefits for retirees.
- In the 2007 contract the UAW agreed to slash wages for new workers by 50 percent to about $14 per hour, and to exclude new workers from the traditional health care and pension plans. The UAW also allowed the companies to outsource cleaning work at even lower rates.
- Under the 2007 contract, beginning January 1, 2010 the liabilities for health care for existing retirees will be transferred from the companies to an independent VEBA fund. Taken together, the changes in the 2005 and 2007 contract reduced the companies' liabilities for retiree health care benefits by 50 percent.

As a result of the 2005 and 2007 contracts, workers have not received any base wage increase since 2005 at GM and Ford, and since 2006 at Chrysler. All of these workers will not receive any increase through the end of the contract in 2011. Workers have also accepted reductions in cost of living adjustments.

- New local operating agreements at many facilities provided dramatic flexibilities and reductions in classifications, and have saved the companies billions of dollars.
- Reforms in the 2007 contract have largely eliminated the jobs banks.
- Since 2003 downsizing by the companies has reduced their workforce by 150,000, resulting in enormous savings for GM, Ford and Chrysler.

Thanks to the changes in the 2005 and 2007 contracts, and changes that have subsequently been agreed to by the UAW, the labor cost gap with the foreign transplant operations will be largely or completely eliminated when the contracts are fully implemented. Industry observers applauded the sacrifices made by workers and retirees, calling the 2007 contract a "transformational" agreement.

The UAW is continuing to negotiate with the domestic auto companies on an ongoing basis over ways to make their operations more efficient and competitive.

We recognize that the current crisis may require all stakeholders, including the workers and retirees, to make further sacrifices to ensure the future viability of the companies. We are willing to do our part. In particular, we recognize that the contributions owed by the companies to the retiree health care VEBA fund may need to be spread out. The UAW has retained outside experts to work with us on how this can be accomplished, while still protecting the retirees. We also recognize that adjustments may need to be made in other areas.

But the UAW vigorously opposes any attempt to make workers and retirees the scapegoats and to make them shoulder the entire burden of any restructuring.

Wages and benefits only make up 10 percent of the costs of the domestic auto companies. So the current difficulties facing the Detroit-based auto companies cannot be blamed on workers and retirees.

Contrary to an often-repeated myth, UAW members at GM, Ford and Chrysler are not paid $73 an hour. The truth is, wages for UAW members range from about $14 per hour for newly hired workers to $28 per hour for assemblers. The $73 an hour figure is outdated and inaccurate. It includes not only the costs of health care, pensions and other compensation for current workers, but also includes the costs of pensions and health care for all of the retired workers, spread out over the active workforce. Obviously, active workers do not receive any of this compensation, so it is simply not accurate to describe it as part of their "earnings." Furthermore, as previously indicated, the overall labor costs at the Detroit-based auto companies were dramatically lowered by the changes in the 2005 and 2007 contracts, which largely or completely eliminated the gap with the foreign transplant operations.

The UAW submits that it is not feasible for Congress to hammer out the details of a complete restructuring plan during the coming week. There is simply not enough time to work through the many difficult and complex issues associated with all of the key stakeholders, including equity and bondholders, suppliers, dealers, management, workers and retirees, as well as changes in the business operations of the companies.

What Congress can and should do is to put in place a process that will require all of the stakeholders to participate in a restructuring of the companies outside of bankruptcy. This process should ensure that there is fairness in the sacrifices, and that the companies will be able to continue as viable business operations. This process can begin immediately under the supervision of the next administration. By doing this, Congress can make sure that the emergency assistance is indeed a bridge to a brighter future.

Contrary to the assertions by some commentators, in the current environment a Chapter 11 reorganization—even a so-called "pre-packaged" bankruptcy—is simply not a viable option for restructuring the Detroit-based auto companies. As previously indicated, research has indicated that the public will not buy vehicles from a company in bankruptcy. It also is doubtful that the companies could obtain debtor-in-possession financing to operate during a bankruptcy. In addition, attached to this testimony is a more detailed analysis prepared with the assistance of experienced bankruptcy practitioners explaining why a "pre- packaged" bankruptcy is not a feasible option for the domestic auto companies because of the size and complexity of the issues that would necessarily be involved in any restructuring, including relationships with thousands of dealers and suppliers and major changes in business operations. Thus, the UAW wishes to underscore that any bankruptcy filings by the domestic auto companies at this time would inevitably lead to Chapter 7 liquidations and the cessation of all business operations.

The collapse of the domestic auto companies would have disastrous consequences for millions of workers and retirees and for the entire country.

- Hundreds of thousands of workers would directly lose their jobs at GM, Ford and Chrysler, and a total of three million workers would see their jobs eliminated at suppliers, dealerships and the thousands of other businesses that depend on the auto industry.
- One million retirees could lose part of their pension benefits, and would also face the complete elimination of their health insurance coverage, an especially harsh blow to the 40 percent who are younger than 65 and not yet eligible for Medicare.
- The Pension Benefit Guarantee Corporation could be saddled with enormous pension liabilities, jeopardizing its ability to protect the pensions of millions of other workers and retirees. To prevent this from happening, the federal government could be forced to pay for a costly bailout of the PBGC. The federal government would also be liable for a 65 percent health care tax credit for pre-65 retirees from the auto companies, at a cost of as much as $2 billion per year.
- Revenues to the federal, state and local governments would drop sharply, forcing cuts in vital social services at a time when they are urgently needed.

- The ripple effects from the collapse of the Detroit-based auto companies would deal a serious blow to the entire economy, making the current recession much deeper and longer.
- There also would be a serious negative impact on many financial institutions that hold large amounts of debt from the Detroit-based auto companies and their auto finance associates. This could pose a systemic danger to our already weakened financial sector.

For all of these reasons, the UAW submits it is imperative that Congress and the Bush administration act next week to provide an emergency bridge loan to the Detroit-based auto companies. The consequences of inaction are simply too devastating, the economic and human toll too costly.

The UAW believes that the recent actions by the federal government to provide an enormous bailout to Citigroup reinforce the case for providing an emergency bridge loan to the Detroit-based auto companies. The total assistance provided to Citigroup will dwarf that being sought by the domestic auto companies.

Citigroup received this assistance without being required to submit any "plan" for changing its operations or demonstrating its future viability. It was not required to change its management. And it is still able to continue paying bonuses and other forms of lucrative executive compensation.

If the federal government can provide this type of blank check to Wall Street, the UAW submits that Main Street is no less deserving of assistance. Since the domestic auto companies have come forward with detailed plans relating to accountability and their future viability, there is simply no justification for withholding the emergency bridge loan that is necessary for them to continue operations.

The UAW also notes that other governments around the world are actively considering programs to provide emergency assistance to their auto industries.

In particular, the European Union is considering a $51 billion loan program for automakers. And there are ongoing discussions with Germany, Great Britain, Sweden, Belgium, Poland, South Korea, China and other nations about steps their governments can take to assist their auto industries. Clearly, other governments recognize the economic importance of maintaining their auto industries. The UAW submits that the economic importance of GM, Ford and Chrysler to the U.S. economy is no less important and no less deserving of assistance.

It is not enough, however, for the federal government to provide an emergency bridge loan to the Detroit-based auto companies, and to oversee and facilitate the restructuring of the companies. The 111th Congress and the incoming Obama administration have a responsibility to pursue policies in a number of areas that will be critically important to the future viability of the domestic auto companies, as well as the well-being of our entire nation.

First, the UAW is very pleased that Congressional leaders and the Obama transition staff are already making plans to move forward quickly with a major economic stimulus package that will create jobs and give a boost to the entire economy. We believe this is urgently needed to prevent the economy from slipping into a deeper and more serious recession. This is particularly important for the auto sector. In order for the Detroit-based auto companies to succeed, it is vital that auto sales rebound from the record low levels we have seen in recent months. The single most important thing that can be done to increase auto sales is to reinvigorate the overall economy.

Second, the UAW believes it is critically important that Congress and the Obama administration move forward quickly with plans to reform our broken health care system, and to put in place programs that will guarantee health insurance coverage for all Americans, contain costs, ensure quality of care, and establish more equitable financing mechanisms. In particular, we believe any health care reform initiative should include proposals to address the challenges associated with providing health care to the pre-Medicare population aged 55-65.

There can be no doubt that one of the major financial challenges facing the Detroit-based auto companies in future years is the cost of providing health care to almost a million retirees. Although the 2005 and 2007 contracts greatly reduced the companies' retiree health care liabilities, they are still enormous and a major problem that hinders the ability of the companies to obtain financing from private lenders.

All of the other major auto-producing nations have national health care systems that spread the costs of providing health care across their societies. As a result, the automakers in these countries are not burdened by retiree health care legacy costs. Accordingly, the UAW is hopeful that the enactment of national health care reform in the United States would help to establish a level playing field among all employers, and alleviate the retiree health care legacy costs facing the Detroit-based auto companies.

Third, during the coming year Congress and the Obama administration are likely to consider major new initiatives dealing with energy security and climate change. The UAW strongly supports prompt action in both of these vital areas.

Specifically, besides requiring automakers to comply with the tougher new fuel economy standards that were enacted in 2007, we believe Congress and the Obama administration should take steps to ensure that fuel economy improvements continue in the years following 2020, and that the companies move expeditiously to introduce advanced technology vehicles. In particular, we support an aggressive program to increase domestic production of plug-in hybrids and their key components, and to expand the infrastructure that will be needed to support these vehicles. To help achieve these objectives, Congress and the Obama administration should make sure that the Section 136 Advanced Technology Vehicles Manufacturing Incentive Program (ATVMIP) continues to be fully funded, and that additional resources are provided to ensure that production of advanced, more fuel efficient vehicles and their key components is ramped up quickly. In addition, the UAW strongly supports the enactment of an economy-wide cap-and-trade program to aggressively reduce emissions of greenhouse gases that are causing climate change.

Although these initiatives pose challenges for the auto industry, the UAW also believes they can provide great opportunities. Properly structured, these initiatives can not only ensure that our nation reduces its consumption of oil and emissions of greenhouse gas but also can ensure that the more fuel-efficient vehicles of the future and their key components are built in the United States by the domestic auto companies and American workers. In effect, these initiatives can be an important part of the restructuring that is necessary to ensure the future viability of the domestic auto companies.

Fourth, Congress and the Obama administration must make sure that our nation's trade policies promote fair trade, not so-called "free trade" that fails to provide a level playing field and instead places our domestic automakers at a significant competitive disadvantage. In particular, prompt action needs to be taken to eliminate unfair currency manipulation by China and Japan. In addition, Congress and the Obama administration should insist that the U.S.-Korea free trade agreement must be renegotiated to require that Korea dismantle the non-tariff barriers that have kept its market closed to U.S.-built automotive products, before it is granted any further access to the U.S. market.

By pursuing all of these policies, Congress and the Obama administration can benefit our entire country. The UAW also believes that these policies can provide a basis under which a restructured domestic auto industry can remain viable and strong in the coming years.

In conclusion, the UAW appreciates the opportunity to testify before this Committee on the state of the domestic automobile industry: Part II. We strongly urge this Committee and the entire Congress to act promptly to approve an emergency bridge loan to the Detroit-based auto companies to enable them to continue operations and to avoid the disastrous consequences that their liquidation would involve for millions of workers and retirees and for our entire nation.

Testimony before the House Select Committee on Energy Independence and Global Warming[*]

Joan Claybrook

President, Public Citizen, Washington, D.C., 1982–2009; born Baltimore, MD, June 12, 1937; BA, Goucher College, 1959; JD, Georgetown Law Center, 1973; research analyst, Social Security Administration, Department of Health, Education and Welfare, 1959–1966; Congressional Fellow, American Political Science Association, 1965–66; special assistant to the administrator, National Traffic Safety Bureau (renamed National Highway Traffic Safety Administration), U.S. Department of Transportation, 1966–1970; founder and director, Public Citizen's Congress Watch, 1973–77; administrator, National Highway Traffic Safety Administration, U.S. Department of Transportation, 1977–1981; author, Retreat from Safety: Reagan's Attack on America's Health, *with the staff of Public Citizen, 1984;* Freedom from Harm: The Civilizing Influence of Health, Safety and Environmental Regulations, *with David Bollier, 1986. Statements and testimonies before the U.S. Congress and numerous private groups, educational institutions and foundations, and various articles for* The Washington Post, USA Today, New York Times, Los Angeles Times, Baltimore Sun *and various other periodical publications. Boardmember, Georgetown Law Center Board of Visitors, Citizens for Tax Justice, Public Justice; Co-Chair, Advocates for Highway and Auto Safety (with the insurance industry); Co-Chair, Citizens for Reliable and Safe Highways; California Wellness Foundation Advisory Board.*

Editor's introduction: A longtime advocate for increased fuel-efficiency and auto-safety standards, Joan Claybrook rebuts Ron Gettelfinger's argument that the auto industry's woes are caused chiefly by the global credit crisis and asks that Congress impose on the industry binding agreements with provisions for accountability in return for public funds. She advises requiring a return on the public's investment and a commitment to increased environmental and safety standards. To support her argument for binding agreements, she presents what she calls "a litany of broken promises" by the auto industry over several decades.

---

[*] Delivered on December 9, 2008, at Washington, D.C.

Joan Claybrook's speech: Chairman Markey and members of the Select Committee, I appreciate the opportunity to testify today. I am Joan Claybrook, president of Public Citizen, and I have worked on auto safety and fuel economy issues for more than 40 years. As the administrator of the National Highway Traffic Safety Administration (NHTSA) from 1977–1981, I issued the first fuel economy standards, which forced recalcitrant Detroit manufacturers to double average car fuel economy to 27.5 miles per gallon by 1985. Since that time I have consistently advocated for tough increases in fuel economy standards to support a national energy policy that promotes conservation and efficiency as a means of insulating the nation from volatile oil prices and to push Detroit to compete with foreign-based manufacturers. I also issued the 1977 passive restraint rule, resulting in airbags that save about 3,000 lives each year and successfully pressed for enactment of five laws since 1991 to force manufacturers to improve vehicle safety.

The industry has tried to make the case that the problems it faces today are a result only of the credit crisis. However, the domestic industry has been in trouble for several years as oil price spikes in 2005 and the summer of 2008 have raised consumer demand for fuel-efficient vehicles and shifted the market away from the SUVs and light trucks that have been Detroit's cash cows—the core of their product lines since the mid-1990s. The domestic industry has fought against increased fuel economy for three decades. The broken promises of the Partnership for a New Generation of Vehicles (PNGV), which was a voluntary arrangement in 1993 between the Department of Energy and the domestic auto manufacturers to build an 80 mpg car by 2004 that never materialized, demand skepticism about automakers' promises.

While it is immutable that the domestic industry is in distress and the consequences of its failure would cause a devastating ripple through the economy, public investment in the Detroit Three provides an opportunity for the industry to make philosophical changes in how it approaches the business of building cars. The public statements made by the industry, and the plans the companies submitted to Congress on December 2, 2008, show some evidence that this perspective is changing, but we ask that Congress make these promises binding. I attach to my testimony a litany of Detroit's prior broken promises.

Public Citizen acknowledges the impact of the larger economic crisis, and we note for the record that the Japanese auto manufacturers saw sales figures drop at almost the same rate as the domestic manufacturers in September and October 2008. We do not take the position that the credit crunch and widespread financial anxiety have not contributed to the severity of the domestic industry's problems. However, foreign manufacturers have not come seeking a bailout, in large measure because long-standing investment in efficient vehicles has put them in a better position before the credit crunch, and will leave them in a better position once economic recovery begins.

Public Citizen disagrees with the choice to provide $15 billion in emergency loans to the auto companies from money that was appropriated to fund the advanced technology vehicle retooling incentives established in Section 136 of the

Energy Independence and Security Act (EISA) in 2007. If this is the source of the funds, they must be replenished, and there must be a clear plan for how this will be achieved in the legislation now being negotiated. We do, however, agree that negotiating the bailout in two steps is prudent, as it allows for careful consideration of further terms and conditions that might be required of the industry.

CONDITIONS

Public Citizen supports taking action to help the Detroit Three companies but we must emphasize that if Congress approves a bailout, the money must be conditioned with clear requirements and accountability for the industry. The financial problems facing domestic manufacturers are largely a result of their failure to adapt to a changing market, their risky reliance on gas-guzzling vehicles, and failure to invest in innovative safety, fuel economy, and emissions technologies until literally forced to do so by regulation or lack of sales. Before the American taxpayers come again to the rescue, the industry must agree under statutory mandate to deliver the fuel economy and safety that consumers want and need, to help regain a prominent position in the global automobile market.

Funds allocated to the Detroit Three are an investment by the American taxpayer, not a simple cash infusion to an industry with a failed business model. It must be well managed to assure a return on the investment in the form of a more viable domestic automobile industry with safer, more fuel-efficient cars that consumers are demanding. Specifically three areas need to be the focus of strict government oversight of a bailout: accountability, a return on the investment, and environmental safety and considerations.

ACCOUNTABILITY

The companies participating in the bailout must provide full transparency of their actions in relation to the funds they receive. Regular contact with government overseers must be maintained and other guarantees must be met including the following:

1. An oversight board with the "car czar" as the chair and with authority to secure and review all industry documentation, and with sufficient funding and staff to keep close track of the Detroit companies' progress. The board can also demand concessions from affected parties.
2. The auto industry should provide equity stakes, membership by government representatives on their Boards of Directors, limit executive pay and bonuses, ban golden parachutes, and prohibit dividend payments until the loans are repaid.
3. Automakers should also be restricted from using government funds or guarantee of funds for lobbying and campaign contributions.

4. A bar on equity investments in foreign firms and domestic mergers and acquisitions in the text of this bailout, unless approved by the oversight board.

5. Bailout funds should be granted senior debt status, to ensure taxpayers are paid back first.

RETURN ON INVESTMENT

Public funding must provide a tangible public benefit. If the Big Three used these monies to invest in more fuel-efficient technologies it would provide a great benefit to the entire country. Such an investment would reduce oil consumption and foreign oil imports, reduce time and money spent at the pump, and reduce harmful greenhouse gas emissions that contribute to global warming. These investments are essential for companies to return to profitability. Specifically:

1. The legislation should require automakers receiving bailout money to implement promised increases in fuel economy, by instructing the oversight board to include the particular plans in each of the loan documents.

2. Automakers who achieve fuel economy above and beyond these promises should get a quarter-point reduction in the interest rate on these loans. Regulation does not quash innovation as some would have you believe, rather, it nurtures it by creating incentives to improve.

3. Automakers must provide energy savings plans to supplement operating plans.

ENVIRONMENTAL AND SAFETY CONSIDERATIONS

The auto industry has fought adamantly against the stricter greenhouse gas emissions standards set by California and other states, even though meeting these requirements would benefit them greatly by making their vehicles more competitive against foreign manufacturers.[1] They have falsely argued that higher fuel economy requirements undercut safety. However, increases in fuel economy have been mainly made using technology, discrediting this argument. The technology exists to meet these standards, as well as improved safety. If the domestic auto industry had the foresight to meet these standards instead of paying lobbyists to avoid them, they might be more like their foreign counterparts, who are not before Congress begging for government handouts. Additional steps for the manufacturers include:

1. Automakers must suspend litigation blocking California and other states from setting greenhouse gas emissions standards.

2. NHTSA must also be required to adopt the more realistic calculation for fuel economy promulgated by the Environmental Protection Agency in 2006.[2]

3. Automakers must support safety improvements including a strong rollover roof crush and ejection standard, a compatibility and aggressivity reduction standard, and new child protection standards.

Consumer and environmental groups, in conjunction with Pew Charitable Trusts, have taken out an ad supporting the retention of environmental safeguards and the protection of the California greenhouse gas emissions standards, which we submit for the record.

A BAILOUT WITH CONDITIONS IS PREFERABLE TO BANKRUPTCY

Public Citizen acknowledges that the auto companies are in significant financial distress and that if Congress does not approve a bailout, it is likely that at least one of the domestic manufacturers will be forced to file for bankruptcy. It is our position that a bailout with strong taxpayer protections is preferable to bankruptcy, in terms of impact on the economy, job losses, and long-term viability of our industrial base.

Conditions that ensure equity, accountability and a commitment to building the safer and more fuel-efficient vehicles the market demands are necessary to protect taxpayers from the risk assumed by investing in the troubled domestic auto industry. To promote compliance with these conditions and assure that taxpayers' interests are paramount in this process, it is essential to establish an oversight board similar to what was described in the testimony of Gene Dodaro of the Government Accountability Office before the Senate Banking Committee.[3] Public Citizen supports the recommendation of House Speaker Nancy Pelosi that such an oversight board be chaired by the "car czar" and include representatives from the Departments of Transportation, Energy, Treasury, Commerce, Labor, and the Environmental Protection Agency. We additionally recommend that a member of the Board of Governors of the Federal Reserve and a representative from the Government Accountability Office be added to the board. An advisory group consisting of members representing consumer, safety, and environmental interests, as well as labor unions, auto supplier companies and financial experts should support the board.

We do not believe that a single overseer would be able to effectively address all of the complex and cross-cutting issues related to restoring the domestic auto industry to profitability. The potential usefulness of a board was admitted even by General Motors Chairman Richard Wagoner in response to questions in a hearing in the Senate Banking Committee December 4, 2008.

The board named to supervise the process in the 1979 Chrysler bailout is described in the act itself:

> There is established a Chrysler Corporation Loan Guarantee Board which shall consist of the Secretary of the Treasury who shall be the Chairperson of the Board, the Chairman of the Board of Governors of the Federal Reserve System, and the Comptroller General of the United States. The Secretary of Labor and the Secretary of Transportation shall be ex officio nonvoting members of the board.[4]

A strong oversight board is clearly needed for the auto industry bailout package. While there is less time for decisions compared to the 1979 bailout, sacrificing quality for expedition will only result in the loss of taxpayer dollars. An advisory group to the board for the bailout should include industry financial specialists to ensure proper business practices are followed so the industry won't return for more money in the future, environmentalists to ensure that fuel economy measures are met that will allow Detroit's vehicles to be more efficient, and safety advocates to make sure safety is not surrendered in the name of a balanced checkbook.

The oversight board would be particularly helpful in guiding the companies in their ongoing plans for restructuring. The domestic manufacturers have already been engaged in or promised substantial restructuring activities including job cuts, labor renegotiations, brand contractions, and plant closures and stoppages. The oversight board, led by the "car czar," would provide assurance that restructuring activities are completed in the long-term interest of the taxpayers.

FUEL EFFICIENCY AND SAFETY

Good energy policy is good economic policy, and it is also good business for the automakers. High and volatile gas prices since 2005, as well as increased public concern about global warming, have driven consumers away from the gas-guzzling vehicles that had been popular since the mid-1990s. While gas prices today are comparatively low, they will jump up again with worldwide economic recovery. The plans released by General Motors and Ford promise increases in fuel economy for the 2012 model year that exceed their obligations in 2015 under the proposed fuel economy standards for model years 2011–2015 released by NHTSA in May 2008.[5] They would also be close to meeting the state greenhouse gas emissions requirements initiated by California and other states.

Congress must be careful when considering how to set higher fuel economy targets for automakers accepting loans. The Energy Policy and Conservation Act (EPCA), which established the fuel economy program in 1975, is a technology-forcing standard with a mandate to set the "maximum feasible" fuel economy standards with the "need of the nation to conserve energy" as a central feature. However, the amendments to EPCA made by EISA substantially weakened the technology-forcing thrust of the law at the urging of the Detroit companies, by permitting the agency to set attribute-based standards "in the form of a mathematical function." This clause is an implicit espousal of NHTSA's restructured fuel economy scheme in which standards are now set for each manufacturer using industry-biased cost-benefit analysis.

The restructured fuel economy scheme was developed as a result of intense, back-room meetings between representatives from NHTSA, the Office of Management and Budget, and the Office of the Vice President.[6] This scheme is fundamentally designed in such a way that it is impossible to meet the requirement of EPCA to set maximum feasible standards. Each manufacturer is assigned a target for its passenger car and light truck fleets, respectively, based on the characteristics of vehicles in each manufacturer's fleets. This results in different compliance requirements for each manufacturer, and undermines the government's ability to enforce the law.

Domestic and Japanese Fuel Economy Performance					
Manufacturer	Domestic Car Fleet (mpg)			Light Truck Fleet (mpg)		
	2008	2012	2015	2008	2012	2015
General Motors	29.4	31.7	34.7	22.5	25.4	27.4
Ford	29.5	32.7	35.5	23.2	26.1	28.8
Chrysler	29.3	29.3	33.6	23.6	26.6	29.1
Toyota	34.7	31.5	34.6	24.0	26.0	28.0
Honda	35.2	33.8	36.4	25.4	27.7	29.6
Nissan	33.5	33.2	35.9	23.2	26.2	28.2

Values for 2008 reflect manufacturer averages as reported by NHTSA's March 2008 "Summary of Fuel Economy Performance." Values for 2012 and 2015 are the targets published in NHTSA's Notice of Proposed Rulemaking for the model year 2011–2015 fuel economy standards.

PROMISES, PROMISES

We have heard fuel economy and safety promises from the domestic auto industry again and again, but too often the gains were never realized. In July 2000, Ford, General Motors and (then) DaimlerChrysler announced a commitment to increase the fuel economy of its SUV fleet by 25 percent in five years. However, in 2002, as NHTSA revised fuel economy standards for light trucks, these companies "clarified" those pledges, urging the agency to disregard the promised increases. Instead of making big, public announcements reneging on their promises, the automakers sent e-mails to relevant staff at NHTSA.[7] In 2003, when NHTSA released its light truck fuel economy standards for the 2005–2007 model years, Ford admitted publicly that it would not honor its prior promise.

The auto industry has shirked other promises related to making safety improvements as well. General Motors promised in 1970 that it would install airbags in all its vehicles by 1975. But the fight to make airbags mandatory stretched to 1991, when Congress mandated them. And in 2003, as part of a supposed effort to improve vehicle compatibility, automakers announced a voluntary plan to develop a standard, but nothing came of it. The manufacturers also promised to test and voluntarily install side air bags in most new vehicles, but this promise has only been partially met. The plan, however, did not make any specific commitment or deadline for redesigning vehicles to improve side impact safety. These improvements will follow the upgraded side-impact standard promulgated by NHTSA in 2007, which the agency recently delayed, so it will not be completely phased in until 2015.[8]

In response to the fuel economy proposal for model years 2011–2015, General Motors said, "We intend to do our best to meet these challenging CAFE standards, but additionally complying with stringent state standards would present us with huge additional costs. . . . We do not believe it is realistically possible to comply with California's CO_2 standards given . . . the extent of technical improvements we believe would be required in the time frame provided."[9]

However, in the plans submitted to Congress last week, General Motors says it would achieve a fleet fuel economy of 37.3 mpg for its passenger car fleet and 27.5 mpg for light trucks by 2012.[10] Ford echoes similar promises, saying it intends to increase its passenger car and light truck fleets' fuel economy by 26 percent by 2012, and 36 percent in 2015. Although Ford and General Motors are still complaining about the cost of meeting the California greenhouse gas emissions standards, an analysis by the Natural Resources Defense Council and verified by the California Air Resources Board and submitted to the Committee suggests that if Ford and General Motors followed through with these promises, they would comply with California standards if they were applied nationally. This deception by the manufacturers is not an auspicious beginning for this bailout.

Passenger Car Fuel Economy Promises and Standards						
Manufacturer	2008 passenger car fuel economy[11]	2012 NHTSA standard[12]	2012 company promise[13]	2012 State CO_2 standards (mpg-equiv)	2015 NHTSA standard[14]	2015 CO_2 standard (mpg-equiv)
General Motors	29.4	31.7	37.3		34.7	
Ford	29.5	32.7	35.5†	37.6*	35.5	40.6[15]
Chrysler	29.3	29.3	N/A‡		33.6	

* Greenhouse gas emissions standards set by the California Air Resources manufacturer.
† Based on 2005 model year fuel economy of Ford as reported by NHTSA, using Ford's promise to get 26 percent increase from 2005 in 2012.
‡ Chrysler did not make specific promises regarding fuel economy performance, instead: "Chyrsler accepts all currently applicable CAFE standards as a condition to the funding."

Congress must make sure that the automakers are bound to their promises to increase fuel economy either by mandating more stringent regulations in the bailout legislation, or instructing the oversight board to include manufacturers' plans in the loan documents. Making good on these promises will help the industry become competitive again. And agreeing to binding agreements will signal that the industry is really serious about changing its tune and abandoning the gas-guzzling vehicles that the domestic industry and the American consumer need to leave behind.

INDUSTRY'S CONTINUED FIGHT AGAINST FUEL
ECONOMY AND SAFETY REGULATION

When the auto industry cannot block mandates from Congress, it fights to weaken and delay regulations as they are promulgated through NHTSA. The industry submitted competing cost estimates for the model year 2011–2015 fuel economy standards proposed by NHTSA this spring. Under the restructured fuel economy program, fuel economy targets are very sensitive to cost estimates, so the industry submitted higher cost estimates to game the system and receive lower targets.

The auto industry should suspend all litigation over the California greenhouse gas standards. Public Citizen supports the position of several states' Attorneys General that Congress should include in the bailout legislation language that makes clear the position of the courts that the greenhouse gas emissions standards for vehicles set by California and 13 other states are not preempted by EPCA or any other law.[16]

Just as the industry has resisted making improvements in fuel economy, it has also resisted improving the safety of its vehicles. These companies should support new safety standards including strong rollover roof crush and ejection standards to help save the 10,800 people who die each year in rollover crashes. They should also support the introduction of a compatibility and aggressivity reduction safety standard, which was included as part of fuel economy bills introduced by Sen. Feinstein in 2006 and 2007. Such standards are beneficial for safety and fuel economy because they encourage closing the weight and size gap between SUVs/light trucks and cars. A compatibility standard would also address other vehicle characteristics related to crash compatibility such as bumper height and front-end geometry. Manufacturers should also support child protection standards to ensure that all occupants in and around vehicles are protected. Hundreds of small children are killed needlessly each year.

ADVANCED VEHICLE LOAN GUARANTEES VERSUS BAILOUT

Public Citizen unequivocally opposes to reallocating for industry cash flow purposes the money allocated in EISA Section 136 for retooling loan guarantees to be overseen by the Department of Energy. These funds are not meant to help companies merely comply with fuel economy standards. They are meant to help manufacturers retool facilities and make capital-intensive investments for the future. Vehicles that Section 136 funds are meant to fund will benefit vehicles and components that are still marketable beyond 2020. On December 7, 2008, the

Washington Post reported that House Speaker Nancy Pelosi would consider the Bush administration demand that the Section 136 money provide $15 billion in temporary assistance to the auto industry, while a more robust long-term plan could be negotiated.[17] Although the money would have to be paid back into the advanced vehicle incentive program, we urge that this be specified in any legislation adopted this week.

We support allocating the bailout money from the $700 billion financial services bailout. But if that is not the source of funding, then it should be from completely separate appropriations. The Section 136 money was intended to be used to build advanced vehicles and to provide funding for retooling of plants to build vehicles and components to get significant improvements in fuel economy. This money should not be used for day-to-day operating funding, or to pay legacy and health care costs.

The domestic manufacturers did not publically lobby for Congress to fund the advanced vehicles loan guarantee program until the fall, when car sales dropped off precipitously. We wonder why the automakers were not more aggressive about getting Congress to appropriate funding for this program, which was enacted in late 2007. In late November 2008, General Motors submitted an application for $3.6 billion in loan guarantees to finance the Chevrolet Volt project, which has been ongoing for several years.[18]

SUPPLIER COMPANIES DRIVE INNOVATION

Under Section 136, auto industry supplier companies are thosethat build "qualifying components," whichare defined as components that are: "(A) designed for advanced technology vehicles; and (B) installed for the purpose of meeting the performance requirements of advanced technology vehicles."[19] For many years, it has been the supplier companies that have driven the development of innovative new technologies. Naturally, it is beneficial for supplier companies to push technology forward. By providing better, more advanced components, supplier companies can stand out and compete for contracts from the manufacturers. Thus, Section 136 funds should not be depleted so that suppliers cannot participate as they should.

Also, suppliers have too often been met with resistance from the domestic auto industry to voluntarily install technologically advanced components. In the case of electronic stability control and laminated glazing, supplier companies have worked with public interest groups to advocate for new regulations to force automakers to install these components. A regulation requiring electronic stability control in all vehicles was required by the 2005 surface transportation bill [the Safe, Accountable, Flexible, Efficient Transportation Equity Act: A Legacy for Users (SAFETEA-LU)]. And although NHTSA has not yet released a proposal, it is likely that the ejection mitigation rule required under the same law will mandate laminated window glazing. The same resistance by manufacturers applies to failure to adopt fuel economy innovation, including turbocharged engines and 6-speed automatic transmissions.

LESSONS FROM CHRYSLER

Almost 30 years ago Chrysler found itself in a similar financial situation. President and CEO John Riccardo came before Congress to ask for $1 billion to keep the company alive after rising oil prices left the company's inefficient cars stagnant on dealers' lots. The company had just posted its worst quarterly loss ever up until that time. Congress initially turned down Chrysler's request, but after months of negotiating and the resignation of Mr. Riccardo in favor of Lee Iacocca, a different approach was settled upon. Congress passed the Chrysler Corporation Loan Guarantee Act of 1979. Instead of granting the request for funds with no strings attached, a $1.5 billion loan guarantee was issued that was coupled with strict oversight and concessions that had to be made. Management, labor, and other stakeholders made $2 billion concessions including Mr. Iacocca's pledge to work for $1 a year until the company turned a profit. A ten-year loan was issued and Chrysler was able to pay it back seven years early, netting the government a gain of $350 million in interest.

This action was successful in returning Chrysler to profitability. We need to closely examine the lessons from this act when crafting the best response to the Big Three's current financial dilemma. The greatest lesson from this experience is that including strictures on the bailout did not cause the company to fail, but rather helped it to succeed as it advanced important goals including compliance with safety and fuel economy rules. The statutory language from the Chrysler bailout provides a strong basis upon which to craft the new bailout bill.

The program included strong oversight protections through a strong board that was given enough authority to intervene in the corporation's decisions. It required compliance with fuel economy and safety standards and limits on executive pay, and encouraged a new CEO determined to turn the company around. The board was successful in protecting taxpayer and consumer interests by forcing Chrysler to drop a plan to build gas-guzzling rear wheel drive vehicles.

CONCLUSIONS

This bailout process is painful because the auto industry has been an engine of domestic manufacturing for more than 60 years, and a large number of Americans are employed directly or indirectly or identify with the industry. The restructuring required to save the companies will also be painful and will require fundamental changes in the corporate and union operating philosophies of what has been one of the most powerful industrial lobbies.

If the industry is willing to step back and seriously contemplate how they will operate in the future, then it might just be salvageable. A strong, committed oversight board that is willing to frankly assess the situation of the industry is vital to any bailout program being successful in turning the industry around. The outcome of this program is far from predictable, so the interest of the taxpayer needs to be considered every step of the way, and frequent and regular reporting to Congress from the board on the progress of the industry will be needed to assure the industry is on the right track.

A revitalization of the domestic auto industry including building fuel-efficient vehicles is central to the companies' recovery. On a longer-term horizon, these companies should consider expanding manufacturing capacity into other mass transportation such as for transit and rail vehicles. Expanding markets for clean, efficient buses, mass transit rail, and intercity heavy rail vehicles will provide new customers for the industry. Successfully diversifying into these areas would make the U.S. auto industry competitive in the world market, while at the same time making vehicles that can provide cleaner, safer transportation for the future.

ENDNOTES

1 States that have adopted the California greenhouse gas emissions standards for light duty vehicles are: Arizona, California, Connecticut, District of Columbia, Maine, Maryland, Massachusetts, New Jersey, New Mexico, New York, Oregon, Pennsylvania, Rhode Island, Vermont, and Washington.

2 See 71 Fed. Reg. 77872, 77969. (December 27, 2006).

3 See Testimony of Gene Dodaro, Acting Comptroller General of the United States, Government Accountability Office before the Senate Committee on Banking, Housing and Urban Development. (December 4, 2008).

4 Chrysler Corporation Loan Guarantee Act of 1979. PL 96–185. Jan 7, 1980. 93 Stat 1324.

5 See 73 Fed. Reg. 24352, 24487 (May 2, 2008) at 24444. General Motors said in its report submitted to Congress that it would raise its car fleet fuel economy to 37.3 mpg in 2012. NHTSA's proposed fuel economy target for General Motors' passenger car fleet is 31.7 mpg, so General Motors' promise would exceed the target by 18 percent. Ford's report to Congress promised at 26 percent increase in fuel economy from its 2005 baseline. We estimated this baseline from NHTSA's Summary of Fuel Economy Performance for October 2006 as 28.2 mpg for its car fleet. From this estimate, Ford is promising a 2012 fuel economy goal of 35.5 mpg, which exceeds the target set by NHTSA for 2012 by 8.5 percent. NHTSA has not yet released a final rule for the model year 2011-2015 fuel economy standards, so these numbers are subject to change.

6 See "Slip Sliding Away: the Cheney Sliding Scale for Fuel Economy." Public Citizen. August 2008. Available at: http://www.citizen.org/documents/cheneyscale.pdf

7 Public Citizen obtained copies of these e-mails in a Freedom of Information Act request.

8 See 73 Fed. Reg. 32473, 32485 (June 9, 2008) at 32477. It is worth noting that this NHTSA rule authorizes an extension of lead time from the final rule published in 2007, giving manufacturers an additional year of lead time, and an additional year to phase-in the requirements.

9 Comments of General Motors to NHTSA Docket No. NHTSA-2008-0089 at 0162. (July 1, 2008).

10 See "Restructuring Plan for Long-Term Viability." General Motors. Submitted to the Senate Banking Committee. (December 2, 2008).

11 "Summary of Fuel Economy Performance." National Highway Traffic Safety Administration (March 2008).

12 See 73 Fed. Reg. 24352, 24487 (May 2, 2008) at 24444.

13 See "Restructuring Plan for Long-Term Viability." General Motors. Submitted to the Senate Banking Committee. (December 2, 2008). & "Ford Motor Company Business Plan." Ford Motor Company. Submitted to the Senate Banking Committee. (December 2, 2008).

14 73 Fed. Reg. 24444.

15 "Comparison of Greenhouse Gas Reductions for the United States and Canada under U.S. CAFE Standards and California Air Resources Board Greenhouse Gas Regulations." California Air Resources Board. (February 25, 2008).

16 The Attorneys General of Vermont, California, Connecticut, Maryland, Massachusetts, Oregon, and Rhode Island sent a letter to Speaker Pelosi and Majority Leader Reid on November 17, 2008.

17 Lori Montgomery and Kendra Marr. "Talks Turn to Terms for Auto Aid." *The Washington Post.* (December 7, 2008).

18 David Shephardson. "Energy Department seeks more info on $16 billion in auto retooling requests." *The Detroit News.* (December 4, 2008).

19 See Energy Independence and Security Act. P.L. 110–140. (December 19, 2007).

Announcement on the Auto Industry[*]

Barack Obama

Editor's introduction: In these remarks delivered from the White House, President Obama describes the plight of the American auto industry and blames the sector's sorry condition on poor leadership. Still, he refers to the auto industry as "an emblem of the American spirit" and asserts that it must be maintained. He explains that Chrysler and General Motors (GM) need to restructure as a condition for emergency government loans of up to $6 billion. As part of this process, at the government's request, Rick Wagoner would resign as chairman and CEO of GM to be replaced by Fritz Henderson; and Chrysler would be required to partner with Italian automaker Fiat. Obama suggests that the bankruptcy process might be used in the restructuring, but only to assist in an orderly transition, and not to break up the companies and sell off their assets. To support the industry, the president states that the government would back the companies' warranties, buy efficient automobiles for the government fleet, and give tax breaks to those who purchase energy-efficient cars, which would later evolve into the widely heralded Cash for Clunkers program. Finally, he announces the appointment of former Deputy Labor Secretary Edward Montgomery as the Director of Recovery for Auto Communities and Workers.

Barack Obama's speech: One of the challenges we have confronted from the beginning of this administration is what to do about the state of our struggling auto industry. In recent months, my Auto Task Force has been reviewing requests by General Motors and Chrysler for additional government assistance as well as plans developed by each of these companies to restructure, modernize, and make themselves more competitive. Our evaluation is now complete. But before I lay out what needs to be done going forward, I want to say a few words about where we are, and what led us to this point.

It will come as a surprise to no one that some of the Americans who have suffered most during this recession have been those in the auto industry and those working for companies that support it. Over the past year, our auto industry has

[*] Delivered on March 30, 2009, at Washington, D.C.

shed over 400,000 jobs, not only at the plants that produce cars but at the businesses that produce the parts that go into them, and the dealers that sell and repair them. More than 1 in 10 Michigan residents is out of work—the most of any state. And towns and cities across the great Midwest have watched unemployment climb higher than it's been in decades.

The pain being felt in places that rely on our auto industry is not the fault of our workers, who labor tirelessly and desperately want to see their companies succeed. And it is not the fault of all the families and communities that supported manufacturing plants throughout the generations. Rather, it is a failure of leadership—from Washington to Detroit—that led our auto companies to this point.

Year after year, decade after decade, we have seen problems papered over and tough choices kicked down the road, even as foreign competitors outpaced us. Well, we have reached the end of that road. And we, as a nation, cannot afford to shirk responsibility any longer. Now is the time to confront our problems head-on and do what's necessary to solve them.

We cannot, we must not, and we will not let our auto industry simply vanish. This industry is, like no other, an emblem of the American spirit, a once and future symbol of America's success. It is what helped build the middle class and sustained it throughout the 20th century. It is a source of deep pride for the generations of American workers whose hard work and imagination led to some of the finest cars the world has ever known. It is a pillar of our economy that has held up the dreams of millions of our people. But we also cannot continue to excuse poor decisions. And we cannot make the survival of our auto industry dependent on an unending flow of tax dollars. These companies—and this industry—must ultimately stand on their own, not as wards of the state.

That is why the federal government provided General Motors and Chrysler with emergency loans to prevent their sudden collapse at the end of last year—only on the condition that they would develop plans to restructure. In keeping with that agreement, each company has submitted a plan to restructure. But after careful analysis, we have determined that neither goes far enough to warrant the substantial new investments that these companies are requesting. And so today, I am announcing that my administration will offer GM and Chrysler a limited period of time to work with creditors, unions, and other stakeholders to fundamentally restructure in a way that would justify an investment of additional tax dollars. During this period they must produce plans that would give the American people confidence in their long-term prospects for success.

What we are asking is difficult. It will require hard choices by companies. It will require unions and workers who have already made painful concessions to make even more. It will require creditors to recognize that they cannot hold out for the prospect of endless government bailouts. Only then can we ask American taxpayers who have already put up so much of their hard-earned money to once more invest in a revitalized auto industry. But I am confident that if we are each willing to do our part, then this restructuring, as painful as it will be in the short-term, will mark not an end, but a new beginning for a great American industry—an auto industry that is once more out-competing the world; a 21st century auto industry that is creating new jobs, unleashing new prosperity, and manufacturing the fuel-efficient cars and trucks that will carry us toward an energy independent future. I am absolutely committed to working with Congress and the auto companies to meet one goal: the United States of America will lead the world in building the next generation of clean cars.

No one can deny that our auto industry has made meaningful progress in recent years. Some of the cars made by American workers are now outperforming the best cars made abroad. In 2008, the North American Car of the Year was a GM. This year, Buick tied for first place as the most reliable car in the world. And our companies are investing in breakthrough technologies that hold the promise of new vehicles that will help America end its addiction to foreign oil.

But our auto industry is not moving in the right direction fast enough to succeed. So let me discuss what measures need to be taken by each of the auto companies requesting taxpayer assistance, starting with General Motors. While GM has made a good-faith effort to restructure over the past several months, the plan they have put forward is, in its current form, not strong enough. However, after broad consultations with a range of industry experts and financial advisors, I'm confident that GM can rise again, provided that it undergoes a fundamental restructuring. As an initial step, GM is announcing today that Rick Wagoner is stepping aside as chairman and CEO. This is not meant as a condemnation of Mr. Wagoner, who has devoted his life to this company; rather, it's a recognition that it will take a new vision and new direction to create the GM of the future.

In this context, my administration will offer General Motors adequate working capital over the next 60 days. During this time, my team will be working closely with GM to produce a better business plan. They must ask themselves: Have they consolidated enough unprofitable brands? Have they cleaned up their balance sheets or are they still saddled with so much debt that they can't make future investments? And above all, have they created a credible model for how to not only survive, but succeed in this competitive global market? Let me be clear: The United States government has no interest or intention of running GM. What we are interested in is giving GM an opportunity to finally make those much-needed changes that will let them emerge from this crisis a stronger and more competitive company.

The situation at Chrysler is more challenging. It is with deep reluctance but also a clear-eyed recognition of the facts that we have determined, after a careful review, that Chrysler needs a partner to remain viable. Recently, Chrysler reached out and found what could be a potential partner—the international car company Fiat, where the current management team has executed an impressive turnaround. Fiat is prepared to transfer its cutting-edge technology to Chrysler and, after working closely with my team, has committed to building new fuel-efficient cars and engines here in America. We have also secured an agreement that will ensure that Chrysler repays taxpayers for any new investments that are made before Fiat is allowed to take a majority ownership stake in Chrysler.

Still, such a deal would require an additional investment of tax dollars, and there are a number of hurdles that must be overcome to make it work. I am committed to doing all I can to see if a deal can be struck in a way that upholds the interests of American taxpayers. That is why we will give Chrysler and Fiat 30 days to overcome these hurdles and reach a final agreement—and we will provide Chrysler with adequate capital to continue operating during that time. If they are able to come to a sound agreement that protects American taxpayers, we will consider lending up to $6 billion to help their plan succeed. But if they and their stakeholders are unable to reach such an agreement, and in the absence of any other viable partnership, we will not be able to justify investing additional tax dollars to keep Chrysler in business.

While Chrysler and GM are very different companies with very different paths forward, both need a fresh start to implement the restructuring plans they develop. That may mean using our bankruptcy code as a mechanism to help them restructure quickly and emerge stronger. Now, I know that when people even hear the word "bankruptcy" it can be a bit unsettling, so let me explain what I mean. What I am talking about is using our existing legal structure as a tool that, with the backing of the U.S. government, can make it easier for General Motors and Chrysler to quickly clear away old debts that are weighing them down so they can get back on their feet and onto a path to success, a tool that we can use even as workers are staying on the job building cars that are being sold. What I am not talking about is a process where a company is broken up, sold off, and no longer exists. And what I am not talking about is having a company stuck in court for years, unable to get out.

It is my hope that the steps I am announcing today will go a long way toward answering many of the questions people may have about the future of GM and Chrysler. But just in case there are still nagging doubts, let me say it as plainly as I can—if you buy a car from Chrysler or General Motors, you will be able to get your car serviced and repaired, just like always. Your warranty will be safe. In fact, it will be safer than it's ever been. Because starting today, the United States government will stand behind your warranty.

But we must also recognize that the difficulties facing this industry are due in no small part to the weakness in our economy. Therefore, to support demand for auto sales during this period, I'm directing my team to take several steps. First, we will ensure that Recovery Act funds to purchase government cars go out as quickly as possible and work through the budget process to accelerate other federal fleet purchases as well. Second, we will accelerate our efforts through the Treasury Department's Consumer and Business Lending Initiative. And we are working intensively with the auto finance companies to increase the flow of credit to both consumers and dealers. Third, the IRS is today launching a campaign to alert consumers of a new tax benefit for auto purchases made between Feb. 16 and the end of this year—if you buy a car anytime this year, you may be able to deduct the cost of any sales and excise taxes. This provision could save families hundreds of dollars and lead to as many as 100,000 new car sales.

Finally, several members of Congress have proposed an even more ambitious incentive program to increase car sales while modernizing our auto fleet. Such fleet modernization programs, which provide a generous credit to consumers who turn in old, less fuel-efficient cars and purchase cleaner cars have been successful in boosting auto sales in a number of European countries. I want to work with Congress to identify parts of the Recovery Act that could be trimmed to fund such a program, and make it retroactive starting today.

Let there be no doubt, it will take an unprecedented effort on all our parts— from the halls of Congress to the boardroom, from the union hall to the factory floor—to see the auto industry through these difficult times. But I want every American to know that the path I am laying out today is our best chance to make sure the cars of the future are built where they've always been built—in Detroit and across the Midwest; to make America's auto industry in the 21st century what it was in the 20th century—unsurpassed around the world. This path has been chosen after consulting with other governments that are facing this crisis. We have worked closely with the government of Canada on GM and Chrysler, as both companies have extensive operations there. The Canadian government has indicated its support for our approach and will be announcing their specific commitments later today.

While the steps I am talking about will have an impact on all Americans, some of our fellow citizens will be affected more than any others. And so I'd like to speak directly to all those men and women who work in the auto industry or live in the countless communities that depend on it. Many of you have been going through tough times for longer than you'd care to remember. And I will not pretend the tough times are over. I cannot promise you there isn't more pain to come. But what I can promise you is this—I will fight for you. You are the reason I am here today. I got my start fighting for working families in the shadows of a shuttered steel plant and I wake up every single day asking myself what I can do to give you and working people all across this country a fair shot at the American dream.

When a community is struck by a natural disaster, the nation responds to put it back on its feet. While the storm that's hit our auto towns is not a tornado or a hurricane, the damage is clear, and we must respond. That is why today, I am designating a new Director of Recovery for Auto Communities and Workers to cut through red tape and ensure that the full resources of our federal government are leveraged to assist the workers, communities, and regions that rely on our auto industry. Edward Montgomery, a former Deputy Labor Secretary, has agreed to serve in this role. Together with Labor Secretary Solis and my Auto Task Force, Ed will help provide support to auto workers and their families, and open up opportunity in manufacturing communities. Michigan, Ohio, Indiana, and every other state that relies on the auto industry will have a strong advocate in Ed. He will direct a comprehensive effort that will help lift up the hardest-hit areas by using the unprecedented levels of funding available in our Recovery Act and throughout our government to create new manufacturing jobs and new businesses where they are needed most—in your communities. And he will also lead an effort to identify new initiatives we may need to help support your communities going forward.

These efforts, as essential as they are, will not make everything better overnight. There are jobs that cannot be saved. There are plants that will not reopen. And there is little I can say that can subdue the anger or ease the frustration of all whose livelihoods hang in the balance because of failures that weren't theirs.

But there is something I want everyone to remember. Remember that it is precisely in times like these—in moments of trial, and moments of hardship—that Americans rediscover the ingenuity and resilience that make us who we are. That made the auto industry what it once was. That sent those first mass-produced cars rolling off assembly lines. That built an arsenal of democracy that propelled America to victory in the Second World War. And that powered our economic prowess in the first American century.

Because I know that if we can tap into that same ingenuity and resilience right now, if we can carry one another through this difficult time and do what must be done; then we will look back and say that this was the moment when America's auto industry shed its old ways, marched into the future, and remade itself, once more, into an engine of opportunity and prosperity, not only in Detroit, and not only in our Midwest, but all across America.

The New General Motors[*]

"Day One"

Frederick A. "Fritz" Henderson

President and chief executive officer (CEO), General Motors (GM), 2009– ; born Detroit, MI, November 29, 1958; B.B.A., University of Michigan, Ross School of Business, 1980; M.B.A., Harvard Business School, 1984; various positions, GM, 1984–1992; president of finance, GMAC Group, 1992–97; vice president, GM, and managing director, GM do Brasil, 1997–2000; group vice president, president, GM-LAAM (Latin America, Africa, and the Middle East), 2000–02; president, GM Asia Pacific, 2002–04; chairman, GM Europe, 2004–06; vice chairman and chief financial officer (CFO), GM, 2006–09.

Editor's introduction: After replacing the ousted Rick Wagoner, new GM CEO Fritz Henderson held his first press conference. In his speech, he pledges that GM will work hard to repay the trust and the money invested in the company by the American taxpayer. He notes his top three priorities: customers, cars, and culture. The company will be "obsessed" with customers and customer service, he says, with a "Tell Fritz" Web site where anyone will be able to send a message to the CEO, and states that customers may soon be able to buy cars at online auction. GM will build fewer cars, he announces, among them the Chevy Volt electric car. Henderson describes a new board and a new organizational structure, including staff reductions.

Frederick A. Henderson's speech: Good morning/afternoon/evening everyone, on what is a very exciting day for the new General Motors.

Today marks a new beginning for our company, one that will allow every single employee, including me, to return to the business of designing, building, and selling great cars and trucks, and serving our customers. And there is nothing we want to do more than that!

A lot of people thought we couldn't move through the 363 sale process as quickly as we did. I want to thank everyone involved for a truly amazing effort to

---

[*] Delivered on July 10, 2009, at Detroit, MI. Reprinted with permission.

make it happen—everyone from GM, our team of excellent advisers, and most importantly, the U.S. and Canadian governments, the Automotive Task Force, and the taxpayers of the U.S. and Canada, who have been the key to making this possible.

We deeply appreciate the support we've received during this historic transformation, and will work hard to repay the trust—and the money—that so many have invested in GM.

The last 100 days have shown everyone—including us—that a company not known for quick action can, in fact, move very fast.

Starting today, we take the intensity, the decisiveness, and the speed of these last several weeks and we transfer it from the battlefield triage of the bankruptcy process to the day-to-day operation of the new company. And this is the new norm at GM.

All of you have copies of our press release, so I won't go into detail about the makeup of the new GM.

Instead, I'd like to talk for a few minutes about my three priorities for the new GM: customers, cars, and culture. Let me take them in that order.

First, "customers"—and I place them first because they are my top priority.

At the new GM, we're making the customer the center of everything we do.

Frankly, for some time now, we haven't been as focused on this simple point as we should have been. Now, we're going to be obsessed with it—because if we don't get this right, nothing else we do is going to work. It's that simple.

In addition, with the quality gap virtually eliminated, one of the new frontiers in the auto industry is customer service—which makes it that much more important that we make the customer the center of everything we do.

Going forward, the new GM is committed to listening to customers, responding to consumer and market trends, and empowering the people in the company who are closest to the customer to make decisions.

And we're seeking out more opportunities for direct communication between our customers and our employees at every level—starting with me.

Beginning next week, we're launching a "Tell Fritz" website for consumers—or anybody—to share their ideas, concerns, and suggestions directly with senior management.

I'll review and respond to a sampling of this input every day.

And of course, other executives and I will continue to reach out to customers through our ongoing Web and Twitter chats.

Starting in August, I'll also go on the road every month to meet with consumers, dealers, suppliers, employees, and others—in the U.S. and abroad—who directly impact our relationship with customers and key partners . . . and I'll be asking other members of my management team to do the same. This is something I've done throughout my career, and I assure you I welcome this opportunity again.

Together and individually, we'll be listening to the questions, ideas, and concerns of the people who matter most—those who own and drive GM cars and trucks.

I am personally committed to being closer and more available to consumers than ever before. More importantly, I'm determined to make GM owners the most excited and loyal consumer base in the industry.

Our focus on customers will also extend beyond GM to our great dealer network.

With a significantly smaller and healthier network, both we and our dealers will be able to focus more resources on providing customers with the best possible service.

Our dealers have committed to make the changes necessary to improve the total customer experience for GM vehicle owners.

We're also working on new ways to make car buying more convenient for our customers, including an innovative new partnership with eBay in California to revolutionize how people buy vehicles online.

Customers will be able to bid on actual vehicles just like they do in an eBay auction, including the option of choosing a predetermined "buy it now" price. Think of it as a physical auction for dealers "reinvented" for the online customer.

We'll be testing this and other ideas with our dealers over the next few weeks, and hope to expand and build upon them in the coming months.

In all cases, our goal is to make the shopping and buying process as easy as possible for GM customers—on their time and their terms. Stay tuned.

The second major focus I have for the new GM is "cars."

As I've said many times over the last 100 days, there has never been a successful turnaround in the global auto industry without a focus on both the cost and revenue sides of the business.

To win, we need to stabilize and grow our business around the globe, and particularly in the U.S.—and that means building more of the gorgeous, high-quality, fuel-efficient cars, trucks, and crossovers that consumers want, and getting them to market faster than ever before.

Toward that end, we plan to launch 10 vehicles in the U.S., and an additional 17 vehicles outside U.S., over the next 17 months.

And we are dropping the word "competitive" from our vocabulary. Going forward, every product has to be judged by consumers as best in class. Anything less is unacceptable.

We begin the new GM with a clear vision: to design, build, and sell the best vehicles in the world.

One way we'll achieve this goal is by focusing on just four core brands in the U.S.—Chevrolet, Cadillac, Buick, and GMC. And spread across these four brands will be just 34 nameplates next year, down from 48 last year.

This emphasis on fewer, better entries will enable us to devote more engineering and marketing resources to each model, like the products we're launching in the U.S. this year—vehicles such as the Chevy Camaro and Equinox, Buick La-Crosse, GMC Terrain, and Cadillac SRX and CTS Sport Wagon.

And you'll see it in the products we're launching around the world, as well… cars like the Chevrolet Agile in Latin America . . . Chevrolet Cruze and Buick Excelle in Asia-Pacific . . . and Opel Astra in Europe.

I should add that a key part of our product focus is an emphasis on environmental technology.

We're road-testing a pre-production Chevy Volt extended-range electric vehicle now, and plan to bring it to market before the end of next year.

We announced a new small car last month to be built right here in Michigan. It will add to our growing portfolio of U.S.-built, highly fuel-efficient vehicles—and restore about 1,400 jobs in this country.

We're making advanced battery development a core competency of the new GM. You can expect additional news later this summer.

In short, the products *and* technologies we're launching this year and next are clear demonstrations of our long-term commitment to exciting design, great fuel efficiency, and world-class quality.

They are the cars, trucks, and crossovers that will put us back on consumers' shopping lists, and on the road to profitability and success.

Finally, we're changing the "culture" at GM, with a big focus on customers and products, speed, accountability, and risk-taking.

There's a lot of work to do, and we're starting at the top.

The new GM will have a new Board of Directors—led by our new Chairman, Ed Whitacre, who is here with us today.

Ed, would you care to say a few words?

[Remarks by Mr. Whitacre]

Thanks, Ed. Let me add my thanks to Board member Kent Kresa for his work as interim chairman, and especially for his work to continue building the new Board of Directors.

I'd also like to thank the prior Board members, and I look forward to working with Ed and the new Board with a renewed and continued dedication to making GM a world-class business.

In addition to a new Board, we're also changing the organizational structure of the company.

Today, GM has two senior leadership forums: the Automotive Strategy Board, a team made up of regional vice presidents and global functional leaders, and the Automotive Product Board, a team made up of product development leaders.

Going forward, these two large groups will be replaced by a single, smaller Executive Committee that will meet more frequently, weekly, to anticipate and respond to customer and market needs.

This team will focus on both business results and products, brands, and customers, and much of our work will be outside the Renaissance Center—at Design, the Milford Proving Ground, and places where we are connecting directly to cars, trucks, technology, and the people who develop them.

This move alone cuts the top-level decision-making team in half.

We're also removing layers of management—reducing the number of U.S. executives by 35 percent and overall U.S. salaried employment by 20 percent by the end of this year—flattening the organization and driving broader spans of control.

And, we're eliminating the matrix structure we've employed—simplifying the organization to establish clear accountability for performance.

Bottom line: business as usual is over at GM.

It's a new era at GM, and everyone associated with the company must realize this and be prepared to change . . . fast.

Another significant change involves our regional structure.

Going forward, I will continue as president and chief executive officer for the new GM, working closely with Chairman Ed Whitacre. I also will take responsibility for our operations in North America.

This means we are eliminating the GM North America President position, and the GM North American Strategy Board—essentially, an entire level of management.

Global functional leaders also will have responsibility for running their part of the business in North America.

For example, Ray Young, Chief Financial Officer, also will have responsibility for North America Finance.

In addition, we are moving from a regional focus in Europe, Asia-Pacific, and LAAM to a country-level initiative that will drive increased accountability.

This means we will be eliminating the positions of regional presidents and, instead, we'll be coordinating our global operations under one group.

To that end, I'm pleased to announce that Nick Reilly will become the executive vice president of GM International Operations, and will report to me. GMIO will be headquartered in Shanghai.

The existing regional strategy boards are being eliminated, removing a layer of management.

The Regional Strategy Boards helped strengthen GM's presence in key markets, but given the changes in the industry and in our company, we're taking a more streamlined approach to running the business.

Details of this new structure, including key leadership moves, will be communicated later this month. All of this is aimed at reducing bureaucracy and driving more accountability and a much stronger customer focus.

To help us put even greater focus on the customer going forward, we're creating a new position at GM: Vice Chairman responsible for all creative elements of our products and customer relationships.

I'm happy to announce that we are "unretiring" Bob Lutz to fill this critical new position. As you may know, Bob had planned to retire at the end of this year.

Bob and Tom Stephens will work together as a team, partnering with Ed Welburn, to guide all creative aspects of Design.

GM's Brands, Marketing, Advertising, and Communications will report to Bob to drive accountability for consistent messaging and results.

Bob has a proven track record of unleashing creativity in the design and development of GM cars and trucks. This new role allows him to take that a step further in other parts of GM that connect directly with consumers. Bob will report to me and will be an active member of the newly formed Executive Committee I spoke of a moment ago.

So, today we launch the new General Motors, and our promise is simple: we will be profitable, we will repay our loans as soon as possible, and our cars and trucks will be among the best in the world.

We recognize that we've been given a rare second chance at GM, and we are very grateful for that.

And we appreciate the fact that we now have the tools to get the job done.

The new GM has flexible and efficient factories, labor agreements that are among the best in the industry, and a design studio that is the best in the world.

We have great cars, trucks, and crossovers today, and a product pipeline brimming with exciting new entries.

Our dealer network is outstanding and continues to sell more vehicles in the U.S. than any other.

Compared to the old GM, we have a significantly stronger balance sheet, a much stronger cash position, and a very competitive cost structure.

In fact, the new GM has U.S. debt of approximately $11 billion, in addition to about $9 billion in preferred-stock.

In total, we've reduced our obligations by more than $40 billion, representing mostly unsecured debt and the VEBA trust fund that provides medical benefits to UAW retirees.

Beyond that, we've pledged to be transparent in our financial and other reporting—as Ray Young has said, we'll be the world's most public private company—and we expect to take the company public again as soon as practical, starting next year.

And while we are required to pay off our government loans by 2015, our goal is to repay them much sooner. At GM, we take these loans personally. They represent an enormous obligation to our fellow taxpayers, and we will pay them off as quickly as we can.

In short, the new GM has what it takes to excel—but no interest in making excuses or debating the past.

From this point on, our efforts are dedicated to customers, cars, and culture—and paying back the taxpayers.

Our goal is to create real value—to make sure the immense sacrifices that have been made have been worth it—and to make GM great again.

5

The American City

A City of Innovation*

State of the City Address

Greg Nickels

Mayor, Seattle, WA, 2002– ; born Chicago, IL, August 7, 1955; attended University of Washington; legislative assistant to Seattle City Council member Norm Rice, 1979–1987; member, King County Council, 1987–2001.

Editor's introduction: On February 19, 2008, Seattle mayor Greg Nickels presented the following State of the City address, in which he touts Seattle as an innovator in environmental policies, job creation, infrastructure, and other areas. He describes his initiative in signing on to the Kyoto Protocol when the Bush Administration did not, and introduces Seattle Climate Action Now—a plan to reduce carbon emissions 80 percent by 2050—and his effort to make Seattle America's green building capital. In this and other ways, he declares, Seattle, and by implication other cities, can show the nation how to move forward.

Greg Nickels' speech: Ladies and gentlemen, members of the City Council, honored guests, friends and neighbors, it is my great honor today to report that the state of our city, Seattle, is stronger than ever.

As I begin, I'd like to welcome our two new Councilmembers, Bruce Harrell and Tim Burgess, and congratulate our new Council President Richard Conlin. I am looking forward to working with you and each member to make this city even better.

It is fitting that we gather here at the Pacific Science Center because it celebrates a trait that runs deep in the foundation of Seattle's soul—innovation. As a city, we are driven to confront the problems we face, no matter the scale. We prosper because we challenge conventional wisdom. And when we put our minds to it, we overcome the intractable.

Our ability to make tough decisions has been rewarded with success. That's innovation.

---

* Delivered on February 19, 2008, at Seattle, WA.

But it's never easy. Every good idea must run a gauntlet of skepticism. The people of Seattle are a feisty bunch. They are protective of all that makes this city a great place to live, work, and raise a family. We don't change for change's sake. Innovation must have a purpose—to make a difference in people's lives.

Today, as I look across this wonderful city, I'm proud to say that the Seattle spirit of innovation is alive and well. We are finding new ways to tackle old problems. And as we succeed, others are taking note. Seattle is showing the world how.

We are showing how one city can turn the tide on global warming and how saving our planet will create jobs and opportunities. We are showing how to build a transportation system that works for the century ahead. We are showing how to create parks and open space. We are showing how to keep our neighborhoods safe. And we are showing how to reach out to those hardest to reach.

In Seattle, we see innovation everywhere.

We see it in the light rail tracks that now stretch from our convention center to the airport. And we see it in the city's first modern streetcar line that carries a thousand people a day through our city with zero greenhouse gas emissions.

We see it at the University of Washington, at the Hutch, and at the Gates Foundation, where every day thousands of people go to work curing the intractable problems that confront mankind.

We see it in neighborhoods such as Northgate, Ballard, Southeast Seattle, and South Lake Union, where new jobs, new homes, and new opportunities are flourishing, in some cases after decades of neglect.

And I saw it recently in the eyes of Ed Myers.

Ed lives at 1811 Eastlake. He was a Vietnam vet and a trucker from Council Bluffs, Iowa. For many years he lived on the streets of this city, battling alcohol. He spent a lot of time in the sobering center or the emergency room. He was the kind of guy you might cross the street to avoid, if you noticed him at all.

Today, Ed will invite you into his tidy studio apartment, show you the framed picture of his mom and dad, show off his new cowboy boots, and tell you about a hard life now on the mend.

Thanks to Ed's courage and the support of the people at 1811, he has been sober for more than six months.

1811 Eastlake is one of Seattle's "Housing First" buildings. It is an innovative approach to helping those who are often hardest to help. They are the chronically homeless, many of whom struggle with alcohol, drugs, or mental illness. It works by giving people a clean, safe place to live first, and then helping them to stabilize their lives.

But the residents at 1811 are not required to be sober. And that didn't sit well with some people. They said it would bring crime and grime to the neighborhood. One critic even called Housing First a "comfy ride for bad behavior."

They were wrong. A study released last month showed that 1811 Eastlake and Plymouth on Stewart, have saved $3.2 million in avoided costs for medical, jail and crisis services. But more importantly than that, it has given human beings something even more valuable—hope.

Last year, I talked about the opportunity I had to visit Judith and Sunshine, two residents at Plymouth on Stewart in downtown Seattle. Judith and Sunshine have had their lives reconnected to their family and community. They have each celebrated their first full year in a real home. For the first time in many years Ed, Judith and Sunshine can see a better future. They have a life again. You can see it in the sparkle in their eyes.

In Seattle, more than 500 Housing First apartments have been built or are on the way. And I'm committed to expanding these life-saving programs as part of our 10-year plan to end homelessness. I want to thank Council member McIver for joining with me in this effort. Some people say that we can't end homelessness. They say it is a problem we can only manage but not overcome. I disagree and in Seattle we are showing the world how.

CLIMATE OF CHANGE

We know our climate is changing. We see it in the drenching rainstorms in December and the windstorm that struck more than a year ago. We see it in our mountains, where snow levels whipsaw between too little and too much. We are committed to turning the tide on global warming and preparing for the change already underway.

Last Saturday, February 16th, we marked an important anniversary in Seattle. Three years ago to the day, the Kyoto Protocol went into effect in 141 countries, but not the United States.

On that day, I pledged that Seattle would meet the goals of the Kyoto Protocol and cut our city's climate pollution emissions by 680,000 tons a year. But I also knew that if we took this action alone, it would be merely symbolic.

So I called on mayors across this country to join with Seattle in taking local action on global warming. Today, 794 cities have signed the U.S. Mayors Climate Protection Agreement. More than 78 million people, one in four Americans, now live in cities that are making a difference by reducing their emissions.

In November, Seattle hosted the largest-ever gathering of mayors devoted solely to climate protection. One hundred and twenty mayors traveled from across the nation to share ideas for protecting our climate, including Michael Bloomberg of New York and Antonio Villaraigosa of Los Angeles. We were joined by former President Bill Clinton and former Vice President, Oscar winner, and Nobel Laureate Al Gore. And one common theme emerged during those two days—an urgent desire to take local action now to save our planet.

What was a symbolic declaration is now tangible change. And the world knows Seattle led the way. Other cities have followed. So have the states. And now, we hear the promise of real action at the federal level in the campaigns of senators Barack Obama, Hillary Clinton, and John McCain. We can create a climate of change in this nation, and Seattle is showing how.

I'd like to thank each Council member for your efforts on behalf of our climate and our planet.

REDUCING WASTE; REUSING MORE

We know that our efforts are making a difference in Seattle. In the days before the mayors' summit, I was proud to announce that Seattle had reached a major milestone. We reduced our carbon emissions by 8 percent below where they were in 1990; we exceeded our Kyoto goal.

It was a moment to celebrate. But more importantly, it was a moment to recommit ourselves to overcoming the challenges ahead. If we do nothing more, we will lose ground over the next few years as more people move to our city. And to truly save the planet, we must go an order of magnitude beyond the goals of Kyoto and cut our emissions 80 percent by 2050.

Skeptics will say again that it can't be done. We will show them how it can.

We call it Seattle Climate Action Now. Our goal is to get every Seattle resident to take action, even if it is as simple as changing a light bulb. But just as important, Seattle Climate Action Now is our city's commitment to provide people with tools to make a difference for our planet.

We know what the problem is—most of our greenhouse gas emissions come from the vehicles and buildings. So we must take steps today to reduce the use of fossil fuels in our cars and our homes and businesses.

That is why I joined with State Senator Ed Murray in Olympia earlier this month to introduce legislation that would reduce carbon pollution by encouraging the use of more fuel-efficient cars.

We called it a *Car*bon Tax and it would require drivers to pay for the cost of carbon emissions based on their car's mileage rating. Someone who drives a gas-guzzling Hummer would pay about $180 a year, next to $60 a year for the owner of a fuel-sipping Prius. The money raised from this Carbon Tax would be used to pay for alternative forms of transportation, such as transit, bikes and walking.

But cleaner cars will only get us so far. The other major source of climate pollution in our region comes from our buildings. Seattle is the nation's leader in new green buildings. But most of the places where we live, work and shop are already built.

To meet our climate goals, we must find innovative ways to unlock the doors to energy conservation in the homes and businesses that exist today.

That is why I'm announcing a new effort to make Seattle America's Green Building Capital. I have three goals for this initiative. The first is to improve energy efficiency in our commercial and residential buildings by 20 percent. The second is to provide real cost-savings for struggling homeowners who will see their heating bills drop as waste is reduced. And the third is to create new green-collar jobs for those working to make our homes, offices, and industry more energy efficient.

Achieving this triple bottom line will not be an easy task. This spring I will call together a diverse panel of community members to help us develop the right approach for achieving these three goals—greater energy savings, lower home energy bills, and more good paying jobs.

Whether it is on the road or in our homes, Seattle will continue to lead the way on reducing greenhouse gases. We will show the world how.

BUILDING THE ROADS AHEAD

When I took office, our streets were a mess. A generation of under-investment and dwindling support from the state and the federal government helped create a $500 million backlog of basic maintenance on our roads, bridges, and sidewalks.

It seemed impossibly large. So we started small. We focused on potholes and promised that we would fill them within 48 hours when someone called 684-R-O-A-D. Some thought it was overly ambitious. But we saw it as basic service.

I believe this: If you show the people that you can take care of the small stuff, they will give you the tools you need to tackle the big stuff. And that is just what happened.

When we asked voters for their support in Bridging the Gap between our transportation resources and our transportation challenges they said "yes." These steps have allowed us to more than double our annual transportation investment from when I took office.

Last week, I announced the first year of accomplishments from Bridging the Gap and they are impressive:

- We paved 27 lane miles of arterials. We used to pave between four and eight miles a year.
- We replaced 1,043 street name signs—some nearly as old as I am.
- For the first time in memory, we completed 27 blocks of new and renovated sidewalks.
- And after years of almost no new bike facilities, we added 20 miles of lanes, trails and sharrows in 2007.

And that is just a start. This year, we will do even more to get Seattle moving.

But the work that is underway is much more than paving streets and painting bridges. We are working to create a transportation system that makes it easier, safer and more convenient to get around by foot, bike or transit.

We are taking innovative approaches to pedestrian safety, including the installation of 30 red-light cameras that will catch bad drivers who threaten pedestrian safety. I'd like to thank Council members Nick Licata and Tom Rasmussen for their commitment to improving safety for pedestrians in Seattle. The Council and I share a commitment to making Seattle the most walkable city in the country.

On December 12 at 12:12 P.M., we accomplished something incredible. We opened the first line of the Seattle Streetcar network. At the time, I said I didn't care what people called it, just as long as they rode it. And they have. So far,

125,000 people have taken the streetcar and the demand to expand the network is growing.

Four years ago, when we started working on the streetcar, some people scoffed. But we didn't back down. We challenged the skeptics, engaged the community and delivered the first new transportation alternative in Seattle in more than 40 years. We showed how it is done.

I'd like to thank Councilmember Jan Drago for her help on both Bridging the Gap and the Seattle Streetcar. Your leadership has been invaluable in Getting Seattle Moving.

We are making it happen. Seattle is showing how.

CREATING JOBS AND OPPORTUNITIES

Six years ago, as I took office, Seattle was experiencing the worst recession in a generation. We were hemorrhaging jobs and we were forced to cut $120 million from the city budget. But Seattle is a resilient and innovative city.

In the midst of that economic darkness, we looked around the city for signs of light.

In Northgate we found a neighborhood poised for growth but languishing in acrimony and indecision. Today there are new jobs, new homes, and a new sense of community.

In the University District we revitalized the Ave and redefined our relationship with the most important generator of new ideas, new talent and new jobs in our city—the University of Washington.

In Southeast Seattle, we are making sure that the people who live in this dynamic and diverse neighborhood today are the ones who benefit tomorrow from our investments in light rail and housing.

And in South Lake Union, we have helped create some 7,000 new jobs and nearly 2,000 homes.

As the nation's economy once again teeters on the brink of recession, we must remember the lessons we learned. We cannot take jobs for granted in our city.

That is why we took action with the Industrial Jobs Initiative to prevent real estate speculators from driving out the 120,000 family-wage jobs that thrive on our industrial lands. That is why we worked to keep one of our biggest employers, Amazon.com, in Seattle. That is why we are helping our neighborhood business districts to prosper.

But something else innovative and amazing is happening in Seattle. By embracing our need to save the planet, we are creating new jobs here at home. They include familiar companies like McKinstry, which started out 50 years ago as a plumbing and heating company, but today is a leader in helping businesses save energy and money. I had the chance to join Senator Barack Obama on a tour of McKinstry recently. He called this Green Seattle company "proof that reducing our emissions isn't a drag upon our economy, it's the future of our economy, it's a job generator." They also include new companies such as V2Green, which is helping power utilities prepare for the coming age of plug-in electric cars.

We are showing how protecting our climate does not destroy our economy—it creates economic opportunity. Let's show the White House how it's done in Seattle.

GETTING PREPARED

Later this month we mark the seventh anniversary of the Nisqually earthquake. It was a wake-up call and a warning that we must heed. When I took office, I pledged to make Seattle the most prepared city in the nation. We are making that happen, thanks to the Fire Levy approved by voters. We are rebuilding or renovating all our fire stations to withstand a major earthquake. We are offering emergency preparedness training to every neighborhood in our city through our SNAP program—more than 8,500 people have taken this class so far.

Later this month, we will dedicate our new Emergency Operations Center. The EOC is the city's nerve center in a catastrophe. It allows us to coordinate our response and inform the public in an emergency. And it will be ready when we need it most.

We can make Seattle the most prepared city in the nation. We are showing how.

KEEPING SEATTLE SAFE

Seattle is a remarkably safe city. Last month, I stood with Police Chief Gil Kerlikowske and Councilmember Tim Burgess to announce that Seattle's crime rate fell 14 percent last year to the lowest it has been since 1968.

When you compare our murder rate to similar-sized cities, the differences are astounding. Last year, Washington, D.C. experienced 181 murders; Milwaukee had 105; and Boston suffered 66. In 1968 Seattle had 45 homicides but last year in Seattle it was 24.

Seattle is a safe city. But if you are the victim, the statistics don't matter. And that is why the murders and attacks we have experienced in recent weeks are so shocking. They aren't supposed to happen here. And when they do, it creates a sense of fear and uncertainty made more alarming by the sensational headlines and television news teasers.

I'd like to take a moment to commend the work of the Seattle Police Department in arresting suspects in the murder of Shannon Harps and of Degene Berecha. It was a clear reminder of the professionalism and dedication the men and women of SPD show every day.

I'm committed to giving them the tools they need to do their jobs. We are taking the strongest steps to reforming the way we protect our city in 30 years as we implement Neighborhood Policing. We will better utilize our officers and make policing stronger, faster and smarter. We are adding 154 additional patrol officers through 2012, a 25-percent increase in our patrol strength.

We are also taking steps to reform our police accountability system, so that both the public and officers have confidence that we are upholding the standards of professionalism that have served this city so well.

But for all the progress we have made we still have our tragedies. Just a few days into the new year, two young men, 17-year-old Allen Joplin and 14-year-old De'Che Morrison, were shot to death. Something is deeply wrong when it is easier for our young people to get their hands on a gun than it is to get a driver's license.

I have pledged to work with the community to reduce the toll of youth and gang violence in our city. We must find ways to arm our children with hope instead of bullets.

And we must start reducing the number of illegal guns on our streets. I have called on the state legislature to pass commonsense laws to close the gun show loophole, require safe storage of guns and ban assault rifles. But they have not listened. That is why we are working with communities across this state to forge a nonpartisan coalition that will create new and innovative ways to reduce gun violence and build support for change.

When it comes to saving lives, we will not take no for an answer. Together, we will show how to get it done.

A LEGACY FOR PEOPLE AND PARKS

A century ago, the Olmsted brothers overcame skepticism to create a magnificent park system for a young city. We are fortunate to have inherited such a rich legacy of parks and open space.

As this city continues to grow, our open space must grow with it.

That starts with making sure that everyone feels welcome and safe in our parks. This year we will see our new Park Rangers, added activities and attractions, more investments, and new security measures in our Center City Parks. I'd like to thank the Council for supporting my program to reclaim these parks as active, exciting, and vibrant places.

We are finding new ways to add open space. Last year, we finalized a deal to buy the U.S. Navy's Capehart holding in Discovery Park, which will add 24 acres of breathing space.

And we saw an innovative opportunity to do much more in an unlikely place—over our reservoirs.

We could have simply put floating covers on our reservoirs and called it good. But in Seattle, good isn't good enough. So we are using this opportunity to create new open space across the city.

By 2010, new parks will sit atop the Beacon and Myrtle reservoirs. When all the remaining reservoirs are covered by 2013, we will have added 100 new acres to our city's park system. That's 2½ times as much new parks acreage as the Pro Parks levy provided.

It is a tremendous accomplishment and a gift to generations to come. That is the power of innovative thinking.

As we think about what we leave to the future, we cannot forget two Seattle legacies in need of investment today—the Pike Place Market and the grounds of the 1962 World's Fair, our Seattle Center.

Later this morning, you will hear about plans for the future of Seattle Center. I want to thank the Century 21 committee for its thoughtful recommendations on how we can prepare this incredible combination of art, culture, entertainment and open space to serve the people of Seattle for the next 50 years.

Last August 17th, the venerable Pike Place Market celebrated its 100th anniversary. What started as a protest against the high cost of onions has become one of the city's most beloved gathering places. More than ever, the Market brings Seattleites together—and brings the world to Seattle.

That is why we cannot allow the Market's age to become its enemy. Although the salmon still fly and the shops and stalls are as vibrant as ever, the bones of this wonderful place are getting brittle. The need to protect the Market from earthquakes and to replace its worn-out wires, plumbing, and heating systems is becoming urgent.

A generation ago, the people of Seattle saved the Market from the wrecking ball. Now it is our turn to save this historic place—for the next generation.

AFFORDABLE SEATTLE

We are fortunate to live in such an incredible city. But for too many working families today, the cost of housing is rising out of reach. We must find new ways to help grocery clerks, nurses, truck drivers, teachers, and other working people who are struggling to find decent, affordable housing in our city.

That is why I launched my Affordable Seattle strategy. It is built around three important elements: renewing the Housing Levy, expanding our Homes Within Reach program, and adopting incentive zoning so that development in our fastest-growing neighborhoods creates housing for all.

This year, we will begin work on renewal of Seattle's Housing Levy in 2009. The levy has funded 1,649 apartments for low-income people in Seattle since 2003 and it will continue to be an important tool in the years ahead.

But today's market is pricing out more and more working families. That is why last year, I proposed Seattle Homes Within Reach. It would expand and update an incentive program so that it helps more people in more places. If we had it, we could create some 1,600 more homes for middle-income workers in developments already underway.

Finally, I have proposed Incentive Zoning. The idea is to require developers in our fastest-growing neighborhoods to set aside homes for working families or pay to support more affordable housing. It is modeled on the center city plan the Council endorsed just a year ago. Our goal is simple: If you work in Seattle, you should be able to live in Seattle.

Let's show what we can do to keep this city affordable for everyone.

SERVING OUR CUSTOMERS

Despite all of Seattle's innovations, there is one place where the city government has not kept pace—customer service.

Some people say government isn't a business; we don't have customers. I think the 600,000 people who live here, pay taxes, and contribute to the life of our city would disagree.

Each year, we get more than 10 million phone calls and thousands more e-mails, letters, and other requests from people looking for help. Many are handled well. But too often, the caller is confronted by a bureaucratic and unresponsive system that does not value their time or their intelligence.

You can see for yourself, right in the blue pages of the phone book. There you'll find more than 1,000 numbers listed under the City of Seattle. It is cumbersome, confusing and impossible to navigate.

Worse yet, if someone does get through to the right person, we often have no way of knowing whether their problem was solved and the loop closed.

This is a city that gave the world the Nordstrom standard of innovative customer service.

We must move from a culture of "sorry, not my problem," to one of rolling up our sleeves and fixing the problem.

That is why in the next few months, I will be asking for the public's help in creating a Customer Bill of Rights for our city. The principles will help to create an open, responsive and accessible government that serves all of our residents, regardless of their language, their income or their neighborhood. I look forward to working with each member of the City Council on this.

Together, we can bring customer service and public service together again. We will show how.

CONCLUSION

It isn't surprising that an innovative city attracts innovation. Sometimes it takes a little time to see how one good idea can change the world.

Few people outside this city took much notice when Bill Boeing started working on an airplane in a red barn on the edge of Lake Union. Or when a little coffee shop called Starbucks opened in Pike Place Market. Or when a couple of kids at Lakeside started tinkering with computers.

That spirit of innovation is the very foundation on which this community has grown and prospered. It has put Seattle's stamp on the world—and, more importantly, put our stamp on the future.

We are showing how one city can make a difference for the future of our planet. How we can create jobs and opportunities by protecting our environment instead of abusing it. How we can begin transforming a transportation system built in the last century into one that works for the next. How we can build a community where people are safe, neighborhoods flourish and everyone can enjoy a better life.

When people say we can't, we just try a little harder. That's why we love Seattle. If we put our minds to it, we can make a difference in people's lives. And that matters. Just ask Ed Myers and Judith and Sunshine.

Thank you and God bless our home, Seattle.

MetroPolicy[*]

A New Partnership for a Metropolitan Nation

Bruce Katz

Vice president, The Brookings Institution, 2002– ; founding director, Metropolitan Policy Program, The Brookings Institution, 1996– ; visiting professor in Social Policy, London School of Economics, 2004– ; born June 21, 1959; B.A., magna cum laude, Phi Beta Kappa, Brown University, 1981; J.D., Yale Law School, 1985; senior counsel, U.S. Senate Subcommittee on Housing and Urban Affairs, 1987–1992; staff director, U.S. Senate Subcommittee on Housing and Urban Affairs, 1992–93; chief of staff, U.S. Department of Housing and Urban Development (HUD), 1993–96; member of President Barack Obama's transition team, and senior advisor to U.S. HUD Secretary Shaun Donovan, 2008–09; editor: Reflections on Regionalism, *2000;* Redefining Urban and Suburban America, Volume I, *with Robert Lang, 2003;* Redefining Urban and Suburban America, Volume II, *with Alan Berube and Robert Lang, 2005;* Taking the High Road: A Metropolitan Agenda for Transportation Reform, *with Robert Puentes, 2005;* Redefining Urban and Suburban America, Volume III, *with Alan Berube and Robert Lang, 2006; author or co-author of numerous editorials in national and regional print media, including* The Christian Science Monitor, Washington Post, New York Times, Los Angeles Times, *and others.*

Editor's introduction: During the heat of the presidential campaign, Brookings Institution scholar Bruce Katz delivered the following speech urging the next president and Congress to think of America less as a country of 50 states than as one of 363 economically integrated metropolitan areas, arguing that the nation's health is dependent on the vitality of its urban areas. A MetroNation, as he calls it, demands a MetroPolicy that allows integrated solutions rather than bureaucratically divided responses to critical problems in infrastructure, housing, and education. We must fundamentally rethink federalism, he contends, to adapt national policies to a global era.

---

[*] Delivered on June 12, 2008, at Washington, D.C. Reprinted with permission.

Bruce Katz's speech: I want to thank Stacy Stewart for that introduction and for the leadership and generous support that Fannie Mae has provided to Brookings over the past decade.

I also want to thank all of you for coming today.

We are here because there is a palpable sense that something big is happening in our country.

Just think about what transpired in this past week alone.

The primary phase of this presidential election ended . . . and the final lap of this historic race began.

And the issues at stake in this election came into sharp focus as gas prices soared, housing prices declined, the stock market tumbled, and the Senate debated meaningful climate legislation for the first time.

The next Administration and Congress, to put it mildly, will have their hands full.

To inform what comes next, we launched the Blueprint for American Prosperity eight months ago with a simple and urgent proposition: More than ever before, our nation's ability to grow and prosper is at risk unless our metropolitan areas are healthy and vital.

Our initiative challenges the nation to fundamentally alter our mental map from a union of 50 states to a network of 363 highly connected, hyperlinked, and economically integrated metropolitan areas.

The blunt tagline of our initiative: We are a MetroNation and it's high time to start acting like one.

Today we go the logical next step and offer a MetroPolicy for our MetroNation during this historic presidential election.

We make the following proposition:

First, metro areas are the engines of national prosperity, and they are at the cutting edge of policy action. Yet, despite all their energy and effort, metros cannot go it alone and ultimately require a dependable national partner to succeed and prosper.

Second, our federal government has gone fundamentally adrift, and is out of step and out of sync with the dynamic changes underway in the country. We are a MetroNation economically, but we do not act like one politically, governmentally, or administratively.

Finally, our MetroNation demands a MetroPolicy. We need to fundamentally re-imagine and remake the partnership between the federal government, states, localities, and the private and voluntary sectors to unleash the unfulfilled potential of metro America and resolve our most critical national challenges.

We desperately need our national government to lead where it must since the big challenges transcend parochial borders and require national vision, direction, and purpose.

At the same time, we need our federal government to empower metros where it should by being flexible enough to reflect the variation across metros, smart enough to enable integrated solutions, and assertive enough to insist that cities and suburbs work together to resolve their common problems.

And, what's more, during a time of severe fiscal constraints, we need our national government to maximize performance. More focus on evidence-based, outcome-driven, and performance measured decisions. More reliance on public/private partnerships, innovation networks, and market mechanisms.

A METROPOLICY FOR A METRONATION . . . THE TIME IS LONG OVERDUE.

So, let's start with our initial frame: broad forces have positioned metropolitan areas as the engines of national prosperity and the cutting edge of policy action.

As we reported in November, the top 100 metro areas pictured here have kept growing and growing to the point where they now constitute 65 percent of our nation's population and concentrate the workers and firms that fuel the economy.

Economists refer to this as agglomeration because the assets that matter most to nations gather and strengthen disproportionately in urban and metropolitan places:

- Innovation . . . the new products, processes and business models that drive economic productivity and sustainable solutions.
- Human capital . . . the education and skills that further innovation and serve as the ticket to the middle class.
- Infrastructure . . . state of the art transportation, telecommunication, and energy distribution systems that move people, goods, and ideas quickly and efficiently.
- And quality places . . . that special mix of distinctive communities and responsible growth that is competitively wise, fiscally responsible, and environmentally sustainable.

Innovation, human capital, infrastructure, and quality places.

These assets and the people and firms that leverage them come to ground in metro America. Our top 100 metropolitan areas alone take up only 12 percent of our land mass but harbor 2/3 of our population and generate 75 percent of our gross domestic product.

More importantly, metros gather what matters and make an outsized contribution on each of the assets that drive prosperity—whether it's indicators of innovation like patents or indicators of human capital like adults with graduate degrees or indicators of infrastructure like air cargo or indicators of quality places like public transit.

Our metro areas constitute a new spatial geography, enveloping city and suburb, township and rural area in a seamlessly integrated economic and environmental landscape.

In the Chicago metropolis, for example, the new geography stretches from the hustle of the downtown Loop to the leafy suburban neighborhoods of Oak Park to the prairie landscape of Goose Lake to the employment center of Schaumberg and to the satellite cities of Aurora and Waukegan.

These disparate places—once fully separate—are now co-joined and co-mingled as people live in one municipality, work in another, go to a sports game or medical specialist or shopping in yet another . . . and share the same air, water and natural resources.

America's metros find themselves on the front lines of dynamic change and confront daily the challenges of our new global order.

Yet they are responding, affirmatively, with energy, invention and creativity.

Challenged by unsettling economic restructuring, metros are finding new ways to bolster innovation . . . whether by financing wind energy and fuel cells in struggling, industrial metros like Cleveland or by connecting new entrepreneurs to money, markets, partners, management and other resources in prosperous metros like San Diego.

Confronted with a diverse, less educated workforce, metros are laboring to elevate human capital by preparing disadvantaged workers to excel in such global hotbeds of employment as logistics in Louisville, life sciences in the Bay Area, and health care in both.

Faced with rising congestion, exploding gas prices, and aging systems, metros are designing and implementing market-shaping infrastructure investments . . . to reconfigure freeways in Milwaukee, modernize water and sewer systems in Atlanta, build out region-wide transit in Denver, and install fiber-optic networks in Scranton.

And, confronted with what Strobe Talbott calls "the existential threat of climate change," metros like Seattle and Chicago are taking ambitious steps to create quality, sustainable places by promoting green building, transit-oriented development, urban regeneration, and renewable sources of energy.

What knits these policy efforts together? It's their embrace of a new style of governance that brings together city and suburban leaders around common purpose; cuts across conventional lines of government, business, and philanthropy; and deploys systemic market- and environment- shaping investments and interventions.

Yet, no matter how much metros focus and innovate, they are learning that they do not have the resources or powers to "go it alone." And they shouldn't have to.

The forces affecting metros are the same ones that are buffeting our nation.

The movements of talent and capital or the drift of carbon emissions take place at the global scale and have impacts and implications that transcend parochial borders.

A rapidly changing world demands that the federal government serve as a strategic, flexible, and accountable partner so that metros can address their central problems, realize their full potential . . . and, in so doing, resolve our most pressing national challenges.

A FEDERAL GOVERNMENT GONE ADRIFT

This leads to our second point: the federal government has gone adrift and is out of sync with metropolitan reality.

The conventional wisdom of two parties in perennial conflict with each other may be true, but it's only part of the story.

Equally important from our perspective is the sharp disconnect between the dynamics of a changing Metro Nation on the one hand and the static nature of federal policy on the other.

Washington, in short, is failing to lead where it must during a period of global transformation.

It is failing to empower metros where it should to reflect the changing and varied nature of metropolitan communities.

And it is failing to maximize performance to ensure that scarce resources have optimal societal impact.

At the broadest level, the federal government is absent where it needs to be present, failing to lead on issues of national significance.

In prior transformational periods, the federal government acted with confidence and purpose:

- Creating advanced economic sectors through investments in health care, scientific research, and defense.
- Extending the education of millions of Americans through the GI bill.
- Radically reducing poverty of older Americans through Social Security and Medicare.
- Constructing an interstate highway system to make us one nation, one integrated network of markets.
- And taking bold steps to conserve the nation's natural heritage through Teddy Roosevelt's system of parks and open lands . . . and, 60 years later, to ensure clean air and clean water.

The return on these smart investments—economically, socially, environmentally—is beyond calculation.

But today Washington lacks any strategic plan to tackle the big stuff that is beyond the scope of metros:

- Burnishing critical assets like innovation in a disruptive economy that has shed close to 3.4 million manufacturing jobs in the past 8 years alone
- Building a world-class labor force when the next generation of workers, African Americans and Hispanics, have education levels that are literally one-third or one-half those of white Americans.
- Rethinking the transportation needs of a MetroNation that is slated to grow from 300 million to 420 million people by the middle of this century.
- Reducing the carbon footprint of a nation that is the world's largest per capita emitter of greenhouse gas emissions, releasing twice the level of emissions as Germany and the United Kingdom.

By contrast, our competitor nations understand full well that the rules have changed and require new purpose and direction from central governments . . . whether it be South Korea's and Finland's attentiveness to innovation, or Ireland's and Singapore's bets on developing talented workers, or Japan's and Germany's campaigns around broadband and high-speed rail connections or Europe's consistent focus on alternative energy and smart metropolitan development.

Now we all remember Harry Truman's favorite maxim, "the buck stops here." It seems at times that we now have a "pass the buck" government . . . routinely shifting the responsibility and, even more significantly, the obligation of funding to lower levels of government for challenges that are simply beyond their control.

The absence of leadership is coupled with a failure to empower metros with the tools they need to thrive and build on their own distinct assets.

Over the past forty years, from Nixon to now, the federal government has experimented with devolution, pushing large responsibilities for program design and implementation down to states and localities.

Yet devolution has failed to keep pace with the evolution of metros, and offers only compartmentalized responses to multidimensional challenges and parochial solutions to issues that cut across artificial political borders and boundaries.

In the real world, families know that issues like transportation and housing and education are inextricably linked. In the specialized, stove-piped universe of federal bureaucracy, these issues are broken apart and kept separate.

Let's take traffic congestion, for example, which is the natural byproduct of land-use patterns that separate where we live from where we work. We know that it is fiscal folly to build or widen roads to mitigate congestion. More roads equal more congestion.

The real solution lies in rearranging the location of housing and jobs and building transit to give people more choices . . . and then introducing pricing schemes to reduce and alter demand.

But federal transportation programs offer only transportation solutions to congestion, making fiscal follies the easy if not only choice.

And efforts to link disparate areas of federal policy like transportation and housing for example run into countless roadblocks . . . such as headache-inducing differences in grant requirements and restrictions.

The federal government has become an ossified network of specialized and balkanized agencies at a time when most challenges require integrated solutions that "join up" related areas of domestic policy.

Federal policies also reinforce governmental fragmentation.

Our top 100 metros may be integrated economies, but most like Chicago have inherited 19th century governmental structures that are highly fragmented and balkanized.

With globalization, the competition is no longer between all these separate jurisdictions but with international metros like Shanghai, Mumbai, London, and Frankfurt.

Cities and suburbs should be encouraged to collaborate to compete globally and resolve common problems rather than compete against each other.

Yet federal programs and policies rarely encourage such collaboration. Rather, federal housing, workforce, transportation, and even homeland security programs, just to name a few, break apart metros by allocating resources to either parochial city or county bureaucracies or distant (and often hostile) state agencies—entities that rarely see the metropolitan area as an economic or environmental whole.

The federal government, of course, is not solely responsible for governmental fragmentation. Cities and suburbs are creatures of states . . . which are often reluctant to alter the geography or rules of local governance, stymied by tradition and vested interests. And localities, as we know, don't work or play well together.

But federal rules and resources make a difference...and are powerful enough to chart a new path and make city/suburban collaboration the norm rather than the exception.

Beyond encouraging fragmentation, the federal government is failing to maximize performance, apparently blind to the revolution in business practice, organization and accountability underway in the best of corporate America.

We all know it hasn't always been this way.

In earlier decades, the typical government agency was organized in ways that looked remarkably similar to the typical state-of-the-art corporation.

In many respects, the mass production corporate economy had its direct analogue in the command and control bureaucracies engendered by the New Deal and Great Society.

The past thirty years have told a different story.

Remember the Great Competitiveness Threat of the late 1980s and early 1990s?

How did we respond? Well, the best corporations retooled and restructured in the face of international competition. Top-down planning gave way to decentralized, "federated" systems that rewarded decisive front-line problem-solving and experimentation.

Businesses deemphasized rule bound control in favor of bottom-up accountability that enshrined systematic measurement, benchmarking, evaluation, and learning.

We all know the success of the Austin-based Whole Foods Markets. This corporation maximizes performance across its 11 regions and 270 grocery stores by combining the radical autonomy it allows its store based teams with data-rich and evidence-driven accountability systems so that performance can be measured and rewarded.

And the federal government?

It barely funds the national census, constitutionally mandated and in operation since 1790.

It has dismantled information systems.

It has degraded our statistical agencies and denigrated program evaluation and assessment.

With a few notable exceptions, most federal agencies have no clear, quantifiable mission and no end game against which to benchmark progress.

Folks, this is not rocket science.

- Measure what matters.
- Track what counts.
- Get what you pay for.

A CALL FOR METROPOLICY

And so we come to our final point: a MetroNation demands a MetroPolicy, a fundamental remaking of federalism and our federalist compact.

We face a sharp contrast.

On one hand, we are a MetroNation, rich in assets, bursting with promise and potential, but incapable by itself of addressing the panoply of challenges shaped by global forces.

On the other hand, we have a powerful federal government (and frankly a level of local governmental fragmentation) that is out of step and out of touch.

We need to end this disconnect.

We need, in short, a MetroPolicy for a MetroNation that recognizes and leverages the core assets that drive prosperity in the nation.

At the core of MetroPolicy is a call for a new federalist compact.

This compact should have three essential components:

First, the federal government should lead where it must. Global challenges, broad in scale and geographic reach, require national solutions. Only the national government can set a strategic vision for the entire country, address issues that naturally transcend state borders and establish a unified framework for smart private and public sector action.

Next, the federal government must empower metros where it should. A nation of our size and diversity displays immense variation. Charlotte is not Cleveland. Phoenix is not Pittsburgh. Denver is not Detroit. Federal policy must enable these and other metropolitan areas to bend national policies to their own distinctive market realities and strengths.

But there is another piece to our federalist puzzle. The federal government must maximize performance and fundamentally alter the way it does business in a changing world. It is time for Washington to Get Smart and become a fact-filled rather than fact-free zone.

- Lead.
- Empower.
- Maximize.

Simple concepts.

We need a 21st century federalism that marries national vision and purpose with local implementation and invention and couples public sector engagement with private sector energy and discipline.

So—our final point—what does MetroPolicy look like in practice?

For the past decade, Brookings has listened carefully to a new class of metropolitan innovators like many here today—elected officials, business and civic leaders, university presidents, environmental activists—who are grappling with the big challenges of our time.

What follows is the initial fruit of our labor . . . organized along the lines of the four assets that drive prosperity—overwhelmingly metropolitan assets: innovation, human capital, infrastructure, and quality places.

As a start, we need a federal government that leads again.

We desperately need a national innovation policy if our metro areas and our nation as a whole are going to stay one step ahead of our competitors.

To lead that effort, we recommend a National Innovation Foundation, to bring together under one roof and ramp up the government's fragmented efforts to boost commercial innovations in fields such as precision manufacturing, information technology, life sciences, and the environment.

Modeled on successful efforts in Japan and Korea, Finland and Britain, the National Innovation Foundation would create an entrepreneurial hot spot that works with states, metros, and the private sector to unleash innovation in firms across our economy.

Now, no matter how much we innovate, we must recognize that many American workers will not be able to make ends meet without government help.

So the federal government must lead on supplementing wages of working families. We will recommend a Metro Raise, a targeted boost in the earned income tax credit, the most successful anti-poverty effort in the modern era that rewards work rather than idleness. It is time to make the EITC go further in rewarding the employment of workers who are currently not benefiting fully from this incentive, such as childless workers, non-custodial parents who still care for a child or families with three children or more.

Beyond innovation and human capital, we propose that the federal government lead again, as in the 1950s, and set forth a national transportation vision that fits the challenges of our time . . . namely, to facilitate the movement of people and goods within and among the metropolitan gateways of international trade and the major corridors of inter-metropolitan travel.

It is economic and environmental suicide to expect our major ports, freight hubs, and rail corridors to do what it takes on their own and to stay one step ahead of global forces.

And it is fiscally irrational and irresponsible to expect that a system of Congressional earmarks will get the job done.

Our response: identify, map, prioritize, finance, and then implement those investments that will have the largest return for the nation, economically and environmentally.

Take politics out of the system and invest in what matters: Intermodal facilities at our congested ports and freight hubs. High-speed passenger rail between key economic centers.

Smart infrastructure is essential to the building of quality places, another driving asset. But the federal government must go further and lead on climate change and create a national framework for smart and sustainable development.

Now we support either a carbon tax or a national cap-and-trade system to lower greenhouse gas emissions through market innovation.

But we think such a system must fully recognize the carbon footprint of the built environment—the residential sector alone contributes a full fifth of greenhouse gas emissions.

That's why we will recommend Washington mandate energy transparency in residential home purchases, promote new efforts to jump-start private markets for the retrofit of older homes and build a new network of discovery innovation institutes to scale up ideas around alternative energy.

But the days of solutions that are exclusively made in Washington, DC, are long over.

Beyond leadership, the federal government must also empower metros where it should by enabling metropolitan areas to tailor national policies to their own realities.

On innovation and human capital, we recommend that the federal government empower metropolitan areas to build on their strengths—distinctive clusters of economic activity that join together webs of for-profit firms, advanced research institutions, suppliers, investors, skills providers, and business associations.

- Energy in Houston.
- Logistics in Louisville.
- Photonics in Rochester.
- Advanced manufacturing in Minneapolis.
- Life sciences in Boston.

These distinct clusters are the foundation of metro competitiveness in the global marketplace . . . and hence the foundation of the nation's ability to compete globally.

We will thus recommend a new CLUSTER effort—Competitive Leadership in the United States through Economic Regions . . . Competitive Leadership in the United States through Economic Regions . . . pretty good acronym right? That took seven months. Anyway, a new CLUSTER effort would reward metro-grown initiatives that help economic sectors undertake common efforts on job training, product and service innovation, networking, and global marketing.

WORKERS BENEFIT. FIRMS BENEFIT. METROS BENEFIT.

And on infrastructure and quality places, we recommend that the federal government empower metros by issuing a Sustainability Challenge.

Just imagine if the federal government said to Greater Denver or Greater Dallas or Greater Cleveland or Greater Charlotte: "Show us a plan to reduce greenhouse gas emissions and lower your carbon footprint from combined changes in housing, transportation, land use, and energy and we will provide additional resources as well new powers to align disparate federal programs."

We think metro areas would rise to such a challenge. Metros might propose to concentrate mixed use facilities and mixed income housing around transit stations. Or they might decide to institute congestion pricing, or extend transit and commuter rail.

These efforts would actually give our residents what they want: more choices in where they live and how they move around their communities.

Let's face it: with rising gas prices and the climate threat, sprawl is no longer an option for people or places.

These and other empowerment proposals flip traditional federal practice on its head and embrace solutions that are bottom-up (reflecting local variation), joined up (rewarding problem-solving across stove-piped bureaucracies), and suited up for global competition (insisting that cities and suburbs work together on issues that obviously cross jurisdictional lines).

So that brings us to another part of the new federalist compact, namely the need to maximize performance of the vast partnership between federal government, states, localities, and the private and voluntary sector.

Our most basic recommendation here is simple, relatively cheap, doable . . . and transformative.

- Set Audacious Goals.
- Use Evidence to Make Decisions.
- Track Performance continuously.
- In a phrase, GET SMART.

Let's create the intricate network of data, metrics, and analytic tools used in Europe and American corporations and measure what really matters: the performance of clusters that drive metropolitan economies; the share of our high school graduates who move on to one-, two-, and four-year degrees; the economic and environmental returns on transportation investments; the changing carbon footprint of our metropolitan areas.

Ask any corporation. Information moves markets. Information creates wealth.

A relatively small federal investment in the tens of millions will ultimately mean that public and private sector investments in the hundreds of billions can be smart and strategic.

These are the policy ideas we have today to lead, empower, and maximize performance. But our work, yours and mine, is not done.

We intend to continue throughout this year and next to offer concrete, legislatable ideas on additional challenges that face our nation and our metros—particularly the challenges that continue to undermine progress in urban school systems and post-secondary education.

As with our current efforts, we will not do this alone . . . but rather in concert with the real experts in this country . . . the metropolitan corporate, civic, political, university, and environmental leaders who are driving change.

CONCLUSION

Let me end where I began.

The United States enters a new century with a new geography and a new face.

We are no longer Jefferson's nation of rural hamlets and small towns, with economies that are internally focused and self-reliant.

Rather we have emerged as the world's preeminent economic power precisely because we are now a network of metropolitan areas that are integrated and connected with their sister economies across the globe.

Our challenge is to get comfortable in our new metropolitan skin and alter the way we govern so that our metro communities can achieve their fullest potential as our engines of national prosperity.

Quite simply, we have come to a point in our nation's evolution where the purpose of national policy—and the roles and relationships between different levels of government to achieve that purpose—need to be fundamentally reexamined and then remade.

Our MetroNation needs a MetroPolicy. Together, let's make it happen.

Addressing America's Shrinking Cities[*]

Jay Williams

Mayor, Youngstown, OH, 2006– ; born Youngstown, OH, September 26, 1971; B.S./B.A., Youngstown State University; examiner, Federal Reserve Bank of Cleveland, 1995–97; vice president, First Place Bank, Warren, OH, 1997–2000; director, Community Development Agency, Youngstown, OH, 2000–05.

Editor's introduction: Addressing the "Revitalizing Older Cities" summit, Youngstown mayor Jay Williams argues that cities have been fundamental to American history and will remain central to the nation's continued prosperity. While the country's industrial cities have fallen on hard times, he points out, they still have amenities that make them, for some, preferable to suburbs. These smaller cities, however, need more support from the federal government, which tends to focus on larger urban areas. With leaner bureaucracies, he argues, smaller cities are also better able to use money more flexibly and with faster results. Williams offers a money-back guarantee to the federal government, promising that if granted federal money, Youngstown will partially match the stimulus funds and guarantee the creation and retention of jobs.

Jay Williams's speech: It was John F. Kennedy who once stated that we will neglect our cities at our peril, for in neglecting them, we will neglect our nation. And if this nation cannot prosper without strengthening its cities it is only logical to conclude that our states will never be greater than their most vulnerable cities.

Even before this country was formed into a union of United States, cities and towns served as the building blocks that were centers of activity and innovation that provided the foundation to eventually help grow the most powerful nation on earth.

Cities served as the port of entry for millions of immigrants who sought to make this country their home. Cities and towns fueled the growth and expansion of a fledging nation as it expanded westward into unexplored territories.

---

[*] Delivered on February 12, 2009, at Washington, D.C.

Cities and towns birthed many of the institutions of higher learning that would prepare our nation's citizens for greatness. Cities house and protect many of our nation's greatest treasures and artifacts in their museums and other cultural and historical institutions.

An urban sociologist once described cities as having both advantages and problems. The city can provide a popular setting for cultural events, diverse commerce, innovative services, and the fine arts. However, cities can also struggle with crime, poverty, and pollution. Ironically, while cities can satisfy a wide variety of human desires, they also produce certain problems that affect a large number of people. It is important to realize that the city should not be ignored nor taken for granted.

The more than 7 million Americans who live in smaller to mid-sized industrial cities are essential to the nation's economic future, cultural vibrancy, and community well-being.

Cities like ours in the Northeast and Midwest once were the backbone that sustained the middle class and helped make America one of the most prosperous nations the world has ever known. Even the names evoke a chronicle of American industrial growth—Cleveland, Ohio; Youngstown, Ohio; Flint, Michigan; Schenectady, New York; Scranton, Pennsylvania; and so many others.

In recent decades, though, these cities have fallen on hard times. Economic and social factors have drained many of these cities of residents and businesses. Residents of these cities are some of the most isolated in our nation, living in neighborhoods that lack good jobs, strong schools, and quality housing.

We can be strong again—and we know what it will take to get us there. We are blessed with rich legacies and the urban infrastructure that comes with it.

In an era of environmental awareness and sky-high gas prices, cities like ours already are built around walkable downtowns, with shops, housing, and businesses within easy reach. Sprawling suburbs are spending millions of dollars to create the kind of community spaces that cities like ours already offer.

These walkable cityscapes are becoming attractive for growing numbers of Americans. Young families, new professionals, and retiring Baby Boomers are increasingly looking beyond the spread-out suburbs in favor of more dense, more pedestrian-friendly areas. With our museums, shops, college campuses, and park spaces, our cities are perfectly suited for many to call home—all on a smaller, more manageable scale than spread-out suburbs or big cities.

A report titled "To Be Strong Again," released by the national advocacy group PolicyLink, proposes ways cities like ours can leverage our existing assets to be stronger and more fair for all our residents. Smaller cities—unlike their larger counterparts—are tailor-made for the kind of flexible innovation required to compete in the new global economy. Bureaucracies are leaner. Results can be seen more quickly. Novel approaches to public and private sector challenges can be kick-started on a manageable scale.

Already, many of these cities are leading the charge for public policy innovation, creating opportunities for all their citizens. For instance, I'll tell you Youngstown's story.

Youngstown was an industrial powerhouse throughout the beginning and middle of the 20th century. Its population peaked, in 1930, at over 170,000. But on a day that became known as Black Monday, September 19, 1977, the closure of a large portion of Youngstown Sheet and Tube was announced, resulting in the loss of 5,000 jobs within 90 days, and 30,000 jobs over the next five years. This was followed by the withdrawal of U.S. Steel in 1979 and 1980 and the mid-1980s bankruptcy of Republic Steel.

This series of events led to an economic, psychological, and emotional collapse. A vacuum of leadership was created and the city fell victim to a cadre of destructive forces, most notably wide-reaching corruption in political leadership. The community also spent an inordinate amount of time "chasing economic windmills" in an effort to find a panacea to replace the once mighty steel mills that had brought so much prosperity.

There was, however, ultimately a community-wide "epiphany"—people saw that there was a need to establish a new vision and a new plan for Youngstown. With the rise of another steel industry unlikely, they saw they had to accept Youngstown as a smaller city. In fact, the population of Youngstown today is closer to 70,000 than to 170,000. However, Youngstown also set out to establish that the notion of a smaller city does not have to equate to an inferior city.

Youngstown continues to take aggressive and innovative measures to redefine its role in a new regional/global economy. The city has established economic development initiatives that are not only greatly diversifying its economic base, but also have landed it in *Entrepreneur Magazine*'s Top 10 places in the country to start a business.

Although typically a part of traditional economic development and/or land-use plans, Youngstown also recognized the necessity of addressing issues to improve the image of the city and the quality of life of its residents.

It was also critical that this new vision and new plan was very pragmatic, action-oriented, and measurable in its approach. It needed to foster a sense of ownership through a broad constituent base in the community. This was necessary so that the vision and plan would be able to rise above any self-serving political agendas or special interests that had been the fatal flaw of so many previous efforts.

One of the most vital elements of the approach involved fostering community engagement and encouraging community ownership at unprecedented levels. The idea was to create a shared responsibility and shared ownership for the destiny of the community. It was an educational process than ran counter to the tradition of "waiting for the future" to be delivered through some mystical transformation that was never going to occur.

In Youngstown, the Business Incubator looks to reverse the "brain drain" by giving home-grown young innovators and entrepreneurs focused on business-to-business software the support and mentorship they need to succeed.

Other cities throughout the nation are recovering in innovative ways from the crash that resulted from the departure of industry.

In Scranton, PA, blighted parks have been reclaimed to provide civic gathering places and to draw families seeking a mix of urban and suburban living.

In Kalamazoo, MI, the Kalamazoo Promise looks to lure young families and promote economic recovery by providing college scholarships to all eligible graduates of the city's public school system.

In New York State's "Tech Valley" region, several small cities are tying job training in underserved communities to the burgeoning tech sector, uniting economic development with workforce development.

Advocates and elected officials like us are working diligently to renew the promise in our cities. But we need the support of the federal government.

The proposed National Infrastructure Bank would be a major boon to smaller cities that are too often overlooked when it comes time to dole out federal money to fix bridges, roads, and water systems—the backbone of a successful economy.

By giving cities like these a fair share, we could leverage our substantial existing strengths. Rebuilding our crumbling infrastructure is a vital step to renewing our cities.

We are not naive. We know the problems facing smaller industrial cities did not appear overnight—and they will not disappear quickly, either. We cannot afford to be photogenic swing-state campaign stops and then become faded memories as policies are developed and implemented.

America cannot afford to leave us in the shadows. Our people have the skills, the tools, and the drive to serve as beacons for just, fair and equitable redevelopment. We can be strong again. However, the economic tsunami sweeping this nation has already begun to unravel any signs of progress as it relates to our nation's cities.

The federal government has recognized the need to act. However, it is critical that those actions are inclusive of, and benefit, our nation's smaller to mid-sized industrial cities.

Our national metropolises have rarely had difficulty attracting the attention of our federal government. Not to say that these large cities are not also in need of assistance, but their sheer size and stature often serve as their calling card when federal government intervention is warranted. However, it is short-sighted to focus resources and attention by placing too much emphasis on size. Aristotle said that a great city is not to be confounded with a populous one.

FEDERAL POLICIES/MESSAGE TO WHITE HOUSE URBAN POLICY DIRECTOR

Partnerships with America's cities must endure.

There is no better way to sense the pulse of the country than by a substantive engagement with cities and mayors.

Community Regeneration, Sustainability, and Innovation Act of 2009 as drafted by Congressman Tim Ryan of the 17th District of Ohio [. . .] would create a new, competitive program within the U.S. Department of Housing and Community Development (HUD) targeted towards cities and metropolitan areas experiencing large-scale property vacancy and abandonment due to long-term losses in employment and population.

The Act would provide assistance to communities to start or expand land banks that establish public control over vacant and abandoned property so it can be used in ways to benefit the public.

The Community Regeneration Act would encourage innovation, experimentation, and environmentally sustainable practices through collaborative efforts to reuse land bank properties in ways that will provide long-term benefits to the public, whether it is through the creation of green infrastructure, economic development, or other strategies.

Implementation of such strategies would create new and sustainable employment opportunities for residents. The Community Regeneration Act would also strongly encourage multi-jurisdictional or regional approaches to addressing the problem of vacant and abandoned property.

These are some of the ways that the federal government can ensure that we have a fighting chance to bring vibrancy back to our country's smaller to mid-sized cities.

As I watch very closely the debate on Capitol Hill, I consistently hear the mantra of jobs, jobs, and jobs. However, I am deeply concerned when I begin to examine where the stimulus money is being directed.

Infrastructure, education, and certain other spending initiatives are important and will provide some limited job creation. However, we must also invest in well-established programs with a proven track record of sustainable job creation; programs which recognize that ultimately long-term job creation must attract private sector investment.

It is imperative that our President and congressional leaders fully appreciate the ability and capacity of our cities to help facilitate job creation.

Youngstown, Ohio's economic development programs are replete with success stories. The programs have help facilitate the creation of thousands of jobs and have been recognized and rewarded by the U.S. Small Business Administration.

STIMULUS MONEY-BACK GUARANTEE

So confident are we in our economic development program's ability to facilitate the job creation so desperately needed to save this country, that I am offering a 5 Million Dollar/2000 Job Stimulus Money-Back Guarantee. It is a return on investment better than anything you will find on Wall Street, and we won't come back hat-in-hand pleading for a taxpayer bailout.

Based on past experience, over the next three years, the City of Youngstown:
- will match 25 percent of the stimulus investment in the City's economic development programs with local funding
- will commit to facilitating and documenting the creation/retention of 2000 jobs

- will commit to multiply threefold the stimulus investment with private investment dollars
- failing to achieve this goal, will otherwise offer to repay the stimulus money

Lest anyone perceive this as a publicity stunt, I can assure you that the City of Youngstown is willing to put its money where its mouth is. Our federal government must be willing to do likewise. If this stimulus bill is really about job creation, then all eyes should be turned toward Youngstown, Ohio, as a model for economic development and job creation for our nation's smaller to mid-sized industrial cities.

CONCLUSION

Whether we're talking about Youngstown, Ohio; Muncie, Indiana; Pontiac, Michigan; Trenton, New Jersey; or Cleveland, Ohio, according to Jennifer Vey, of the Brookings Institution, in her "Restoring Prosperity" report, these cities weren't always in such a tenuous position.

To the contrary, they were once the economic, political, and cultural hubs of their respective regions, and the engines of the nation's economic growth.

They were vibrant communities where new ideas and industries were conceived and cultivated, where world-class universities educated generations of leaders, where great architecture and parks became public goods, and where glistening downtowns grew up within blocks of walkable, tree-lined neighborhoods where the middle class swelled and thrived. They were, in short, physical testaments to the innovation and spirit that shaped the nation and its citizens. And so they can be again.

Business leaders, citizens, community organizations and activists, local officials, state officials, and certainly the federal government all have a stake in the condition of our cities, large and small.

All these actors need to work together to set aspirational goals for city renewal, gauge their progress over time, and continually adjust their strategies to overcome new challenges and seize new opportunities, as they arise.

Moving a real reform agenda for older industrial cities will naturally be an organic, messy, and frustrating process that will demand the patience, flexibility, and commitment of many diverse constituencies.

Success won't come easy, it won't come soon, and it won't come to every city. But given the positive trends now afoot, there's little excuse not to try—and no better time to get started.

"We will neglect our cities at our peril, for when we neglect them, we neglect our nation."

The State of the Borough[*]

Adolfo Carrión Jr.

Director, White House Office of Urban Affairs Policy, 2009– ; born New York, NY, March 6, 1961; B.A., Kings College, NY, 1985; masters degree, public planning, Hunter College, 1990; associate pastor at a Bronx church; public school teacher, West Bronx; New York City Councilman, 14th Council District, The Bronx, 1998–2002; borough president, The Bronx, NY, 2002–08.

Editor's introduction: Adolfo Carrión, Jr., who had been selected to serve as the director of President Obama's Office of Urban Affairs Policy, delivered his final State of the Borough address as Bronx Borough president. In evoking the "hemorrhaging of jobs, foreclosures on homes, reduced business activity, and a slowing of our construction boom" in the Bronx, he could have been describing the situation in cities across America. Carrión also looks forward to his new post, arguing that since "the top 100 metro areas generate two-thirds of our jobs [and] nearly 80 percent of patents, and handle 75 percent of all seaport tonnage," and because "42 of our metro areas now rank among the world's 100 largest economies," cities are too important for the federal government not to embrace a strong urban policy.

Adolfo Carrión Jr.'s speech: I didn't think I would have one final opportunity to address you in the context of a State of the Borough Address. People say, sometimes it's better to be lucky than good.

Today I get to thank you for your partnership and collaboration in moving the Bronx forward. In preparing for today I had a chance to look back and review what we focused on in the last seven state-of-the-borough addresses. In the first year, in the wake of the September 11th terrorist attacks, we focused on coming together as a city and community to rebuild; on fiscal austerity, having lost 100,000 jobs in 3 months; and getting back to basics in education.

In the second year I presented the three Es—economic development, environment—in the large sense of good neighborhood development—and education

* Delivered on February 20, 2009, at The Bronx, NY.

as we continued our recovery from 2001. In the third year I argued that the best social program is a job and we launched the Bronx at Work program, insisting that any developers doing business in the Bronx had to do business with the Bronx. In partnership with Cablevision, with the help of our Secretary of State Lorraine Cortes-Vasquez, back then at Cablevision, we installed high-speed internet access in every Bronx school and with Con Edison we put every community board on the web. That year we launched the Bronx Domestic Violence Advisory Council and opened 30 new schools.

In year four, we announced the plan for the redevelopment of the Yankee Stadium neighborhood and crafted an historic agreement with a host of community benefits which set the standard for host communities around the city and even as far away as the City of Houston. We announced the creation of 21 more new schools and the start of the Bronx Children's Museum. In year 5 we focused on public-safety initiatives, the Team Up to Clean Up the Bronx community service program that enlisted hundreds of volunteers in every neighborhood of the borough, and negotiated the largest tenant purchase of housing in Bronx history, 1,865 units in the Soundview section of the Bronx—the Lafayette/Boynton Coops. In year 6 we focused on greening initiatives, including the planting of thousands of trees; a green roof on the Bronx County Courthouse and many other buildings around the borough; a Health and Wellness campaign to combat obesity, diabetes, and unhealthy lifestyles; and the Bronx Veterans Advisory Council. In year 7 we launched an aggressive quality of life campaign and the Bronx Historic Preservation Task Force that this year published a report identifying historic sites throughout the Bronx worthy of preservation and in some cases landmark status.

With the help of every Bronx elected official and community board we ushered in an unprecedented period of growth and development that includes a new Yankee Stadium neighborhood, the new Gateway Center along the Harlem River, millions of square feet of office and retail space, more than 40,000 units of housing for families of every income, unprecedented parks development, modernization of schools and community facilities, a large expansion of funding for senior programs, healthcare facilities, and enhancements to schools in the form of science and computer labs, and libraries, and an investment of almost $24 million through Bronx Federal Empowerment Zone loans and grants for commercial and green projects. Altogether we invested nearly $210 million, just from borough president funds. When we add everything up, including city, state, federal, and private investment, we are looking at an investment of more than $10 billion . . . this has been a truly unique time of partnership between the public and private sector.

And now we enter a moment of great difficulty and challenge. Today we gather at a moment of great opportunity and newness because of the election of President Obama and a new generation of leaders, but also a moment of great distress and gravity because of an unmatched global economic crisis. If someone would have told me on January 1, 2002, when I first walked—that would be hobbled on crutches—into the borough president's office, that a 47-year-old young man named Barack Obama would be our President, and that that President along with a Congress led by Democrats in both houses would pass a $787-billion stimulus bill, followed quickly by a $275-billion housing rescue operation, in order to get our economy out of an almost unprecedented crisis, rivaled only by the actions of another President and Congress to dig us out of a Great Depression . . . that major banks would go out of business or have to be bailed out by the taxpayers, that US automakers would have to be rescued, that we would have seen the loss of 3.6 million jobs and more than 2 million foreclosures in one year, that our state, city, and borough would be experiencing such distress, and that I would be addressing you for the last time as Borough President and going to work for the 44th President of these United States, I would probably dismiss you as someone with a fairly loose grip on what we purport to know as reality.

I guess this constitutes, yet again, the vindication of those who insist that anything is possible. Once again you and I are called upon to believe that we are in fact able to set our course, and that the limits we imagine are set only by us. Two hundred years after the birth of Abraham Lincoln and Frederick Douglas and 45 years after a 39-year-old preacher from the South called our nation to rise up to all it could be, we open a chapter of new promise and potential for our nation and our community here in the Bronx. I am more proud than ever to be from a special American community called the Bronx. I ask you to do yourself and me a favor, today. The next time you encounter a self-loathing pessimist who dwells on the negative and emphasizes the unaccomplished, as opposed to how far we've come, and how promising the future is, please cast them aside and move forward with optimistic fervor. I believe nothing can keep us back . . . nothing.

It is true that in our short 233-year history we have not faced many moments like the one we face today. It is also true that every time we've had to overcome adversity, the American people have prevailed. Whether it was a civil war that almost destroyed the Union, reconstruction, a great economic depression, world wars, civil and social unrest at home, wars abroad, no matter . . . we have overcome. The Bronx is no different. Today, we face a time, after years of growth and development, when we will see the effects of a global financial crisis here in our 61 neighborhoods. We are already experiencing the hemorrhaging of jobs, foreclosures on homes, reduced business activity, and a slowing of our construction boom. We know this will get worse before it gets better . . . in part because we have yet to see the full effects of the global financial meltdown and in part because it will take time for the impact of the stimulus package to get to households and businesses. So, while we were able to see great progress in the last seven years, we must now brace ourselves for tough days again. But we know that the people of the Bronx, probably more than most counties in America, know adversity and know how to overcome it. Al Pacino, who grew up on 174th Street in the Bronx, was once told by some handlers he needed protection . . . to which he responded, "I don't need bodyguards. I'm from the South Bronx." We know how to overcome obstacles.

Let me be clear . . . we know this crisis is not due to the greed and irresponsibility of the hardworking 90 percent of the people who simply get up every day and go to work, school their kids, worship in their communities, participate in civic activities, simply believing that if they play by the rules they will get ahead. No, we are in this bind because of the greed and irresponsibility of the few—the result of a banking and government culture that has rewarded excess and discouraged responsibility and stability . . . promoting an obscene view of what it means to succeed . . . measured not by added value, but by the trappings of wealth. Well, once again, just like we've done in the past, the hardworking people of our city and country will set things right. We will do it by insisting that our government behave responsibly . . . that it set the right priorities . . . and that we elect the right leaders with the right motivations . . . Just this week President Obama, in announcing his plan to stem foreclosures and keep millions of American families in their homes, called on the country to return to our core values of responsibility and common sense . . . a return to the basics of investing in the areas that build communities of aspiration and opportunity.

While I am very proud of what we've accomplished, now we must turn our attention to unfinished business and new opportunity. The historic American Economic Recovery and Reinvestment Act offers the next borough president and all officials a fresh opportunity to address our areas of natural strength. The Bronx is known as the borough of parks, universities, and hospitals. It is no secret that at a minimum, one-quarter of the Bronx workforce is in the healthcare industry, and almost one in five in education. These are the building blocks. If we educate and promote wellness and build the connections for paths to careers in these areas of strength, we will make great progress in addressing the needs of this borough. So outside of everything else you will be able to do, I encourage the next borough president and all Bronx and city officials to tee up those projects right away, and let's link the healthcare and education institutions to the schools, colleges, and job-training programs, some of which will be expanded with funds from the federal government, and let's get people on successful career tracks. There is no valid reason we should be importing healthcare workers and teachers when we have a growing population and young people in our neighborhoods that are uneducated or undereducated, and consequently unemployed or underemployed because of our collective failures. We need to create the local synergies that take more time but make more sense—Back to Basics. We cannot continue in the mode that took our economy into the tank . . . that quick fix, get-what-you-can-while-you-can, approach. Again, a return to the core values of responsibility and common sense.

Today I am addressing you for the last time as Bronx borough president and I've accepted the invitation of the President of the United States to be director of the White House Office on Urban Affairs. After spending time talking to people around the country about the possibility of resetting our priorities and returning to the basics of building strong communities, and carefully considering what President Obama said to the nation's mayors as a candidate, I agreed that this was the approach we needed toward cities and metropolitan areas.

Let me share with you, from much of what the President said to America's mayors last summer, why I am going to Washington to work with him.

President Obama acknowledged that in this country, change comes not from the top down, but from the bottom up.

- That when a disaster strikes—a Katrina, a shooting, or a six-alarm blaze—it's City Hall we lean on, it's local government we call first and depend on to get us through tough times;
- That because local leaders are on the front lines in our communities they know what happens when Washington fails to do its job;
- That when Washington puts out economic policies that work for Wall Street but not Main Street, it's towns and cities that get hit when businesses close their doors, and workers lose their jobs, and families lose their homes because of unscrupulous lenders.

The President believes local governments need a partner in the White House because,

- When Washington makes promises it doesn't keep and fails to fully fund No Child Left Behind, it's our teachers who are overburdened, our teachers who aren't getting the support they need, and our teachers who are forced to teach to the test, instead of giving students the skills to compete in a global economy;
- When Washington succumbs to petty partisanship and fails to pass comprehensive immigration reform, many communities are forced to take immigration enforcement into their own hands, cities' services are stretched, and our neighborhoods see rising cultural and economic tensions;
- When Washington listens to big oil and gas companies and blocks real energy reform—our budgets get pinched by high energy costs, and our schools cut back on textbooks to keep buses running; it's the lots in our towns and cities that become brown-fields;
- Even with the absence of leadership in Washington over the last eight years, we're seeing a rebirth in many places . . . we shouldn't be succeeding despite Washington—we should be succeeding with a hand from Washington.
- And this president understands what we know in the Bronx . . . that neglect is not a policy for America's metropolitan areas.

I agree. What we need is a partner who knows that the old ways of looking at our cities just won't do; who knows that our nation and our cities are undergoing a historic transformation. The President reminded the mayors that the change that's taking place today is as great as any we've seen in more than a century, since the time when cities grew upward and outward with immigrants escaping poverty, and tyranny, and misery abroad. And that while this population has grown by tens of millions in the past few decades, it is projected to grow nearly 50 percent more in the decades to come . . . not only in our cities but throughout larger metropolitan areas.

We know that nearly 80 percent Americans live in metropolitan areas that are increasingly inter-dependent. The President recognizes this is creating new pressures, but it's also opening up new opportunities—because our metropolitan areas, not just the central cities—are hotbeds of innovation. He explained it's not just Durham or Raleigh—it's the entire Research Triangle. It's not just Palo Alto, it's cities up and down Silicon Valley. The top 100 metro areas generate two-thirds of our jobs, nearly 80 percent of patents, and handle 75 percent of all seaport tonnage. The fact is 42 of our metro areas now rank among the world's 100 largest economies.

He recognized that to seize the possibility of this moment, we need to promote strong cities as the backbone of regional growth. We need to promote a new urban agenda that will not only tackle areas of concentrated poverty . . . we need to make sure kids get the right start . . . we need to create public-private business incubators. . . . we need to fund the COPS program . . . we need to restore funding for the Community Development Block Grant program . . . we need to recruit more teachers to cities, pay them more, and give them more support.

In June President Obama told America's mayors he would put forth a plan to provide real relief for struggling homeowners and help them keep their homes and avoid foreclosure; this week he made good on that commitment. President Obama made good on his commitment to help us build more affordable housing by ensuring funding in the stimulus package.

I agree with the President that we need to stop seeing our cities as the problem and start seeing them as the solution. We in the Bronx believe that strong cities are the building blocks of strong regions, and strong regions are essential for a strong and competitive America. This new national urban agenda has to be as much about South Florida as it is about Miami; about Mesa and Scottsdale as much as Phoenix; about Stamford and Northern New Jersey as much as New York City.

And, I agree with the President that our children will grow up competing with children in Beijing and Bangalore and Berlin. President Obama reminded the mayors that China is developing an advanced network of ports and freight hubs, and an advanced network of universities modeled after our own. And that Germany has launched rail and telecom projects to connect its major metro areas. We cannot compete in this global economy if we don't show the same kind of leadership.

So the President's agenda aims to unlock the potential of all our regions by connecting them with a 21st century infrastructure—a world-class transit system . . . re-committing federal dollars to strengthen mass transit . . . reforming our tax code to give folks a reason to take the bus instead of driving to work, and making metro areas more livable in order to help our regional economies grow. He said we'll partner with mayors to invest in green energy technology and ensure that your buses and buildings are energy efficient. We'll invest in ports, roads, and high-speed rails—I agree that we don't want to see the fastest train in the world built halfway around the world in Shanghai; we want to see it built right here in the United States of America.

The President talked about change during his campaign . . . I believe as he does that if we can bring about change in our neighborhoods, then change will come to our cities. And if change comes to our cities, then change will come to our regions. And if change comes to our regions, then change will come to every corner of this country we love.

For these reasons the President said he would appoint the first White House Director of Urban Affairs. I am thrilled to be called into service to our country from the village of the Bronx.

So I conclude with this. In about a month you will hear the national anthem, followed by the famous words "PLAY BALL" in a new state-of-the-art Yankee Stadium. On a hopefully sunny April afternoon you will hear the crisp crack of a wood baseball bat meeting a leather baseball and the roar of a stadium full of Yankee fans, the start of a new era that will usher in a period of construction of a new regional park. On the waterfront you will see a tennis center and ice-skating concession, and a new mall next to a waterfront park, teeming with families who will be able to take their kids to the Bronx Children's Museum or join tourists from around the world who will be visiting the new International Museum of Hip Hop, or thanks to the advocacy of my friend Freddy Ferrer, your former borough president, people will be visiting from around the country and the world to participate in the world's largest marathon and Latin music fest. We will build it, and they will come.

Again, I thank my family, my friends and the supporters who helped put me in position to get elected to do this job, and my colleagues who helped to carry forward a Bronx agenda. Thank you to my staff . . . a team of people who each in their own way, with the limits of time, experience, and politics, forged ahead and tolerated me while I tried to build a stronger Bronx.

It's been 2,602 days since I hobbled on crutches down the center aisle of Veterans Memorial Hall to be sworn in as the 12th president of the Borough of the Bronx. This community has done more for me than I will ever be able to claim I have done for it. When I come home from a tour of duty in our nation's capital, I will continue working right here in our city with the optimists who believe our best days are always before us because we can always do better. This city, that has been the incubator for people like Al Smith, a poor Irish immigrant from the Lower East Side; Fiorello LaGuardia, an Italian Jew who did more for our infrastructure and the garden of skyscrapers we are still building; FDR; and so many others, is my beloved city. This is the city that when pushed to describe it James Joyce could only say, "Here comes everybody." This is the city that defies convention and beckons us into the future with the same sense of awe and daring that ring in the words of Emma Lazarus, that 34-year-old German-Jewish poet who had grown weary of the anti-Semitism and persecution in Russia, and in 1883 submitted a 14-line poem to help the faltering fundraising campaign for the pedestal of the Statue of Liberty. And in her still haunting and quite prophetic words suggests the following:

> Not like the brazen giant of Greek fame,
> With conquering limbs astride from land to land;
> Here at our sea-washed, sunset gates shall stand
> A mighty woman with a torch, whose flame
> Is the imprisoned lightning, and her name
> Mother of Exiles. From her beacon-hand

Glows world-wide welcome; her mild eyes command
The air-bridged harbor that twin cities frame.

"Keep ancient lands, your storied pomp!" cries she
With silent lips. "Give me your tired, your poor,
Your huddled masses yearning to breathe free,
The wretched refuse of your teeming shore.
Send these, the homeless, tempest-tost to me,
I lift my lamp beside the golden door!"

I will come back to our beloved New York, but for now I will join our President in helping to rebuild the promise of America.

God bless you . . . God bless the Bronx and New York City . . . and God bless these United States of America!

Cumulative Speaker Index: 2000–2009

A cumulative speaker index to the volumes of Representative American Speeches for the years 1937–1938 through 1959–1960 appears in the 1959– 1960 volume; for the years 1960–1961 through 1969–1970, see the 1969–1970 volume; for the years 1970–1971 through 1979–1980, see the 1979–1980 volume; for the years 1980–1981 through 1989–1990, see the 1989–1990 volume; and for the years 1990–1991 through 1999–2000, see the 1999–2000 volume.

Index